"It's Bristol, Baby!"
— Dale Earnhardt Jr.
August 2004

BRISTOL
Stories of Oval and Drag Racing in Thunder Valley

David McGee

CarTech®

CarTech®

CarTech®, Inc.
838 Lake Street South
Forest Lake, MN 55025
Phone: 651-277-1200 or 800-551-4754
Fax: 651-277-1203
www.cartechbooks.com

© 2018 by David McGee

All rights reserved. No part of this publication may be reproduced or utilized in any form or by any means, electronic or mechanical, including photocopying, recording, or by any information storage and retrieval system, without prior permission from the Publisher. All text, photographs, and artwork are the property of the Author unless otherwise noted or credited.

The information in this work is true and complete to the best of our knowledge. However, all information is presented without any guarantee on the part of the Author or Publisher, who also disclaim any liability incurred in connection with the use of the information and any implied warranties of merchantability or fitness for a particular purpose. Readers are responsible for taking suitable and appropriate safety measures when performing any of the operations or activities described in this work.

All trademarks, trade names, model names and numbers, and other product designations referred to herein are the property of their respective owners and are used solely for identification purposes. This work is a publication of CarTech, Inc., and has not been licensed, approved, sponsored, or endorsed by any other person or entity. The Publisher is not associated with any product, service, or vendor mentioned in this book, and does not endorse the products or services of any vendor mentioned in this book.

Edit by Wes Eisenschenk
Layout by Monica Seiberlich

ISBN 978-1-61325-348-9
Item No. CT600

Library of Congress Cataloging-in-Publication Data
LC record available at: https://lccn.loc.gov/2017010576

Written, edited, designed, and printed in the U.S.A.
10 9 8 7 6 5 4 3 2 1

CONTENTS

Acknowledgments 7
Introduction 9

Chapter 1: The Early Years 11
    World's Finest Speedway 12
    First Race, First Sellout 17
    Weekly Modified Showcase 22
    First Cackle 26
    Lorenzen Rises to the Top 28
    MovingM ountains 32
    Drawing Rave Reviews 38
    NASCAR Influences 44
    The Thrillo f Victory 48
    Ushering in Funny Cars 55
    Crowning the King 59
    Pearson Finds the Bristol Groove 60
    Turbulent, Tumultuous AHRA 65
    1970 Spring Nationals 71

Chapter 2: Racing into the 1970s 72
    Don Garlits: Big Daddy's Comeback 72
    Second Event, No Second Fiddle 75
    Bristol, the IHRA Flagship 79
    Junior Johnson: Dominance Defined 87
    Relief Is Where You Find It 92
    Financial S truggles 96
    Dale Earnhardt Sr.: The Breakthrough 97

Chapter 3: Taking Center Stage in the 1980s 101
    Bristol Has the Buck$ 102
    Darrell Waltrip: Seven, Here Comes Eleven 105
    Midwest ASA Magic 109
    Larry Flickinger: Fastest Ever 113
    Candies & Hughes: Cajun-Spiced Nitro 115
    Dale Pulde: War Eagle to Warrior 119
    Speedway Ownership Shuffle 122
    Rusty Wallace: My Favorite Track 124
    Top Sportsman Takes Over 127
    Mountain Motor Mastery 130

Chapter 4: Raising the Bar in the 1990s 135
    HomeC ooking 135
    Valleydale Meats 500 140
    Jim Ruth: *Party Time* 144
    Alan Kulwicki: Special K 147
    Mark Martin: The Stupidest Thing Ever 150
    Doug Herbert: DougZilla Reigns 151

Johnson and Hill: Pro Stock's Professors 155
Jeff Gordon: Rainbow Warrior 160
Building the New Bristol 164
John Force: Superman Wins Showdown 168
Terry Labonte: Rattle His Cage 171

Chapter 5: The 2000s and Beyond **175**
Dirt Weeks 175
Wood Brothers: A First 179
Dale Earnhardt Jr.: It's Bristol, Baby! 182
Busch Brothers: Snow Angels and Dominance 185
Johnson & Johnson: In Search of the Win 189
Matt Hagan: Hunting the Groove at Bristol 191
Fast Women 194
Kyle Busch: A Clean Sweep 204
World's Fastest Half-Mile 206
Rickie Smith: Tricky Rickie 208
Dustups and Nail-Biting Finishes 213

Appendix I **221**
Bristol Motor Speedway NASCAR Cup Series Winners 221
NASCAR Xfinity Series Winners 223
NASCAR Truck Series Winners 224

Appendix II **225**
Bristol Dragway National Event Winners 225

Index **229**

Frontispiece: *Dale Earnhardt Jr. celebrates in victory lane after winning the 2004 Sharpie 500. Asked why he was so excited, Earnhardt was the first to utter, "It's Bristol, baby!" The win came exactly five years after his father's final Bristol win. (Photo by David Crigger, Courtesy Bristol Herald Courier)*

Title Page: *Don Carlton won the 1973 Spring Nationals Pro Stock title in Ted Spehar's vaunted Mopar Missile Plymouth Duster. The victory was part of an amazing five-race IHRA win streak for the team. An MPC model kit of the car pictured it at Bristol. (Photo Courtesy John Beach)*

Back Cover Photos

Top: *Dale Earnhardt and Terry Labonte got together off the final corner of the final lap of Bristol's 1995 night race. But that time Labonte held on to take his battered, steaming Chevrolet to victory lane. He was less fortunate in the rematch. (Photo Courtesy Bristol Motor Speedway)*

Bottom: *Rows of dragster drivers wait their turn on the "hot car" fire-up road near the finish line at the 1965 Springnationals. In those days dragsters and many other faster class cars were push started up the racetrack then turned around to race down the quarter-mile. (Photo Courtesy Author Collection)*

Publisher's Note: *In reporting history, the images required to tell the tale will vary greatly in quality, especially by modern photographic standards. While some images in this volume are not up to those digital standards, we have included them, as we feel they are an important element in telling the story.*

ACKNOWLEDGMENTS

A book of this magnitude would have been impossible without the assistance of an incredible number of people as passionate about this subject as the author. A heartfelt thank you to the team at Bristol Motor Speedway and Dragway, especially Jerry Caldwell, Julie Bennett, Becky Cox, Anthony Vestal, Chris Lawyer, Ben Trout, Drew Beddard, Brandon Cross, Jack Cocklin, and Trey Hatcher for support and encouragement. It is an honor to work with you.

Thank you to CarTech editor Wes Eisenschenk, who cajoled me to tackle this project and refused to let me put it down. It was a challenging project but more than worth it.

I have extensive files on Bristol racing history and a library of racing books, but even that wasn't enough to accurately document every detail. Additional information was found and verified through multiple published sources, including *Bristol Herald Courier, Car Craft, Circle Track, Drag Racing, Drag Review, Hot Rod,* NASCAR annual yearbooks, *NASCAR Illustrated, NASCAR Scene, National Dragster, Speedway Illustrated, Stock Car Racing, Super Stock & Drag Illustrated,* and Greg Fielden's remarkable series *Forty Years of Stock Car Racing.*

A simple thank you cannot begin to cover all the stories, advice, encouragement, interviews, photographs, and other contributions provided by a host of people along my Bristol journey. For this I say thank you to David Allio; Gene, Alberta, and Chris Barker; Coy Bays; John Beach; Bobby Bennett; Steve Blevins; Brian and Lorie Bradley; Tommy Byrd; Mark Carrier; Shirley Carrier; David Crigger; Harold Denton; Charles Earhart; Phil Elliott; Greg Fielden; Larry Flickinger; John Force; Bob Frey; Dale Funk; Mark Garrow; Don Gillespie; Don Good; Allen Gregory; Van Greer; Chris Haverly; Debbie Helton; Robbie Henry; Drew Hierwarter; Roy Hill; Dave Huber; Allen Johnson; Lisa Johnson; Ted Jones; Richard Keesling; Winston Kelley; Bret Kepner; Brownie King; Mike Lester; Paul Lewis; Randy "Crusher" Lewis; Buz McKim; Joey Millard; Carl Moore; Randy Moore; Tony Morton; Earl Neikirk; Tom Netherland; Richard Petty; Bill Pratt; Wes Ramey; Doug Rice; Christine Riser; Bob Rogers; Curt and Sally Smith; Freddy Smith; Rickie Smith; Steve Smith; Geoff Stunkard; Tom Swabe; Andre Teague; the Tennessee State Library Archives; Joe Tennis; Kevin Triplett; Melanie Troxel; John A. Utsman; Darrell Waltrip; Red Whitmore; Deb Williams; and Lori Worley.

Websites I relied on and highly recommend include Bristolmotorspeedway.com, Competitionplus.com, Draglist.com, Hemmings.com, IHRA.com, NHRA.com, Racing reference.info, UltimateRacingHistory.com, vintage-nitro.com, and wediditforlove.com.

INTRODUCTION

Bristol Speedway and Dragway founders Larry Carrier and Carl Moore audaciously declared their rural racing complex, built on a former Appalachian dairy farm, as the "Racing Capital of the World" on a 40-foot-tall sign that greeted fans for the March 1965 Southeastern 500 NASCAR Grand National race. The new marquee also boasted an impressive row of symbols for sanctioning organizations: National Association for Stock Car Auto Racing (NASCAR), United States Auto Club (USAC), Fédération Internationale De L'Automobile (FIA), Sports Car Club of America (SCCA), and National Hot Rod Association (NHRA), which sanctioned a $1 million state-of-the-art dragstrip still under construction. A championship road course was on the drawing board but was never completed.

That spring, the NASCAR race was rained out for the first time in Bristol history. When fans returned in May, the sign had been conspicuously repainted to read "Action Center of the Racing World," after NASCAR founder Bill France demanded the change.

Racing capital of the world? Action center of the racing world? More than five decades later, both claims ring true. Both oval and dragstrip were established amid fanfare of being world class and have weathered waves of economic challenges to provide some of racing history's most defining moments. Racing fans from all 50

Erected prior to the 1965 season, this impressive track sign displayed several sanctioning-body symbols and claimed Bristol was the "Racing Capitol of the World." That wording changed almost immediately, at the insistence of NASCAR founder Bill France, to read "Action Center of the Racing World." (Photo Courtesy David McGee Collection)

states and around the globe have visited and continue to journey to this corner of East Tennessee, boasting countless memories from one track or both. The Bristol experience included a record string of 55 consecutive sold-out NASCAR Cup races from 1982 to 2009, extending across four different ownership groups and accompanied by persistent increases in seating capacity.

Today's Bristol Motor Speedway and Bristol Dragway rank among the world's premier motorsports venues due to the vision and Midas touch of Speedway Motorsports Executive Chairman O. Bruton Smith. After acquiring both facilities in 1996, Smith and his team embarked on massive reconstruction projects, establishing a bar few attempted to match. A manmade eighth wonder of the world, Bristol Motor Speedway is one of the world's 10 largest sports stadiums, with 160,000 seats and upper rings of nearly 200 suites rising 10 stories above the rolling countryside. Now billed as the "Last Great Colosseum," it is large enough that Neyland Stadium, the 102,000-seat home of the University of Tennessee football program, could easily fit inside.

NHRA founder Wally Parks described the original Bristol Dragway as the "world's most beautiful drag racing facility." Its modern incarnation continues to blend the amphitheater atmosphere with modern amenities amid a serene mountain setting that instantly transforms into the world's largest surround-sound system when a pair of nitro cars reach full song.

Parks is credited with coining the term "Thunder Valley" for the dragstrip, but that moniker is often applied to the entire complex, which is set in a quaint community of less than 45,000 residents that straddles the border of Tennessee and Virginia. It is smaller than either of its Tri-City brethren, Kingsport and Johnson City, which combined scarcely crack the nation's top 100 media markets.

How does this modest area boast two of the world's great cathedrals of speed? Through the steely determination of a series of visionary owners, great timing, a dash of luck, and a certain magic found only in the mountains. Bruton Smith has often said that he could build Bristol's facility anywhere, but it is the host region that cannot be duplicated.

CHAPTER 1

Fred Lorenzen waves to the crowd after winning the 1964 Southeastern 500. It was his second-straight victory at the Bristol oval and he was the first driver to score multiple wins there. Beauty queens surround Lorenzen, including Miss Bristol Phyllis Shipley (third from left) and Miss Firebird Linda Vaughn (right). (Photo Courtesy Bristol Motor Speedway)

THE EARLY YEARS

Auto racing's popularity grew by leaps and bounds in the 1960s as new ovals and dragstrips opened across the United States. The modest East Tennessee community of Bristol garnered national headlines with its 1961 unveiling of a gleaming new oval track (featuring two annual NASCAR race dates) followed in 1965 by a dragstrip that was home to a new NHRA national event. Both facilities were constructed amid unique circumstances to meet seemingly impossible deadlines yet delivered copious action for patrons.

World's Finest Speedway

Just three races remained in the 1960 National Association of Stock Car Automobile Racing (NASCAR) Grand National season when the circuit made its second appearance at the new Charlotte Motor Speedway. Rex White had all but wrapped up the points championship before the green flag waved over that weekend's National 400. Good thing, since track officials threatened to reject White's entry after he criticized the track surface following a prerace practice session.

Controversy was no stranger to Charlotte founders O. Bruton Smith and Curtis Turner, whose grand-opening World 600 was delayed from May to mid-June because the landmark 1.5-mile track wasn't completed. Some parts of the track surface broke apart during practice, but repairs were completed and the race went to its advertised distance.

A Seed Planted

Despite those controversies, or perhaps because of them, some 29,000 fans filed into Charlotte's grandstands that October Sunday afternoon to watch a 50-car field battle it out. Among the spectators were Larry Carrier and Carl Moore, two East Tennessee entrepreneurs from Bristol. A homebuilder and bowling alley operator, Carrier had attended the previous day's practice and was witnessing his first NASCAR race. His attention was drawn to how many people enthusiastically spent their hard-earned money to watch cars race in circles.

Carrier's hometown was surrounded by cramped, little dirt-oval tracks where daredevils in souped-up cars regularly crashed into each other while small clumps of people looked on from sagging wooden grandstands. The magnificent Charlotte facility was a sight to behold, with rows of spectators filling concrete grandstands that extended the length of the frontstretch, with additional seating along the backstretch. Crisply painted lines separated three full lanes, making the asphalt racing surface resemble a high-speed highway.

Carrier was so impressed on Saturday night that he called Moore and convinced his friend to join him.

"I flew over to Charlotte the next day, and we sat in the stands and watched that race," Moore recalled. "It was a long race with plenty of crashes, and more than once I asked Larry if we could go. Larry kept saying no."

Blown tires and multicar wrecks sent one driver to the hospital and marked a contest where only half the field was running at the end. The pair was intrigued by the spectacle and, despite his protestations, Moore also recognized opportunity. After returning home, they met for dinner at the former Bennie's Drive-In Restaurant and agreed to give motorsports a whirl.

"We thought it would be a good venture," Moore recalled in an interview decades later, "but only if we could get NASCAR to come."

Meeting "Big Bill"

Armed with enthusiasm but lacking money, land, and motorsports experience, they secured an appointment to meet with NASCAR founder and president William H. G. "Big Bill" France at his Daytona Beach, Florida, office.

"We got in to see Bill France," Moore recalled. "We talked, and he sent us to talk to Pat Purcell, who was his executive manager. He was a carnie, an old carnival promoter. I didn't smoke, but we went to dinner and smoked an old, green cigar and had drinks. Well, Pat said he believed we could build a track. We go back the next day and Pat said, 'If you guys are crazy enough to build a racetrack in the East Tennessee hills, what dates do you want?' Just like that! We picked our own dates out and it didn't cost us a penny. Today those dates would cost you $100 million apiece if you could get them. But he just asked us, so we picked July 30 and October 22."

Jubilation was soon tempered by the reality that they had less than nine months to find a site, arrange financing, construct a racetrack, and promote their first event.

"We wanted to build something smaller than Charlotte but bigger than a half-mile, maybe three-quarters of a mile or up to a mile in length," Moore said. It was one of their selling points to France, as 30 of the 44 races on NASCAR's 1960 schedule were run on tracks less than a mile in length. Eighteen were half-mile ovals, and nearly all of them sported a dirt surface.

Finding a Site

"Larry's dad was in real estate and he found us some land in Piney Flats, halfway between Bristol and Johnson City. We really liked it and took an option on it, but a couple of local preachers wanted to stop it. So we had a meeting to listen to what the community had to say," Moore recalled. "Most everybody there was for us, but there were two preachers who didn't like it. They thought racing would bring in all kinds of undesirable elements, drinking and gambling and loose women, so we decided if Piney Flats didn't want us, we'd go someplace else."

It was November 1960, and NASCAR's 1961 season had already started. Local NASCAR driver Paul Lewis suggested they consider land near the Johnson City,

After struggling to find a location, Larry Carrier and Carl Moore decided to build their NASCAR-sanctioned half-mile speedway on a 100-acre former dairy farm located about 5 miles south of Bristol, Tennessee. They announced the project and began construction in January 1961. (Photo Courtesy Bristol Motor Speedway)

Tennessee, airport, but city fathers were also unimpressed with the prospects of a rowdy, raucous race crowd coming to their community. Soon after, Carrier's father found a 100-acre dairy farm a few miles southeast of Bristol that owner Winnie Carter was ready to sell.

Finding Money

"We figured it would take $600,000 to buy the land and build the track," Moore said. "But we didn't have any money, and nobody would talk to us. It was my job to get the money, but we went to every bank around and couldn't even get a seat to sit down."

Growing desperate, they contacted Bill France, who suggested they speak with the Berlo Vending Company, a concessionaire for professional sports stadiums and drive-in movie theaters. Carrier and Moore traveled to New Jersey to present their plans.

"The guy asked us how much we needed, and we said $600,000. He said he would loan it to us, but the interest rate at that time was 5 percent, and he would charge us 10 percent. And we had to give him the concession rights for 15 years," Moore said. "We didn't have any choice. We had to do it."

With the property secured, Carrier, Moore, and their new partner, construction company owner R. G. Pope, began designing their track on paper napkins, quickly realizing that the nearly one-mile track they'd envisioned wouldn't fit on their land,

By February 1961, speedway partner R. G. Pope's construction crews were carving the hillside to form the frontstretch grandstands. Work continued at a breakneck pace to get the facility ready for its first Grand National race that July. (John Beach Photo)

which was bound on three sides by a creek, with a highway along its northern border and two steep hills in the middle. What it would hold was a half-mile oval.

"It was all we could build," Moore said. "It was all we had room for, with the creek and the highway. But it worked out pretty good because we could cut the concrete stands into those hills."

Architect Gene Rawls ultimately translated their ideas into formal designs that were unveiled to the public and Bristol-area news media on January 17, 1961.

Building the Track

Construction began on January 27, 1961, a month before the Daytona 500 and just 184 days prior to Bristol's first scheduled race. After visiting other short tracks in Martinsville, Virginia, and Asheville, North Carolina, the partners agreed that Bristol's paved surface should feature banked corners and wide straightaways for an exciting show. Concrete walls would run along the frontstretch and backstretch beneath some 18,000 grandstand seats to improve spectator safety and create a walkway, much like the Charlotte track. Seats would be terraced into the facing hillsides, and fans would have ample concession and restroom facilities, paved walkways, and onsite parking near the highway and in the meadow between the creek and frontstretch grandstands.

Workers moved more than three-quarters of a million yards of dirt to create the speedway. They used dirt and rock from the top of one hill to form the base of the banked turns and to fill in parking areas.

In June, as NASCAR scorched across the Carolinas, Pope's crews poured Bristol's asphalt racing surface, a process that included chaining the heavy paving machine and roller to a tractor to keep it from toppling over on the 22-degree banked turns. Poured atop a 6-inch rock base, the asphalt varied from 8 inches to 3 feet deep.

Ticket brochures for the inaugural Volunteer 500 touted Bristol International Speedway as the "finest track in the world" and "the world's fastest high-banked half-mile track." Inside, the brochure declared, "All roads will lead to the Bristol International Speedway on Saturday, July 29, for time trials and Sunday, July 30, for the first annual Volunteer 500. Your racing year will not be complete if you don't make it."

Carrier and Moore didn't deliver the one-mile track they'd envisioned, but NASCAR still found a home on their sparkling new half-mile oval, which has hosted the premier series twice annually and virtually all of its other series in the decades since.

After crews had prepared the track's foundation, they poured the layers of asphalt that would comprise the original half-mile racing surface. Plans originally banked Bristol's turns at 22 degrees; the signature high-banked turns didn't arrive until 1969. (Photo Courtesy Bristol Motor Speedway)

Former Tennessee governor Buford Ellington (seated) signed a proclamation for Bristol Speedway's first race in 1961, making it Volunteer 500 Auto Racing Week in the state. Left to right are Bristol founding partners R. G. Pope, Larry Carrier, and Carl Moore. (Photo Courtesy Bristol Motor Speedway)

First Race, First Sellout

As work wrapped up and bills mounted for the new Bristol International Speedway, promoters Larry Carrier and Carl Moore placed a new goal at the top of their to-do list: sell out the tickets for their first race. As an added incentive, NASCAR executive Pat Purcell bet track manager Hal Hamrick a new cowboy hat that they couldn't, and wouldn't, reach that goal.

"We sold some advance tickets, but we didn't come close to selling out," Moore reflected. "So before the race, we went out and started giving tickets away. We figured it was better to get people in and fill up those grandstands, and maybe they would come back to the next race and buy a ticket. Well, I guess everybody waited until the morning of the race. Men came in their suits and women in their nice dresses, and we had all these people waiting in line to buy tickets."

Fans from 26 states and Canada snarled the region's mostly winding two-lane roadways for miles in every direction, overwhelmed the speedway's parking areas, and filled adjoining fields the morning of that first race. Some eager fans were in their seats by 7 a.m.; others struggled to make it before the green flag flew at 1:30 p.m. The official NASCAR race report claims 24,000 people attended the inaugural Volunteer 500; photographs show full grandstands, with people clinging to fences, clustered on still-grassless hillsides around the track, and even climbing trees for a better vantage point.

A newspaper advertisement promotes the all-new Bristol Speedway's inaugural Volunteer 500 race in July 1961, featuring eventual winner Jack Smith and other stars of the era. Reserved seat tickets cost $6, $7, and $8. (Photo Courtesy Author Collection)

Chapter 1: The Early Years   17

Aerial Seats

A handful of lucky fans received a unique perspective of the sold-out show courtesy of an East Tennessee helicopter company that provided brief flights above the track.

This vintage patch marked the creation of Bristol International Speedway, annual home of two NASCAR premier series races since opening in 1961. (Photo Courtesy Carl Moore)

Forty-two cars raced around the gleaming new Bristol Speedway during the inaugural 1961 Volunteer 500. In the center of the new track's infield was a football field where an NFL exhibition game occurred later that year. (Photo Courtesy Carl Moore)

Among that crowd was 21-year-old Fred Hayter, a Bristol resident who'd regularly driven by to monitor track construction. He and his father paid $8 each for tickets to their first race. "We bought our ticket the day of the race and got a top-row seat," Hayter recalled decades later. "It was really amazing, watching all those cars go around a little half-mile track."

He also clearly recalled the post-race traffic jam, noting that it took three hours to exit the parking lot, as fans who had parked in the meadow behind the frontstretch grandstands attempted to leave.

Bristol attracted large crowds all three days of its opening weekend. Despite intermittent showers, about 11,000 people attended Friday afternoon's qualifying session, where Fred Lorenzen grabbed the first pole with a lap of 22.72 seconds at 79.225 mph (22.72/79.225).

Drivers were effusive in their praise.

"I've been in racing 15 years, and I've never been treated as nice anywhere," two-time NASCAR champion Buck Baker told sportswriters. "This is a great layout. I know the track is new, but so what? I don't find it any rougher than some others I've been on, and these people are going to make it better. These people are hungry for racing. It will be a real pleasure to drive for them. And the rain didn't chase the fans. Some of them didn't even leave their seats. Yes, sir, this Bristol track is going to be a real good one."

On Saturday night, an estimated 8,000 people filled the frontstretch stands to watch Rebecca Lee Barnett emerge from a field of 38 contestants to win the first Miss Volunteer 500 beauty pageant, with Martinsville Speedway Promoter H. Clay Earles and Darlington Raceway promoter Bob Colvin among the judges. The program included a concert by 17-year-old rockabilly music sensation Brenda Lee and The Casuals and concluded with fireworks.

The Starting Field

The rumble of the 42-car field replaced the final strains of "The Star-Spangled Banner" on Sunday as Lorenzen's Ford and Junior Johnson's Pontiac led the way to the green flag. David Pearson, Richard Petty, Buck Baker, 1960 champion Rex White, DeWayne "Tiny" Lund, points leader Ned Jarrett, Tommy Irwin, and Bob Welborn rounded out the first 10 starting spots.

Sprinkled throughout the field were fan favorites Glenn "Fireball" Roberts, Joe Weatherly, Buddy Baker, Everett "Cotton" Owens, Jim Paschal, Wendell Scott, Nelson Stacy (driving a Ford owned by Bristol car dealer Ron Henard), and many East

A sellout crowd looks on as David Pearson (No. 3) and Richard Petty (No. 43) race off the backstretch pit road during the inaugural Volunteer 500. Petty finished 4th in Bristol's first race; Pearson finished 30th. (John Beach Photo)

With a sellout crowd looking on, relief driver Johnny Allen wheeled Jack Smith's Pontiac to the checkered flag in Bristol's inaugural Volunteer 500 NASCAR premier series race. Allen jumped in during a pit stop on lap 290 after Smith sustained burns on his feet. (Photo Courtesy Bristol Motor Speedway)

Tennessee drivers, including Paul Lewis, Bill Morton, George Green, Herman Beam, and three members of the Utsman family, Dub, Layman, and Sherman.

Public-address announcers Bob Montgomery, Chris Economacki, and Barney Hall kept fans at the track updated on the action, although Hayter recalls that it was difficult to hear them unless a caution flag slowed the race. In addition, a track-organized network of radio stations, with a separate team of announcers that included Earl Kelley of Charlotte, North Carolina, broadcast the event to listeners in a dozen states.

Racing Action

The hard-charging Johnson led the first 124 laps but was temporarily forced to the pits after a hard crash with Joe Weatherly and Tiny Lund peeled away his driver's door. Johnson soldiered on and later recaptured the lead. Welborn inherited the point from Johnson and led 26 circuits before Jack Smith took over the top spot for 10 laps. Richard Petty, whose father, Lee, was still recovering from a serious Daytona 500 crash, led briefly, but Johnson stormed past to lead lap 180 before eventually falling out with mechanical issues.

Two Winners, One Car

Jack Smith passed Rex White for the lead just past the race's midway point and quickly built a three-lap cushion over 2nd place. Heat was coming through his Pontiac's floor and burning his right foot. A pioneer in two-way communication, Smith radioed his crew to request a replacement; veteran Johnny Allen, who dropped out with mechanical issues, was standing by when Smith pitted on lap 290.

"I'd driven his car before at Darlington, and we'd raced together," Allen said years later. "He had led a couple of laps or so when I jumped in the car, and I was still in the lead when I got back on the track. I was able to maintain it for the rest of the race."

Despite a broken sway bar, Allen built the margin to six laps over 2nd-place Fireball Roberts. It shrank to two laps during a pit stop on lap 419, but Allen finished two laps and 22 seconds in front of Roberts, driving a Pontiac prepared by Smokey Yunick. Ned Jarrett ran 3rd and extended his points lead over Rex White, who blew an engine and was relegated to 25th. Richard Petty, Buddy Baker, Joe Weatherly, Emanuel Zervakis, Jim Paschal, Sherman Utsman, and Tiny Lund rounded out the top 10 finishers. Less than half the field was running at the finish.

After the race, both Allen and Smith climbed onto the hood of the still-steaming Pontiac to accept the winner's trophy, kisses from the beauty queens, a wreath of flowers, and a handshake from a beaming Carrier.

Race winner Jack Smith (right) and relief driver Johnny Allen celebrate in Victory Lane after claiming the Volunteer 500 trophies and a $3,025 payoff. The winning duo finished two laps ahead of 2nd-place winner Fireball Roberts. (Photo Courtesy Bristol Motor Speedway)

Weekly Modified Showcase

One week after the NASCAR Grand National Series moved on from Bristol's inaugural Volunteer 500, track owners Larry Carrier and Carl Moore reopened the gates to welcome the machines of NASCAR's Modified and Sportsman divisions and a crowd of 8,000 to watch them.

Bristol only operated a weekly program for less than 2½ seasons, but the races often attracted some of the country's biggest names, including Ralph Earnhardt, the 1956 NASCAR national Sportsman champion; Virginia's Eddie Crouse, who finished 3rd in the 1961 national points and won the 1962 Modified championship; Glen Wood; G. C. Spencer; Joe Lee Johnson; and Tiny Lund, a transplanted Iowan who relocated to South Carolina and later won the 1963 Daytona 500.

A field of NASCAR Modified coupes and Sportsman cars race into Turn 1 at Bristol during the 1961 season. Bristol hosted regular weekly races featuring the two divisions during its first two years of operation and attracted many of the nation's top drivers. (Photo Courtesy Tony Morton)

NASCAR's newest track scheduled eight weeks of competition in 1961. Modified-division cars typically featured 1930s-era coupe bodies and were allowed more engine modifications; the Sportsman cars were mostly based on 1950s-era cars and were restricted to a single carburetor. Both divisions ran together on the track, and both awarded points based on finishing position. Best of all, Bristol offered guaranteed payouts, while many area promoters paid a percentage of the gate receipts, a number that was often in dispute.

Paul Radford Owns Bristol, Kinda

The field for the first weekly show on August 5, 1961, included Jimmy Thompson of Monroe, North Carolina, the winner of that season's Daytona Modified race, and a host of drivers from Tennessee, Virginia, North Carolina, and West Virginia. Paul Radford of Ferrum, Virginia, wheeled his 1937 Ford to victory in the 100-lap feature race. Radford took the lead on the opening lap and held off Grand National driver George Green of Johnson City, Tennessee. Sherman Utsman of Bluff City, Tennessee, fresh off a 9th-place finish in the Volunteer 500, steered a 1955 Ford to 3rd place. Radford and Utsman won the 15-lap heat races; Grand National Series regular Bill Morton of Church Hill, Tennessee, was the fastest qualifier, with a lap of 73.17 mph.

Radford swept the second weekend, setting fast time and winning his heat race and the 100-lap feature in his 1937 Ford. Charlie Williamson of Roanoke, Virginia, finished 2nd but returned to win week three, steering his 1937 Ford Modified to a $500 victory over Radford and eventual Bristol and Tennessee state champion Earl Hatcher of Mount Airy, North Carolina.

Football at Bristol

Racing took a back seat to football that Labor Day weekend, as the speedway hosted a National Football League preseason game between the Washington Redskins and the Philadelphia Eagles. The Eagles won, 17 to 10.

When racers returned, North Carolinian Perk Brown and Bill Morton collected victories.

On October 6, Sherman Utsman appeared to have the field covered by leading the race's first 99 circuits, but his Ford experienced tire trouble on the white-flag lap. Perk Brown squeezed by for the win, with Utsman hanging on to finish 2nd.

Bill Morton claimed the track's first Modified championship; Earl Hatcher won the Sportsman title over George Green.

Driver Bill Morton (right) celebrated winning his second-straight Bristol Speedway Modified track title in 1962 with car owner Jimmy Dishner. Morton was also a regular in NASCAR's premier series during the late 1950s and early 1960s. (Photo Courtesy Tony Morton)

Southeastern Championship Modified Race

Bristol hosted the 200-lap Southeastern Championship Modified race on the evening of Saturday, October 21, as a companion to its Southeastern 500 Grand National race. A sizable $5,700 payout attracted 67 cars and prompted promoter Larry Carrier to increase the field size from 25 to 40 cars.

After rain delayed qualifying, Charles "Red" Farmer shattered the track's Modified track qualifying record by 6 mph, putting his 1934 Chevrolet on the pole with an 88-mph lap that edged Bobby Allison by .04 second. The field also included eventual national champion Johnny Roberts of Baltimore, Maryland; Tennessee stars Friday Hassler, Clifton "Coo" Marlin, Malcolm Brady, and Bob Reuther; North Carolina's Bobby Isaac and Ralph Earnhardt; and Connecticut's Eddie Flemke.

Once the green flag flew, Farmer and Allison established a blistering pace, lapping the remainder of the field by lap 70 and trading the lead three times before Farmer asserted control on lap 120. He finished eight laps ahead of Allison's Chevrolet as a crowd of 9,000 looked on. Farmer pocketed $1,000 for the victory with a $50 bonus for the pole; Allison earned $725.

Charles "Red" Farmer poses beside his F-97 coupe after dominating a 200-lap NASCAR Modified race at Bristol in October 1961. Farmer bested traveling mate Bobby Allison by six laps. (Photo Courtesy Bristol Motor Speedway)

Weekly Racing Resumes in 1962

Bristol scheduled nine races for the Modified and Sportsman classes for the 1962 season, including some on Sunday afternoons. Joe Bill Adams of Mount Airy, North Carolina, was that season's biggest winner, claiming two straight races in July and two more in August. His victories included a 100-lap feature run caution free. Despite that success, Adams wound up seventh in the track's final Modified standings.

Bill Morton claimed his second Modified title by finishing 2nd to Adams in the last race of the season. Grand National regulars Nelson Stacy and Junior Johnson also competed occasionally during Bristol's weekly shows, and Bobby Isaac picked up one victory in weekly action.

Former NASCAR Grand National and Convertible series regular Herman "Brownie" King of Johnson City, Tennessee, drove a Ford to the Sportsman title and the overall track championship.

1962 Modified Championship 400

Bristol's Grand National schedule shifted to March and July in 1962, so the track's Modified championship became a standalone race on Sunday, September 9, and expanded to include another 200-lapper for NASCAR's short-lived Modified Special cars.

Defending race winner Red Farmer entered both contests but was unable to repeat. Bristol regular Joe Bill Adams set the quick time during Modified qualifying but spent most of the race chasing Grand National driver Johnny Allen at the front of the 33-car field. With 11 laps remaining and sporting a huge lead, Allen crashed while passing a slower car. Adams took over and captured the victory. Sportsman cars ran in the race, as well, with Brownie King finishing first in that division.

Friday Hassler of Chattanooga, Tennessee, set a new track record of 86.12 mph for the Modified Specials and appeared to have that race well in hand before a pit accident. The rear of Hassler's Chevrolet caught fire during a pit stop, and two crewmembers sustained burns attempting to extinguish the blaze.

Farmer took the lead on the restart, but mechanical problems sidelined his Chevrolet. Malcolm Brady of Columbia, Tennessee, inherited the lead on lap 167 and held on to claim the checkered flag.

1963 Modified and Sportsman Races

Bristol opened the 1963 season with a return of its Modified and Sportsman classes, plus NASCAR's new Hobby division. Pee Wee Griffin of Miami, Florida, captured the Modified feature, inheriting the lead when Paul Radford's car

Former NASCAR Grand National and Convertible Series regular Brownie King shows off the trophies he won as Bristol's 1962 champion while surrounded by photos of his remarkable racing career. (Earl Neikirk Photo, Courtesy Bristol Herald Courier*)*

suffered a blown head gasket. North Carolina's Jim Freeman won Bristol's first Hobby feature.

Ken Rush of High Point, North Carolina, started on the pole and dominated the 50-lap May 18 Modified feature before a crowd of 2,500. Bristol's weekly racing program then ended abruptly and never returned. Track manager Hal Hamrick announced that it would be suspended until at least July 28 so that officials could complete a series of track improvements; however, the program never resumed.

First Cackle

Thirty-eight stock cars comprised the field of Bristol's second Grand National race, the 1961 Southeastern 500, but early arriving fans noticed 40 cars on the grid that race morning, and two of them certainly didn't fit in.

One, aptly named *Mad Dog IV,* was a Frankensteinish cross between an airplane and an Indianapolis speedway roadster, with stubby wings on either side of the driver's compartment and an airplane-style tail stabilizer. Its white, hand-formed body began as a Kurtis Kraft open-wheel racer, but jutting from its hood was the supercharger atop a 450-ci Chrysler engine producing 800 hp on methanol fuel, a hefty load for its 100-inch wheelbase and hard-sidewall 3.5-inch-wide Firestone tires.

The bizarre machine was the creation of Bob Osiecki, a NASCAR car builder and owner with the distinction of being among some 40 people in the room at Daytona's Streamline Motel in December 1947 when Bill France organized what we now know as NASCAR. Osiecki created *Mad Dog IV* expressly to win the $10,000 that France posted for the first car to exceed 180 mph at his Daytona International Speedway.

Bob Osiecki (standing, left) helps push driver Art Malone's Golden Rod *Top Fuel dragster onto Bristol Speedway's pit road. No duck out of water, Malone entertained oval-track fans prior to the 1961 Southeastern 500. (Photo Courtesy Bristol Motor Speedway)*

Nearby was another supercharged machine, the *Golden Rod* Top Fuel dragster of Florida's Art Malone. Its 392-ci Chrysler Hemi engine produced more than 1,000 hp and sat inches in front of the driver's compartment that was Malone's office on race days. The handcrafted machine was capable of speeds nearing 200 mph on a dragstrip, only there wasn't one around for miles.

Bristol's promoters brought *Mad Dog IV*, Malone, and Osiecki to Bristol, expecting them to establish a new closed-course world record for a half-mile track, just as they had a few months before, when Malone piloted the machine to a lap of 181.561 mph around the Daytona track. After claiming that honor, the duo began cashing in on the attention by making appearances and displaying the unique craft, which prompted a phone call from Tennessee.

Newspaper ads leading up to the race promised that fans would see history made. Photographs of Malone and the car appeared in the souvenir program above the words, "The car that holds the world record for a closed racetrack is slated to appear at Bristol International Speedway in quest of a new record for a half-mile track."

A front-page story in the *Bristol Herald Courier* the morning of the race claimed that Malone would kick off prerace festivities at noon by hotlapping *Mad Dog IV*, which typically lived up to its name and was nearly impossible to steer when its substantial power and light weight overwhelmed its tires. During Malone's Daytona thrill ride, the stubby machine regularly spun out on the corner exit.

Bristol's course was much narrower and more confined than Daytona, offering no margin for error. A spin at Bristol would almost certainly send the car careening into the concrete walls or shiny new steel guardrails, either of which could easily have dislodged one of the wings mounted next to the driver and potentially decapitated Malone.

Art Malone blasts down Bristol Speedway's front straightaway with his dragster's tires boiling smoke in a demonstration run that gave many NASCAR fans their first taste of a nitromethane-fueled dragster. (Photo Courtesy Author Collection)

Common sense ultimately prevailed, and Malone and Osiecki merely displayed the one-of-a-kind car during prerace festivities. To appease the promoter, they unloaded Malone's dragster and agreed to serve the fans a prerace nitromethane cocktail.

First Burnouts at Bristol

Osiecki pushed *Golden Rod* onto pit road as Malone donned his fire-retardant uniform and helmet and then push-started the dragster until its Hemi engine belched to life. Malone then pulled onto the racing surface, stopped momentarily at the exit of Turn 4 as if staging for a drag race, and unleashed the monster. Its rear M&H Racemaster tires struggled for traction, spewing thick trails of white smoke as the car rocketed down the 650-foot-long front straightaway. Malone lifted well past the start-finish line and coasted onto the apron of Turn 1.

Their Top Fuel virginity lost, the large crowd cheered boisterously.

The ultimate credit for Bristol's original dragstrip goes to the visionary men willing to take a massive gamble: speedway owners Larry Carrier and Carl Moore and NHRA founder and president Wally Parks, who, like stock car racing patriarch Bill France Sr. before him, scheduled a race before the first blade of grass was disturbed.

Give a nod also to Malone and Osiecki. On a sunny October afternoon in East Tennessee, where Joe Weatherly grabbed the headlines accompanying victory, they briefly entertained fans and gave two aggressive promoters another opportunity to ponder.

Lorenzen Rises to the Top

Blown engines and tires, spectacular crashes, and feuds between superstar teammates punctuated a dramatic three seasons in which Fred Lorenzen emerged as Bristol's first dominant driver.

Fred Lorenzen looks on as a Holman-Moody crewmember works inside his No. 28 Ford. Lorenzen was the first driver to sweep both Bristol races in a single season, claiming both checkered flags in 1964. (Photo Courtesy Bristol Motor Speedway)

Fred Lorenzen (No. 28) chases Tiny Lund (No. 21) during Bristol's 1963 Southeastern 500. Lund fell out with a blown engine in the Wood Brothers Ford, and Lorenzen narrowly lost a controversial finish to Holman-Moody teammate Fireball Roberts. (John Beach Photo)

The Illinois native known as NASCAR's "Golden Boy" won the pole for Bristol's inaugural Volunteer 500 but suffered mechanical failure after 175 laps. Engine problems negated his 1962 Volunteer 500 run, after qualifying second fastest. Lorenzen truly flexed his muscles at the 1962 Southeastern 500, qualifying 4th, leading 117 laps, and rubbing fenders with Richard Petty and Jim Paschal for the top spot. Paschal eventually passed Lorenzen with 26 laps remaining and held on for his first win in his first start for Petty Enterprises. Lorenzen finished 2nd amid a shower of sparks, after his Holman-Moody Ford pitched a wheel on the final lap.

In 1963, Bristol switched the names of its races, moving the Southeastern 500 to March and running the Volunteer 500 in July, but this time it was Lorenzen who arrived with a new teammate and in search of better luck. Car owner John Holman had lured Fireball Roberts away from Pontiac, and his first start came in the Southeastern 500. Roberts responded by qualifying third fastest, trailing pole winner Lorenzen and Daytona 500 winner Tiny Lund aboard the Wood Brothers Ford.

Lorenzen wrestled the lead from his teammate on lap 328 and appeared headed for his second win of the 1963 season when his white and blue No. 28 Ford sputtered, out of gas with eight laps remaining. Lorenzen headed to pit road for a splash of fuel but could only draw within 5 seconds of the top spot before the checkered flag fell on Roberts, who ran out of fuel crossing the start-finish line. Lorenzen later fumed to the press, claiming he got 25 fewer miles on his final fuel run, sparking speculation that his crew put less gas in the tank to help Roberts win.

Lorenzen Captures His First Bristol Crown

The fortunes of the two Ford stars were reversed when the series returned to Bristol in July, as Lorenzen became the first driver to win Bristol from the pole. Lorenzen, second qualifier Roberts, and Junior Johnson all broke Roberts's previous track record, but Roberts claimed the times were bogus. Asked how soon Lorenzen's new 82.229-mph record might be broken, Roberts said, "Hell, it will take 30 years to go that fast." Later that weekend Lorenzen agreed, claiming all three cars were likely slower than their official times.

In the race, Roberts made a dramatic exit on lap 312 when his lavender Ford slammed the wall between Turn 1 and Turn 2, flipped end over end multiple times, and skidded on its top before landing on its wheels. He suffered a minor back injury. After the caution, Richard Petty took the top spot, but Lorenzen passed him and rode the upper groove to victory, finishing 3 seconds ahead of Petty.

"By going high, I could really get going while coming down the inclines. I really got up a head of steam down the straightaways," Lorenzen told the media. He led four times for 336 laps, and his $4,590 payday became part of NASCAR's first-ever season where one driver's winnings topped $100,000.

Back-to-Back

The following spring, Lorenzen became the first driver to win Bristol back-to-back, posting his first victory of the 1964 season in a chilly Southeastern 500, although he nearly didn't finish. After qualifying second, Lorenzen took the lead on lap 6 and led the final 494 laps. The 427-ci engine in his Holman-Moody Ford dropped a cylinder with 30 laps remaining. That allowed 2nd-place teammate Fireball Roberts to erase most of a 5-lap lead before Lorenzen sputtered beneath the checkered flag at 50 mph, with Roberts a half lap behind.

"I had to really back off. My car's engine was turning only about 4,000 rpm for the last 15 miles. Every time I gunned the engine, the car would slow down and

Fred Lorenzen poses beside his iconic Holman-Moody Ford. The NASCAR Hall of Fame driver won the pole position at Bristol's first two races and became the first driver to win two and three consecutive times at Bristol. (Photo Courtesy Bristol Motor Speedway)

sputter," Lorenzen told reporters after the race. "I thought for a while I had lost a horseshoe."

Three Consecutive

An engine failure also played a role in the 1964 Volunteer 500, but this time Lorenzen was the beneficiary. Lorenzen claimed his third consecutive Bristol victory by leading just the final circuit after Richard Petty's engine expired. It was a star-crossed weekend for Lorenzen, who was making his first series start in three weeks after suffering an injured wrist in a qualifying crash for Daytona's Firecracker 400. At Bristol, he was the last car on the track for qualifying and a favorite for another pole, but the rear of his Ford stepped out exiting Turn 4, forcing him to lift and relegating him to an 8th-place starting spot.

Richard Petty earned the pole by breaking Lorenzen's track record. He dominated the race, leading twice for 442 laps and holding a 3-lap lead over Lorenzen, when his Hemi engine erupted in smoke with 4 laps remaining. Petty circled the track until the 499th lap, but the car finally coasted to a stop. Lorenzen, who needed midrace relief help from Ned Jarrett, claimed the victory; Petty took 2nd place.

Lorenzen's remarkable Bristol winning streak ended early in the rain-delayed 1965 Southeastern 500, but he received a consolation prize by helping fellow Ford pilot Junior Johnson score his lone Bristol win as a driver.

Almost Four in a Row

With the race rained out from its originally scheduled March date, NASCAR's stars returned May 2. Marvin Panch grabbed the pole in the Wood Brothers Ford, and Lorenzen started on the outside of the front row. Lorenzen's run ended when he slammed the wall trying to avoid a crash involving Paul Lewis, Tom Pistone, and

Panch. When race leader Johnson's team called for relief, Lorenzen climbed aboard his rival's yellow Ford on lap 213.

A green-flag pit stop to replace a flat tire left the Johnson/Lorenzen machine 1 lap down, but Junior climbed back aboard on lap 360 and chased down leaders Dick Hutcherson and Ned Jarrett, bumping fenders with Hutcherson to take the lead on lap 438. A late caution bunched the field and set up a 9-lap shootout among the three Ford pilots. Johnson edged Hutcherson by one car length at the stripe, with Jarrett glued to Hutcherson's rear bumper. Hutcherson and car owner Ralph Moody filed a protest that wasn't upheld. "I'll always think I won that race," Hutcherson said. "I'll accept the decision, although I don't agree with it."

Moving Mountains

Attendance at Bristol's oval-track races was solid, but other events, including an NFL exhibition football game, country music concerts, and other types of racing, all fell short at the turnstiles. When Larry Carrier and Carl Moore went searching for new worlds to conquer, organized drag racing got their attention.

At that time, drag racing's fastest cars were running 200 mph, and tracks were springing up across the country. The California-based National Hot Rod Association (NHRA) was the drag racing equivalent of NASCAR, sanctioning about 125 tracks and hosting two major events annually. There were plenty of options. The American Hot Rod Association (AHRA) was quickly gaining credibility, the United Drag Racers Association (UDRA) began staging events outside its Midwest base, and even NASCAR looked to get involved, ultimately forging a brief alliance with an East Coast group.

Dragstrip, Too?

Fascinated by speed, Carrier and Moore considered building a dragstrip adjacent to their Bristol Speedway. Not just any dragstrip, but one with fan amenities on par with the oval and superior to other facilities. They contacted the NHRA in October 1964, and President Wally Parks dispatched Buster Couch, NHRA's chief starter and the newly appointed Southeastern Division director, to visit Bristol and evaluate the proposal.

Couch was immediately impressed with the detailed plans for a spectacular facility on more than 100 acres across the creek from the oval track. A photograph of Couch, Carrier, and track manager Hal Hamrick examining those plans appeared in the sports section of the October 9, 1964, edition of the *Bristol Herald Courier* with the caption, "Speedway officials are considering construction of a dragstrip that *might* be

The men responsible for the original Bristol Dragway are (from left to right) NHRA president Wally Parks, NHRA's Buster Couch, Bristol Dragway owners Carl Moore and Larry Carrier, and manager Hal Hamrick. Carrier and Moore convinced Parks to gamble on a seemingly impossible project to establish NHRA's third major race, the Springnationals, in 1965. (Photo Courtesy Bristol Motor Speedway)

used for an NHRA national event. Carrier said construction of the track will depend on whether an NHRA national event can be scheduled for Bristol, adding there is a possibility the track might be built with an American Hot Rod Association sanction."

The plans were ambitious, and both sides knew Parks needed the facility to gain a foothold with eastern fans and racers, but Carrier dropped rival AHRA's name in the press to ensure he got what he wanted. As with the oval track, the timing was again ideal because Parks was already working to expand NHRA's 1965 national-event schedule, and an agreement was quickly reached.

NHRA Springnationals

In early December, Carrier, Moore, and Hamrick traveled to Detroit to meet with Parks, sign the contracts, and make the formal announcement. The banner headline of the December 18, 1964, edition of NHRA's *National Dragster* newspaper proclaimed, "Spring Nationals Set; Bristol Dragway Will Host."

"We plan to have the finest drag racing plant in the world," Carrier told the press. "Race fans have shown they want and expect the best when they come to Bristol, and that's what they will receive. The huge success and vote of confidence shown by the acceptance of the oval track and the growing need for more and better drag racing facilities were the deciding factors in going ahead with such a tremendous undertaking."

Facility Specs

The facility's dimensions were staggering. Located within a long valley, plans called for seating for 30,000 fans (a third more than the oval); a mile-long 60-foot-wide racing surface; staging lanes to accommodate at least 100 cars; and pit capacity for 1,500 racing machines and support vehicles. The track's signature element would be a spacious, four-story control tower a full decade ahead of its time. In an era when most tracks crammed officials into buildings resembling shacks on stilts with little to no provision for guests, sponsors, or the media, Bristol's tower would feature an expansive second-floor control room, ample space for the news media, a broadcast studio, offices, seating for dignitaries, and emergency medical facilities.

Turning those plans into reality would require a breakneck pace similar to the rapid construction of Bristol's oval track because only initial site work occurred prior to the December 7 announcement, and the Springnationals were then six months away.

"Bristol International Dragway plans may be greeted with doubt by skeptics, but Carrier and his crew have been doubted before," Parks said. "When the speedway plans were announced in early 1961, many people doubted that a modern racing plant could even be built in the area selected, let alone in the short period of time allotted for the project." Any reservations Parks had were never expressed publicly.

"The Springnationals will round out our national championship program and give drag racers both a geographical and calendar balance of competition," Parks said. "We intend to make the Springnationals one of the greatest drag races this or any other country has ever held."

Originally announced as a six-day event for May 11–16, all sides subsequently agreed that June 3–7 would give work crews the extra time needed to complete the daunting project. Longtime speedway employee Fred Markwalter often voiced amazement about the journey transforming the densely wooded valley into a world-class dragstrip.

Work crews spent weeks clearing a natural box valley adjacent to the speedway. Once they had the valley opened up, they terraced concrete seats into one hillside, much like at the oval track, and constructed the track's iconic four-story control tower. (Photo Courtesy Bristol Motor Speedway)

"Larry, Hal, and I came back in here about when it got cold. We had a couple axes, a shovel, a chain saw, an old Jeep, and a bucket truck. The first tree we cut down fell right on the Jeep," Markwalter laughed, recalling the incident years later.

Contract workers arrived in January 1965 and began removing hundreds of trees. They bulldozed and leveled the land, improved drainage to reroute a stream, and dealt with numerous natural springs. By the time the work was completed, they had moved 1.5 million tons of earth and granite. Work on the control tower started early in the process, and it was placed to face straight down the track. The topography forced some unique solutions, including a right-hand dogleg in the uphill shutdown area that became an integral component of Bristol's layout.

"When we got down to building the actual racing surface, the hills and creek got in the way, and we had to make changes. We tried to head the shutdown right up the hill but couldn't figure out a way to get the cars back down," Markwalter said. "The slight turn is more than a quarter mile past the finish line, and we figured it would be fine."

Concrete Grandstands

Borrowing from the oval-track design, workers terraced the dragstrip's hillside to accommodate row upon row of concrete grandstand seating. A series of black-and-white photographs touting the progress appeared that February in *National Dragster*. The track also featured another drag racing first, a concrete wall, designed to keep cars on the course and serve as extra protection for fans. The idea was straight from the Bristol oval, where a high concrete wall lined both the front and back straightaways and provided a spectator walkway.

This aerial view shows Bristol Dragway carved into the valley, with the NASCAR oval track visible in the background. Bristol Dragway provides one of the most iconic settings in all of motorsports. (Photo Courtesy Bristol Motor Speedway)

Racers planning to compete at Bristol likely choked when viewing another photograph in the *National Dragster* April 30 issue showing unfinished grandstands, work just beginning on the racing surface, and the control tower's shell in the background. Rumors flew that workers couldn't finish the track in time and that the event might be canceled or rescheduled. Workers toiled from daybreak to nightfall at an unrelenting pace without days off.

"Nationwide Field For Bristol; Strip Nears Completion," was the top headline in the May 14, 1965, edition of *National Dragster*.

The program cover for the inaugural 1965 Springnationals shows the landmark control tower and sign welcoming fans. Much like the speedway, construction of the drag racing facility had been hasty, with work completed just as the first event began. (Photo Courtesy David McGee Collection)

The story claimed the "super strip was rapidly nearing completion" and touted the $20,000 payout for the second "Triple Crown" race of the NHRA season.

"The night before we opened for the Springnationals, the Barker brothers were trying to finish paving everything. Well, they got into an argument about something and got in a fight right out there in the staging lanes," Carl Moore recalled years later. "They were so tired, they stopped fighting and just laid down and went to sleep right there."

Somehow they finished, but Top Fuel racing legend Conrad "Connie" Kalitta recalls seeing paving work still under way in the pit area as racers rolled in on opening day.

"The supreme being I believe in put mountains on this earth for man to move," Hamrick wrote in the 1965 Springnationals souvenir program. "When the Bristol International Dragway was first conceived in the minds of Larry Carrier, Carl Moore, and myself, most people thought that the sheer magnitude of a venture of this size in the hills of East Tennessee, in such a short period of time, was impossible. I must admit that there were plenty of times in the past six months that we felt the same way. It was night-and-day work. This country is great because men have moved mountains."

Rows of dragster drivers wait their turn on the "hot car" fire-up road near the finish line at the 1965 Springnationals. In those days, dragsters and many other faster-class cars were push-started up the racetrack, then turned around to race down the quarter-mile. (Photo Courtesy David McGee Collection)

Drawing Rave Reviews

From the tire-blazing national speed record established by Top Fuel runner-up Connie Kalitta and the first time the NHRA offered a separate national-event category for what eventually became Funny Cars to the massive crowds and rave reviews about the facility, Bristol's first drag race, the 1965 NHRA Springnationals, was a walk-off home run.

Journalists covering the event exhausted their supply of adjectives describing the grandeur. "Nestled amid the beautiful scenic wonderland of eastern Tennessee is the most magnificent drag racing plant in the United States, bar none," wrote *Drag Racing* magazine editor John Durbin. "In addition to the fine layout and abundant natural beauty furnished by the green hills are acoustics which defy description."

National Dragster associate editor Dan Roulston heaped on the praise, writing in NHRA's in-house publication, "Bristol's big bite and breathtaking beauty of both the super strip and the surrounding Tennessee countryside provided the main ingredients for the Springnationals championship drag races, a meet that is destined to go down in drag racing history as super unreal."

Filling the House

The event's four-day attendance was substantial, reported at about 52,000 by *National Dragster*; the hometown *Bristol Herald Courier* reported about 50,000, with 25,000 viewing Sunday's final eliminations. By comparison, NASCAR announced that about 58,000 people attended that season's Daytona 500 and about 50,000 attended major NASCAR races in Atlanta and Charlotte. Announced attendance for Bristol's Southeastern 500 NASCAR race in May was 18,500.

The only place the Springnationals fell short was in participant numbers, attracting fewer than 400 racers, including many of the nation's finest from about 40 states and Canada. Then, as now, cars were separated into classes, and the gold standard was winning class and advancing to Sunday's eliminator bracket.

Officials blamed low turnout on uncertainty about the facility being ready, rumors the event would be rescheduled, and a race-week weather forecast that included the likelihood of rain. Car count likely mattered little to spectators, who quickly dispelled the prerace prediction that a steady diet of stock car racing meant local fans would favor waves of stock-appearing cars. They liked them all right, especially a familiar blue *43 Jr.* Plymouth Barracuda wheeled by southern son Richard Petty. Many found a new love when the initial pair of Top Fuel dragsters were pushed, popping and cackling, out of the hot car pits and up the track like bulls ready to charge from a rodeo

Danny Ongais (left) was the quickest qualifier on opening day of the Springnationals in the Mangler *Top Fuel dragster. Here, he charges down the track in front of Marvin Schwartz in* Garlits Chassis Special. *(Photo Courtesy Bristol Motor Speedway)*

chute.

If a carbureted, gasoline engine sings tenor, supercharged nitro-burners emit a rich, resonant bass. The sensory overload created by two of those monsters racing side by side through the valley, with that resolute roar echoing off the hillsides, was unimaginable. Excited fans stood and stared when the kings of the sport were on the track.

Figuring Out Bristol

Californian Danny Ongais was quickest during Thursday's early runs, posting a 7.84-second run aboard the Broussard-Davis-Ongais *Mangler* fueler, a run that was well off the car's typical pace. During the first two days of qualifying, other top drivers also struggled to even approach their normal pace. Many theorized that the track was too good, coining the term "big bite," as many fell out with broken differentials, clutches, and other components. Tuning confusion was multiplied by Bristol's mountainous elevation of about 1,500 feet above sea level, and sticky southern humidity meant internal combustion engines had less oxygen to convert into horsepower.

"The bite is out there, all right," Top Fuel car owner Ray Godman said. "All you've got to do is get control of it."

After qualifying concluded that Friday, Texan Jimmy Nix paced the field at 7.65 seconds at just 191.88 mph in his first outing aboard the Texas-based Carroll Brothers & Oxman machine, which held the national record at that time at 7.54 seconds. Michigan's Maynard Rupp was second quickest, followed by Don Westerdale aboard the Ramchargers dragster, Ongais, and Chicagoan Cliff Zink who produced the day's top speed of 199.54 mph.

Conspicuous in his absence was the South's most famous drag racer, "Big Daddy" Don Garlits, who was suffering through a very un-Garlits-like season. Earlier that

Connie Kalitta thundered to a string of 209-mph clockings in his Ford-powered Bounty Hunter *dragster that established a new national speed record. Kalitta finished as Top Fuel runner-up in Bristol's original 1965 Springnationals. (Photo Courtesy Bristol Motor Speedway)*

spring, the Florida native crashed in a match race and was struggling to make his new 426-ci Dodge Hemi engine perform. He skipped the Springnationals after an uncompetitive outing in Maryland the previous weekend.

Records Falling

Chris "the Greek" Karamesines recorded Bristol's first 200-mph Top Fuel pass, a 202.70-mph lap, on his first run of the weekend. All eyes shifted quickly to Connie Kalitta, who eclipsed his previous national speed record with a blast of 209.78 mph in his 427-ci Ford "Cammer" *Bounty Hunter*. However, Kalitta's 7.72-second elapsed time (ET) wasn't quick enough for the top spot, as Rupp ran 7.64 aboard the Logghe Brothers, Steffey, and Rupp *Prussian*.

Twenty cars answered the call for Saturday's AA/Fuel Dragster class runoffs, with Rupp picking up easy wins when foes Tex Randall and Art Malone each fouled trying to outrun the top qualifier. Three machines advanced to the semifinals as Rupp ran 7.64 seconds at 183.28 mph to beat Kalitta's 7.72 and a thundering top-end charge of 208.80 mph. Karamesines earned a bye run when his competition failed to appear. Both cars encountered problems in the class final, with Rupp limping to a 7.99/142.40 victory over the Greek's even slower 8.74/121.13.

Saturday's class victory earned Rupp the coveted "sit-out winner" slot for Sunday, meaning that he would only have to run Sunday's final round. Rupp and crew chief Roy Steffey hauled the dark-blue slingshot dragster back to their motel and swapped in a new engine. Other than doing a brief engine warm-up on Sunday, Rupp's team sat patiently in the pits while the competition battled.

Eliminations

On race day, Bristol's first Top Fuel field consisted of Rupp, Nix (who qualified and drove two different cars), Tom Hoover, Ron Goodsell, Kalitta, Joe Schubeck, Westerdale, Ongais, Marvin Schwartz, Malone, Canadian Fred Farndon, Glen Woosley, Ray DeNoble, Val LaPorte, and two alternates. Tex Randall replaced the broken car of Karamesines and rookie Charley Peacock replaced Zink.

In the quarter-finals, Kalitta uncorked another 209.78-mph blast against Westerdale and the Ramchargers, who wasted a 204.54-mph pass with a foul start. It was a surprising error for Westerdale, who had recorded a 7.51, the meet's lowest ET, in a second-round trouncing of LaPorte. In the other pairing, Hoover suffered a frightening engine explosion and fire at the finish line but still upended Nix 7.56/199.54 to 7.66/192.70.

With Hoover's damage too extensive to repair, Kalitta advanced to the final with an opportunity to avenge his Saturday loss. A quicker Rupp prevailed for the second consecutive day, running 7.59/203.16 to Kalitta's 7.82/205.94. Rupp relied on one of the older 1950s-era Chrysler Hemi engines displacing just 360 ci, which meant his car was allowed to weigh far less than Kalitta's larger, more powerful Ford.

"That's the fastest my car has ever run, and that's my first victory since I started competing in the nationals in 1960," the 24-year-old Rupp told the assembled news media. "That big Ford of Kalitta's kind of scares me, so I never let up off my gas pedal until I hit the finish line."

Rupp and his partners earned $3,000 plus about $700 in sponsor awards for

Maynard Rupp (third from left) and the Logghe, Steffey, and Rupp Prussian *team celebrate in the Winner's Circle after claiming Bristol's inaugural Top Fuel title. Rupp swept the AA/Fuel Dragster class runoffs on Saturday and returned to win the eliminator category on Sunday. (Photo Courtesy Bristol Motor Speedway)*

the victory; Kalitta took home $1,000. Prior to racing in Top Fuel, Rupp wheeled a Top Gas dragster, then the sport's second-quickest class.

In Bristol's Top Gas battle, Georgia racer Pete Robinson emerged victorious from Saturday's 15-car AA/Gas Dragster class run-offs but wasn't so lucky on Sunday. He lost in the finals to archrival and top qualifier Gordon Collett of Portsmouth, Ohio. Collett's supercharged Chrysler-powered dragster posted a winning 8.47/185.94. He earned $1,000 for the victory over the eight-car eliminator field after rebuilding his damaged engine on Saturday night in a motel parking lot.

Funny Car Eliminations

"Strickler Dodge Wins 'Funny Car' Bash" was the *National Dragster* headline after Dave Strickler of York, Pennsylvania, powered his Dodge to the Match Bash victory at the Springnationals. It marked NHRA's initial acknowledgment of the rapidly evolving Funny Car movement. The cars, in this case all Dodge and Plymouth products, featured aluminum parts to reduce weight, a wheelbase altered to improve weight transfer, and ever-increasing horsepower.

The class was a last-minute addition to the lineup because Carrier recognized the potential fan appeal and lobbied for its inclusion. Although only six of the machines made it through technical inspection at Bristol, the class proved to be instantly popular with fans who realized these were much more than typical stockers.

In the opening round, Strickler defeated Lee Smith, running 10.64/131.57 to Smith's losing 10.95/129.12, even after Smith removed his car's parachute to save 35

Dave Strickler (near lane) wheeled his altered-wheelbase Dodge to the Match Bash title at Bristol, NHRA's first attempt at recognizing the rapidly evolving Funny Cars. Here, Strickler dispatches Lee Smith's similar Plymouth in round one of the Springnationals. (Photo Courtesy Bristol Motor Speedway)

pounds. Ronnie Sox triggered a redlight in the next pairing, losing to Bob Harrop's *Flying Carpet* 1965 Dodge that ran 10.47/132.35. Sox had previously set the tone during qualifying with a 10.47-second run in the red, white, and blue Gate City Motor Company–sponsored Plymouth Belvedere.

Bud Faubel's *Honker* 1965 Dodge then dispatched Al Eckstrand's *Golden Commandos* Plymouth, 10.75/131.96 to 10.98/126.58, in a rematch of the AHRA Winter Nationals final, also won by Faubel. Strickler earned the solo run through the semifinals; Harrop defeated Faubel on a holeshot, 10.91/134.55 to a quicker but losing 10.81/132.35. Harrop attempted to leave first in the final but fouled, giving Strickler the win. Strickler ran 11.31/130.05 and collected $300 plus $300 in sponsor bonuses.

The rest of NHRA's outrageous Factory Experimental machines were also out in force, holding a class runoff and then competing in the mundane-sounding Top Stock Eliminator. "Dyno Don" Nicholson's Mercury earned the A/FX class win over Dick Brannan's *Goldfinger* Mustang in a group that also included Phil Bonner, Shirl Greer, Al Joniec, Bill Lawton, Roger Lindamood, Winternationals champion Herb McCandless, and "Fast Eddie" Schartman.

Nicholson's *Comet Cyclone* was off its normal record-setting pace, and he lost via a first-round redlight to Ohioan Ray Christian in Top Stock eliminations. Reigning NHRA world champion Mike Schmitt captured the Top Stock trophy, coaxing record-matching runs from his 427 High Riser–powered AA/Stock Automatic Ford to defeat Shirl Greer, Dallas Kelly, and John Ulrey before besting Robert Borkes' Ford to claim the eliminator title.

Among other classes, world champion Bill Hoefer wheeled his California-based, 3,800-pound 289-powered C/FX Ford past Floridian Doug Patterson's *Brand X Eliminator* F/Stock Automatic Plymouth Barracuda in the Junior Stock final. T. J. Cunningham of Wichita, Kansas, drove his roadster past Ohioan Dick Shroyer to win Street Eliminator.

The weekend's strangest outcome occurred in Competition Eliminator where a timing system malfunction showed that both cars recorded identical ETs of 10.05 seconds and speeds of 141.50 mph. Rather than rerun, NHRA declared Pete Shadinger and Glen Blakely co-winners. Prior to the finals, Shadinger's 6-cylinder Buick dragster had been running in the 10.20 range and Blakely's Chevrolet-powered altered-class car was solidly in the 9.80 range.

Wheelstanding at Bristol

For all that weekend's competition, one car that didn't win anything later appeared in nearly every national and regional publication that assigned a

The 1965 Springnationals marked the debut of Hurst's remarkable Hemi Under Glass *Barracuda, a wild midengine creation that original pilot Bill Shrewsberry wrestled to a series of fan-pleasing bumper-scraping passes. (Photo Courtesy Bristol Motor Speedway)*

photographer to the event. *Hemi Under Glass,* a creation of Hurst Performance, was a black and gold 1965 Barracuda with a 426-ci Chrysler Hemi engine sandwiched behind the driver's seat and beneath the large rear window.

It was originally conceived to compete in the Factory Experimental class, but once original pilot Bill Shrewsberry attempted to hook up all that torque and power, the car's front end shot skyward and remained there until it was about halfway down the quarter-mile. The crowd screamed its approval, and the sport's second exhibition wheelstander (after Bill "Maverick" Golden's *Little Red Wagon*) was born. Originally run with two carburetors, the engine became fuel starved running at that awkward angle, and it was later converted to fuel injection.

A photo of *Hemi Under Glass* appeared in the August 1965 issue of *Hot Rod,* which also included a column by editor Bob Greene, who described Bristol as the "dragstrip of tomorrow" with a "country club atmosphere." He wrote that this was what drag racing needed to grow and attract a new, younger audience. "From Bristol's streamlined entry to the end of its 3,000-foot shutoff strip, it is immediately obvious that the pattern for a new era has been cut, hopefully one that others will follow."

NASCAR Influences

Richard Petty and David Pearson forged Hall of Fame careers driving NASCAR stock cars, yet both were part of Bristol's inaugural 1965 NHRA Springnationals, the most visible of many instances where the two sports crossed paths that weekend. Both drivers were in Bristol rather than competing in a 200-lap Grand National stock car race at Nashville Fairgrounds Speedway, due to Chrysler's decision to boycott

NASCAR in a dispute over its Hemi engine. In December 1964, just days after plans for Bristol Dragway and the Springnationals were unveiled, NASCAR announced it would ban the 426-ci Hemi engines that powered Petty to the 1964 championship and ban the automaker's intermediate-size cars from competition on its largest tracks for 1965.

"It looks as though we've been put out for good," Ronny Householder, Chrysler's racing director, said, after NASCAR released its 1965 rules package. "It looks like we'll have to go drag racing."

It was no bluff.

"We ran in drag racing for about six months," Petty recalled decades later. His father, Lee; crew chief Dale Inman; and the Petty Engineering team had already constructed a Hemi-powered Plymouth Barracuda in their Level Cross, North Carolina, shop, testing the car as early as September 1964 at Piedmont Dragway in North Carolina.

In Spartanburg, South Carolina, NASCAR team owner Cotton Owens took delivery of a radical rear-engine Hemi Dodge Dart station wagon constructed by Michigan's Dick Branstner and Jay Howell, the same guys who turned *Little Red Wagon* into drag racing's first wheelstander.

Pearson and Cotton Picker

Owens replaced the rear suspension on the canary yellow *Cotton Picker* with the same truck arm suspension technology employed in the team's stock cars. Aluminum covered the front grille and headlight openings to reduce drag, but the car's high center of gravity and excessive rear weight made it difficult to steer. *Rodder* and *Super Stock* claimed the car ran 10.33 seconds at 143 mph during testing at Spartanburg Dragstrip in South Carolina.

Circle burner David Pearson also went straight at Bristol, wheeling the Cotton Owens–owned **Cotton Picker** *Dart wagon to a series of 10-second exhibition runs at the 1965 Springnationals. (Photo Courtesy Bristol Motor Speedway)*

"The strips we've run *Cotton Picker* on so far haven't been long enough to really open it up," Pearson told reporters upon his arrival in Bristol. "But we'll run the dragstrip just like we run the round track, flat out. It'll seem funny going straight at Bristol." Pearson recorded a series of 10-second 140-mph exhibition passes at Bristol, but the radical machine didn't fit into any available NHRA class.

Petty and 43 Jr.

Richard Petty, on the other hand, came to race his trademark blue machine with distinctive "43 Jr." markings. The car's Hilborn fuel-injected Hemi engine and 2,500-pound weight ultimately placed it in the B/Altered class within Competition Eliminator. The Barracuda raced at Bristol was the second built by the Petty clan. The first carried the "Outlawed" moniker on its doors, was match raced across the Southeast, and competed at the 1965 AHRA Winter Nationals in Arizona. It came to a tragic end that February while match racing Arnie Beswick at Southeastern Dragway in Dallas, Georgia.

After an uneventful time-trial run, Petty staged in his first of three scheduled races. As Beswick easily pulled away, Petty's car stumbled off the starting line and began accelerating down the right lane. Eyewitnesses estimate he reached 60 mph before a broken tie-rod end sent the car swerving across the track, up an embankment, and onto a fence where fans stood. Eight-year-old Wayne Dye was killed, and six other people were taken to a local hospital.

Petty was also taken to the hospital for observation but was uninjured. He later described that tragedy as one of the most difficult times of his career. The team had commitments, so they readied another Barracuda that debuted at Lassiter Mountain Dragway in Birmingham, Alabama, on April 24, where Petty recorded a paltry best of 10.79 seconds, losing three of five races to Hubert Platt.

Richard Petty's Bristol drag racing debut attracted fans from the oval track, where he first unloaded the 43 Jr. Barracuda for technical inspection. For these new drag racing fans, Petty served as a familiar connection. (John Beach Photo)

Richard Petty buckles his helmet's chinstrap before making a run at the 1965 Springnationals in his injected Hemi Barracuda. In addition to winning the B/Altered class, Petty ran quicker and faster than the class record. (Photo Courtesy Bristol Motor Speedway)

The first place Petty went upon his arrival at Bristol was the oval track, because NHRA staged technical inspection for all cars in its pit area. With paved, level land at a premium on the complex, the *43 Jr.* drag racer was first unloaded on the familiar confines of the oval track's backstretch with a curious crowd looking on.

Petty's car was much quicker at the Springnationals, where he posted a string of 10-second passes and a best speed of 144.12 mph, nearly 10 mph faster than the class national record. He took the class win with a run of 10.62/131 and advanced into the 13-car Competition Eliminator field, where he nearly missed the call.

"That's how dumb we were about drag racing," Petty said decades later. "Our shows were usually match races where we'd go somewhere, and they'd get one of their drag stars to come out, and we'd drag with him two out of three, and that was it. We came up to Bristol for the big show, went through inspection, and we'd never done anything like that, and then run and won our B/Altered class. We were sitting in the grandstand watching the race, and they said, 'Petty, you're supposed to be out there.' We didn't have any idea. The car wasn't ready, and we just jumped in it and ran, but we didn't know what we were doing. But it was a lot of fun."

In round one, Petty defeated Charley Seabrook's D/Altered machine 10.56/135.73 to 10.56/120.16. Petty ran quicker than the national ET record in the second round, at 10.35/135.54, but lost to eventual Springnationals cowinner Pete Shadinger's dragster at 10.27/132.74.

Petty's drag racing career was nearly over. Days before the Springnationals, NASCAR reversed its decision and announced that it would soon allow the Hemi-powered cars to compete on short tracks and road courses. Petty and Pearson returned to Bristol in July 1965 for the Volunteer 500 aboard their factory-supported Chrysler stock cars.

Paul Norris, a Holman-Moody employee, flexes the muscles of his potent, new A/FX Mustang during Springnationals action. The Charlotte-based team was best known for its winning ways in stock car racing, but it also made a big splash in drag racing. (Photo Courtesy Bristol Motor Speedway)

Holman-Moody

Ford also had a significant NASCAR connection at the 1965 Springnationals, as components for all three of the 427 Ford overhead-cam engines used by Top Fuel teams, including speed king Connie Kalitta, came through Ford's North Carolina–based racing headquarters run by John Holman and Ralph Moody. They had prepared and fielded NASCAR race-winning machines for Fred Lorenzen, Ned Jarrett, and Fireball Roberts.

Ford also directed Holman-Moody to prepare 10 altered-wheelbase 1965 Ford Mustangs for NHRA's new A/Factory Experimental class. Many competed at Bristol, including Clester Andrews, Phil Bonner, Dick Brannan, Al Joniec, Bill Lawton (in the Tasca Ford-sponsored car), and Paul Norris. Both white Mustangs of Andrews and Norris prominently displayed Holman-Moody signage on the front fenders; this was no coincidence for Norris because his day job was working as a Holman-Moody mechanic.

Drag Racing on the Air

That inaugural Springnationals also marked another first for drag racing and one that came directly from the Bristol oval: a live radio network broadcast. Twenty radio stations in an eight-state area stretching from Daytona Beach, Florida, to Louisville, Kentucky, carried the four-hour Sunday afternoon broadcast. Previously, all of Bristol's NASCAR races had been broadcast live to a similar multi-state network through the facilities of WJCW-AM in Johnson City, Tennessee.

The Thrill of Victory

On the heels of Bristol's spectacular opening Springnationals and a successful 1965 weekly drag racing program, the greatest challenge facing the 1966 event seemed to

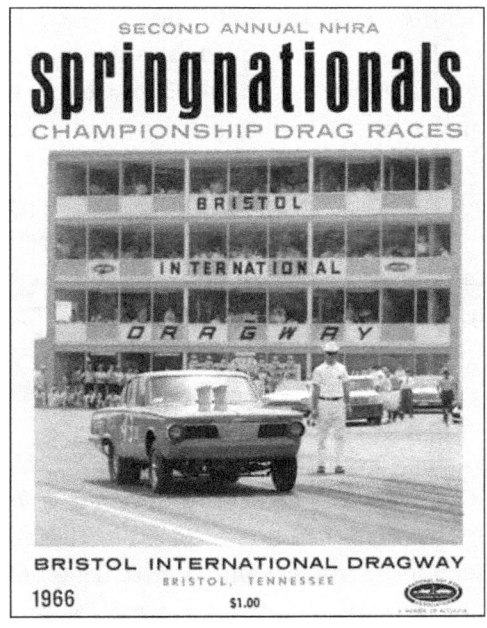

The NHRA Springnationals returned to Bristol Dragway in 1966, where the souvenir program cover showcased Richard Petty's racer framed by the Bristol tower. (Photo Courtesy David McGee Collection)

be exceeding lofty expectations. At least part of that goal was fulfilled six weeks prior to the event when ABC television announced that it would broadcast highlights of the Springnationals on its *Wide World of Sports* program.

Wide World of Sports *at Bristol*

At a time when most U.S. households could choose from just three network channels, ABC's *Wide World of Sports* beamed the "thrill of victory and the agony of defeat" into living rooms across the country. Sandwiched between quirky rattlesnake roundups and Mexican cliff-diving shows was groundbreaking motorsports coverage, including the first Indianapolis 500 television broadcast in 1961, highlights of the 1962 Daytona 500, and the 1963 NHRA Winternationals, the first drag race to appear on network television.

NHRA president Wally Parks later described ABC's Bristol presence as "one of the event's important extras" because that program "introduced drag racing to countless

Fans again flocked to Bristol for the 1966 Springnationals, where the cameras for ABC TV's Wide World of Sports *(foreground, left lane) captured all the action. At the time, the NHRA conducted four national events annually. (Photo Courtesy Bristol Motor Speedway)*

newcomers via the magic of TV." The Bristol event also marked the first time a television broadcast placed a camera inside a helicopter to gain overhead views of the action, after the Federal Aviation Administration temporarily grounded the Goodyear blimp. According to *National Dragster*, "Interference difficulties prevented getting a clear picture, but the high-altitude footage and stop-action sequences were used."

Detroit's deepening involvement in the ever-quicker staggered-start Stock and Super Stock classes elevated a group of drivers and teams to cult-hero status. Fans lined the fences and jammed into the grandstands for every matchup featuring Sox & Martin, Bill "Grumpy" Jenkins, Dick Landy, Don Grotheer, and Arlen Vanke, all who became stars years later in Pro Stock.

Jere Stahl Dominates in 1966

The 1966 event also provided a new working-class hero for the masses: Jere Stahl. *National Dragster* featured Stahl's white 1966 Plymouth Belvedere on the cover of its June 17, 1966, issue following a Bristol win, which appeared to be an omen for the rest of that season. Starting at Bristol, Stahl didn't lose another round of national-event competition all season, sweeping titles at the Springnationals, NHRA Nationals, and World Finals. One magazine subsequently called the car the "most successful" of its kind in the sport's history.

1966 Springnationals

Stahl, an exhaust-header manufacturer from Pennsylvania, and engine builder Bill Stiles prepared the 426-inch Hemi to compete in the A/Stock class, where they tangled with Bill Jenkins's lightweight red-and-white-striped Chevy II powered by a diminutive 283-ci small-block engine. Stahl topped Jenkins's vaunted Chevrolet 11.96/117.03 to a redlight start of 12.25/116.42 in Bristol's A/Stock class final.

Stocker standout Jere Stahl drove his A/Stock Hemi Plymouth to the class victory and Top Stock Eliminator title at the 1966 Springnationals. Bristol kicked off a remarkable streak for Stahl, as he remained unbeaten in national-event action for the rest of the 1966 season. (Photo Courtesy Bristol Motor Speedway)

A smiling Jimmy Nix accepts the 1966 Springnationals Top Fuel trophy from Miss Springnationals Linda Cole. Nix won the AA/Fuel Dragster class runoff and the eliminator title, defeating Ray Marsh in the finals. (Photo Courtesy Bristol Motor Speedway)

Stahl later claimed Top Stock Eliminator with his quickest run of the day, 11.80/119.20, denying Mike Schmitt a repeat final-round victory.

That outcome also kept Schmitt from having a shot at becoming the sport's first driver to win two eliminator categories at a single event; he had already claimed the Street Eliminator final by defeating Al Joniec's Mustang.

In the Junior Stock final, teammates Arlen Vanke and Bill Abraham squared off, with Vanke's GTO getting the win. Mark Pieri was awarded the Top Gas victory after officials disqualified apparent winner Dick Vest when they found unsecured ballast inside his dragster. Michigan's Al Bergler captured the popular new Super[charged] Eliminator title.

In Top Fuel, charismatic Jimmy Nix didn't arrive in Bristol until Saturday morning, but he still emerged victorious. After qualifying during the first round of AA/Fuel class action, Nix swept Saturday's class runoff, defeating Californian Chuck Griffith in the final. After taking the sit-out spot for Sunday, Nix won the eliminator title over Ray Marsh with the day's low ET and top speed, 7.463/213.88.

Marsh, wheeling the same Logghe Stamping Company *Prussian* dragster that won the 1965 Bristol trophy, suffered breakage in his fourth-round win over Danny Ongais. So, too, did Julius Hughes in his victory over R. L. Peyton. Hughes could have pushed to the line and won by default against Marsh, but he opted not to, giving Marsh the round and Marsh's crew extra time to repair their car so someone could face Nix. In a unique twist, the NHRA awarded Hughes co-runner-up honors for his show of sportsmanship.

Bristol was a busy weekend for "Gentleman Joe" Schubeck, who wheeled the *Ramchargers* dragster to top speed of the meet after being called at the last minute when regular driver Don Westerdale couldn't get time off from his job at Ford. Schubeck also thrilled Bristol fans with runs in his regular ride, *Hurst Hairy Oldsmobile*, an ill-handling four-wheel-drive Olds Tornado exhibition car powered by two supercharged engines on nitromethane feeding two transaxles, one in front and the other behind the driver.

The act featured Schubeck, in his tuxedo-style, silver, aluminized-asbestos Bell firesuit, walking up to the car at the starting line and climbing in; newly crowned Miss Hurst, Linda Vaughn, exchanged his top hat for a helmet. The car featured two throttles and two shifters and proved to be incredibly challenging to drive, dinging the right-lane guardrail on one run as smoke boiled from all four tires.

1967 Springnationals

The only things hotter than the temperature at the third-annual Springnationals were the Top Fuel dragsters, as the Bristol field became racing history's quickest and fastest at that time. "Sneaky Pete" Robinson topped qualifying for the second straight year, nabbing the top spot with a 7.11-second run in his Ford-powered dragster. His pole speed from 1966, 7.44 seconds, wouldn't have made the 1967 Bristol show. Tom McEwen wheeled Don Johnson's colorfully striped *Beachcomber* Chrysler dragster to top speed of 223.23 mph.

"The Snake" in the 6s

Don "The Snake" Prudhomme's California-based Baney-Pink-Prudhomme machine marched to the Top Fuel title with four consecutive 6-second elimination runs, the first time ever in drag racing. In his first Bristol appearance, Prudhomme established low ET at 6.92 seconds in the final round, running 222.76 mph to defeat fast qualifier Robinson. Fans hoping for the sport's first side-by-side 6-second race were disappointed when Robinson's supercharger failed at the 1,000-foot mark, slowing him to a losing 7.20/170. The race marked the first national-event victory for engine guru Ed Pink and the third for Prudhomme.

That edition of the Springnationals marked only the second race where the NHRA didn't use Saturday class runoffs for Top Fuel and Top Gas, relying instead on qualifying to set the field, and thus eliminating the sit-out position.

In Top Gas Eliminator, Gordon Collett set low ET at 7.79 seconds, but a final-round redlight gave the victory to Californian Bob Muravez, who raced under the alias

Bob Muravez, alias Floyd Lippencott Jr., wheeled the Freight Train *twin-engine dragster to the Top Gas title at the 1967 Springnationals. He raced under an alias to keep his father from finding out, but the secret was out when the race appeared on television. (Mike Montgomery Photo)*

Floyd Lippencott Jr. to keep his dad from finding out. The secret was exposed when he and the twin-engine *Freight Train* dragster owned by John Peters appeared on ABC's *Wide World of Sports*.

Challenging the dragster classes for fan popularity was a revamped Super Stock eliminator, boasting a field that included Sox & Martin, Bill Jenkins, Jere Stahl, Ron Mancini, John Hagen, Arlen Vanke, Dick Arons, Hubert Platt, Don Grotheer, Tony Pizzi, Tom Myl, Judy Lilly, and Barrie Poole. Sox stormed to the eliminator title over Mancini, who appeared to lose to Arons but was reinstated after Arons ran too quick compared to his class record (a confusing new aspect of the sport, designed to create parity). Sox and his traditional red, white, and blue 1967 Hemi Plymouth mowed down Jenkins, Vanke, and Mancini for the overall win.

Malco Gasser

The event also marked the debut of "Ohio George" Montgomery's revolutionary *Malco Gasser* Ford Mustang. After dominating the AA/Gas Supercharged class, Montgomery advanced to the semifinals of Super Eliminator where he lost to 1966 race

"Ohio George" Montgomery debuted his revolutionary AA/ Gas Supercharged Malco Gasser *Mustang at the 1967 NHRA Springnationals where it ran .4 second under the national record. Some strange circumstances kept it from the Winner's Circle. (Mike Montgomery Photo)*

winner Al Bergler amid strange circumstances. Both cars were shut off twice when officials mistakenly sent other cars down the track toward the starting line. Then, the elapsed-time difference of the two cars wasn't correctly programmed into the starting system and Montgomery ran too quick, for which he was disqualified. NHRA officials rejected his pleas for a rerun. Bergler then lost in the finals to Sonny Adkins aboard Raymond Godman's Tennessee-based dragster.

In its 1967 yearbook, *Hot Rod* editors opined, "Tennessee's Bristol Dragway is not an ordinary dragstrip. The asphalt is laid between beautiful green hills in a setting that would be worthy of the finest summer resort" and noted that fans rarely used their seats, preferring to stand for "90 percent" of the show.

What's in a Nickname?

Bristol Dragway, or its original incarnation, Bristol International Dragway, has long been known as Thunder Valley. It is the most obvious, most applicable nickname for the iconic real estate, given the pathway carved into its original natural box valley and the acoustic bounce produced when screaming internal-combustion engines traverse it. Today, even casual race fans comfortably use Thunder Valley nearly as often as the track's proper name.

More than one person claims to have been the first to coin the now universally recognized handle. Written accounts of Bristol's early events in both local and national publications turn up no evidence until 1967. A Bristol sportswriter dubbed it "Echo Valley" in his coverage of the 1967 Springnationals, but it was NHRA founder Wally Parks who first used the term "Thunder Valley." In the introduction of the 1967 Springnationals event program, Parks wrote, "Top-ranking contestants come from all parts of the United States and Canada to meet the challenge of this modern 'Thunder Valley.'"

Flamboyant sportscaster Keith Jackson wasted no time adopting the name, using it repeatedly during his coverage of the 1967 NHRA Springnationals on ABC's *Wide World of Sports*.

The dragway's nickname became so popular that it quickly spilled over to Bristol Motor Speedway. Former owner Larry Carrier formally changed the dragstrip's name to Thunder Valley Dragway in the 1970s but changed it back in 1984.

Although one nickname stuck, another never did.

Seeking to piggyback on 1960s pop culture, founders Larry Carrier and Carl Moore intended Bristol's informal name be "Drag City U.S.A.," borrowing the title of a popular Jan & Dean song about drag racing that ranked 10th on *Billboard* magazine's 1964 pop-music chart.

Bristol's founders intended Bristol Dragway to be known as "Drag City U.S.A.," but the nickname that stuck is "Thunder Valley." They commissioned this marble marker prior to the 1965 event, and it remains on display today. (David McGee Photo)

Advertising for the first Springnationals included the Drag City nickname. A large, brightly colored sign across the bridge leading to the dragstrip welcomed fans to "Drag City U.S.A., Home of the Spring Nationals, Bristol International Dragway."

The promoters went so far as to secure a political proclamation and have it carved in stone.

On May 12, 1965, Tennessee Governor Frank G. Clement issued a proclamation declaring, "The location of the new Bristol installation shall be known from this time forth as Drag City U.S.A." The promoters commissioned a large granite marker, resembling a tombstone and carved with the date and "Drag City U.S.A.," and displayed it prominently.

Yet news accounts from those initial events, both in local newspapers and racing enthusiast magazines, revealed only occasional, passing mentions of "Drag City U.S.A." and its use quickly faded.

Ushering in Funny Cars

The Funny Car three-year metamorphosis from ragged, altered-wheelbase caterpillar to sleek, flip-top butterfly transpired before the eyes of Bristol fans. A year after Dave Strickler slayed the ballyhooed altered-wheelbase Match Bash class at the 1965 Springnationals, so-called Funny Cars were all the rage from coast to coast. Fuel injection and superchargers replaced carburetors and the fuel evolved from gasoline to nitromethane, the same yellow-tinged pop propelling Top Fuel dragsters to once-unimaginable 210-plus-mph speeds in 1966.

The 1966 Springnationals was the first major race for NHRA's freshly announced Super Experimental Stock classes created specifically for the radical, supercharged full-bodied cars. Listed as A/XS through E/XS, classes were separated by minimum

Bristol was at the center of the 1960s Funny Car revolution, hosting the initial Match Bash class in 1965. Here, Bud Faubel's altered-wheelbase, injected **Hemi Honker** *Dodge (far side) defeats Al Eckstrand's similar* **Golden Commandos** *Plymouth in a side-by-side 10.9-second race. (Photo Courtesy Bristol Motor Speedway)*

weights, with the A class representing the alpha male.

At the 1966 Springnationals, Tommy Grove defeated Ronnie Sox in Saturday's A/XS class final round, but the winning ET was neither announced nor recorded. Grove's stretched *Ford Charger* fiberglass-bodied Mustang recorded a speed of 164.83 mph to trounce Sox & Martin's injected Hemi *Baccaruda*. The speed was more than 8 mph faster than Sox, who ran 9.17 seconds at 156.79 mph and trailed by eight car lengths at the finish line.

Grove previously registered an 8.74 at a nearly identical 164.87 mph to defeat Texan Gene Snow's Dodge Dart, prompting widespread speculation. One published report suggested that Grove may have run as quick as 8.40 seconds after filling the Ford's fuel tank with 92-percent nitromethane. NHRA regulations placed no limits on fuel percentage, but Grove

Tommy Grove's **Ford Charger** *Mustang was cutting edge when it won the 1966 Springnationals, but it appeared hopelessly outmatched against the wave of new flip-top Funny Cars at the 1967 race. Nevertheless, Grove pushed the overweight, outdated hulk past a host of flip-top cars to win Bristol's first Funny Car eliminator title. (Photo Courtesy Bristol Motor Speedway)*

went on to post runs of 8.8 and 8.7 seconds later in the event, both at 162 mph.

In other 1966 Experimental Stock divisions, Illinois racer Lee Smith wheeled a Sox & Martin–prepared Plymouth to the B/XS trophy over Dave Koffel and Gale Mortimer; Al Joniec (C/XS), A. J. Lancaster (D/XS), and Tom Sneden (E/XS) also won. Because they didn't yet merit their own eliminator, all advanced to the Competition Eliminator field, which featured 13 class winners. On Sunday, Grove continued to make noise with a string of 8-second runs to reach the finals, where he turned back Dan Slitten's New York–based dragster for the trophy.

Bill Lawton's gleaming Tasca Ford Mustang was among the top contenders in the new Funny Car category at the 1967 Springnationals. Here he defeats Ed Burnett's Camaro in the first round. His day ended via a second-round redlight against eventual winner Tommy Grove. (Mike Montgomery Photo)

Fans hung on the fences at Bristol to watch the Funny Car spectacle of Tommy Grove (near lane) taking down Maynard Rupp's gleaming-new orange STP Cougar in NHRA's second-ever Funny Car eliminator final round. (Mike Montgomery Photo)

A Wave of Floppers

At Bristol's 1967 Springnationals, sleek, new flip-top fiberglass Ford and Mercury bodies draped across tubular chassis seemed to be everywhere. The gleaming new cars made Dave Strickler's Dodge and Tommy Grove's altered-wheelbase Mustang seem downright docile. That race marked only the second national event where NHRA ran Funny Car as a standalone class (after the 1966 World Finals), and nearly all the Ford factory-backed teams arrived with their new cars sporting fuel-injected Cammer engines. The lineup included pioneer Don Nicholson's red *Eliminator II* Mercury, Art Chrisman's red Kendall GT-1 Oil–sponsored Mercury, Maynard Rupp and Roy Steffey's bright-orange STP Cougar, Bill Lawton's Tasca Ford Mustang, and Eddie Schartman's blue Mercury.

Grove's Old Piece Dismantles the Competition

By contrast, Grove's new car wasn't finished, so he trekked to Bristol with the same supercharged *Ford Charger* Mustang that won the 1966 Competition title. Expecting to again run in the A/XS class, Grove was dismayed to learn that it wasn't on the schedule because all those cars would fit in the new eliminator. Weighing a bulbous 300 pounds more than its sleek, gleaming competition, Grove's blue and gold beast with its opening driver's door appeared outclassed. It wasn't.

The California veteran again tipped the nitro can, increasing the percentage above 90 while relying on his engine's higher compression ratio to compensate for Bristol's higher altitude. Four rounds and four vanquished factory-fresh flip-top cars later, Grove again clutched the Bristol trophy. Nicholson qualified atop the field at 8.23 seconds but was the first to fall as Grove used a holeshot advantage to edge Nicholson's quicker-but-later 8.36 with an 8.44-second run. Lawton posted the quickest run of the first round at 8.33, but he fell to Grove in round two as Grove clocked 8.38/168 to defeat the redlighting Mustang. Rupp posted a winning 8.30 over Bobby Woods's stretched *Palomino* Chevelle, and Schartman made a single when Chrisman couldn't complete repairs.

With an uneven number of cars remaining, Rupp drew the semifinal bye run while Grove continued to amaze, kayoing Schartman with an 8.29/169 to Schartman's losing 8.34/167. Grove's final-round opponent, the gleaming, new, fuel-injected Rupp & Steffey entry, was soon featured on the cover of *Car Craft* and reproduced as a model-car kit. On a sweltering 100-degree day in Bristol, Grove handily defeated him 8.34/170.13 to 8.41/163.

Richard Petty (No. 43) battles Darel Dieringer (No. 26) en route to claiming his first NASCAR premier series victory at Bristol during the 1967 Volunteer 500. The two drivers qualified 1st and 2nd, but Petty had to overcome a cut tire and pit-stop issues to earn the win. (John Beach Photo)

Crowning the King

Richard Petty's 1967 season was one for the ages: 27 victories in 48 starts, a streak of 10 consecutive wins, 40 top-10 finishes, and a record $150,000 winnings. It was a season that branded Petty the "King" of NASCAR and catapulted him to the top of the premier series all-time win list, a spot from which he likely will never be dethroned.

Amazingly, all 27 victories came aboard a single Plymouth Belvedere, a car updated from its original 1966 configuration and competing against as many as 10 Ford factory-backed teams. Eleven of those victories came during the first half of the season, including short tracks at Hickory, North Carolina, and Martinsville and Richmond, Virginia, plus the Carolina superspeedways of Darlington and Rockingham. The majority occurred during the summer and fall, kicking off with three in a row during a 10-day July stretch that included the half-mile dirt oval in Fonda, New York; the tiny .2-mile track at Islip, New York, on Long Island; and Bristol's Volunteer 500.

Petty's Bristol victory was the 16th of his record-smashing season, just 2 shy of the 18-win mark established by Tim Flock, and came in his 14th start on Bristol's half-mile oval.

"We knew now that this was probably a season that none of us would ever see again," brother and engine builder Maurice Petty told reporters that season. "We knew that if we put that car together right and Richard drove that car the way he knew how, we were going to win the race."

Prior to that July afternoon, Petty was shut out at Bristol, finishing in 2nd three times, posting three other top-five finishes, and then suffering a heartbreaking 1964

Richard Petty's summer Bristol win was his 16th of 27 during a landmark 1967 campaign that cemented his reputation as the king of NASCAR. (John Beach Photo)

loss when he won the pole and led 442 laps but finished in 2nd due to mechanical failure. In March 1967, Petty was leading when he drove through oil dumped by another car and slammed into the outside guardrail, ending his day after just six laps.

Petty's blue Plymouth again won the Volunteer 500 pole with a lap of 86.621 mph and took the green flag waved by honorary starter Marty Robbins, but it seemed that fate would intervene again. Petty led the first 56 circuits before coming down pit road with a cut tire that put him two laps behind leaders David Pearson and Dick Hutcherson after his crew changed all four tires.

Engine issues soon sidelined Pearson, and by lap 181 Petty had unlapped himself and retaken the lead from Hutcherson. Petty's crew then left the gas cap loose on the ensuing pit stop, prompting NASCAR to hold the blue Plymouth, which cost him the lead. He and Hutcherson exchanged the top spot on the track once more before Petty took command of the race with just over 40 laps remaining, winning by three-quarters of a lap.

"He [Hutcherson] was running just about as fast as I was," Petty said afterward. "We were both in the same groove, and I had to make a new groove each time to get around him. Then I could settle back in my normal groove and pull ahead of him."

Perhaps the change in luck could be attributed to the ride his helmet received just prior to the race. New Orleans stuntman Jerry Comeaux, billed as the world ski-kite champion, arrived without a helmet and convinced Petty to lend his for the pre-race aerobatic display. Comeaux later established a Guinness record for his speedboat jump in the 1973 James Bond thriller *Live and Let Die*.

Pearson Finds the Bristol Groove

David Pearson made only 20 starts at Bristol during his Hall of Fame career, a number that magnifies the accomplishments of his five wins and three poles on the half-mile Tennessee bullring, primarily during its first decade of operation.

David Pearson claimed his first Bristol pole aboard the Cotton Owens Dodge (No. 6) at the 1966 Southeastern 500. A broken timing chain ended his day after he led 330 of the race's first 362 laps, but Pearson came back to win the following year. (John Beach Photo)

David Pearson (left) listens to advice from crew chief Dick Hutcherson while sitting in the office of his Holman-Moody Ford Torino prior to the 1968 Southeastern 500. (John Beach Photo)

He claimed his initial Bristol pole in March 1966 aboard a Dodge prepared by Cotton Owens and collected his first win aboard another white and red Owens Dodge in March 1967. Pearson's greatest Bristol success came behind the wheel of a series of Ford Torinos prepared in the Charlotte, North Carolina, shop of John Holman and Ralph Moody, home base of Ford's NASCAR fleet during the 1960s. Pearson wheeled the blue-and-gold machines to a sweep of the 1968 Bristol races before finishing 3rd in the spring of 1969. Then track owner Larry Carrier transformed the racetrack, significantly increasing the banking in the turns and on the straightaways, which brought an accompanying rise in speeds. Pearson was the first to conquer that configuration.

His Bristol breakthrough came during the 1967 Southeastern 500, easing the pain of the previous year when he started on the pole and led 330 laps, only to have a timing chain break late in the going. "I just wanted to win so bad after last year," Pearson told reporters, admitting that he had been uncertain whether he or Cale Yarborough was leading down the stretch. "I didn't know whether I was ahead. I wasn't going to take any chances." Yarborough's team thought that its driver was a lap ahead, but the passenger-side rear tire on his Ford went down late in the going, and he finished the race riding on the rim.

Pearson made only four more starts for Owens before jumping to Holman-Moody when the tour reached Darlington, South Carolina, in mid-May 1967. The new team struggled, and Pearson went winless for the remainder of the season. That frustrating streak ended the following spring at Bristol, as Pearson took the Southeastern 500 for the second straight year, lighting the fuse on a 16-win season that brought his second NASCAR championship.

Pearson Sweeps Bristol for 1968

Richard Petty started on the pole in spring 1968 with Pearson's Ford on the outside and Ford drivers Cale Yarborough and Lee Roy Yarborough making up row two. The four of them exchanged the lead 21 times that afternoon before Pearson passed Yarbrough on lap 469 and paced the field to the checkers.

"It has been so long since I've won one that this feels about as good as my first win ever," a grinning Pearson told reporters. He credited some of the win to luck and the rest to preparation. "We didn't have as many tire problems as some of the guys," Pearson said. "We checked with the weather bureau Friday and found there was a good chance of rain Saturday, so we scuffed in all our tires Friday afternoon. The all-day rain on Saturday kept a lot of guys from scuffing in tires, and they had some problems since the water had washed all the rubber off the track from earlier practice runs."

Bristol's summer Volunteer 500 followed the season's midpoint Daytona race by two weeks, a race where Ford executives agreed to fund Pearson to run all the races and compete for the championship. After a trio of 2nd-place runs, Pearson scored his ninth victory at Bristol, thanks in part to a unique cool suit that pumped cold water through plastic tubing sewn into the material to help cope with 95-degree temperatures.

"The cool suit quit working with about 50 laps or so left in the race, but my pit crew had flashed me a sign that I had a two-lap lead over Cale [Yarborough] at that point, so the heat didn't bother me much. You don't mind things like that when you've got a big lead," Pearson told reporters afterward, adding that the heat may have prompted more aggression on the track.

"There was as much bumping going on as I've ever seen here. It seemed like everybody on the track, even the guys who were several laps behind, were driving like they were fighting for 1st place," Pearson said, citing a protracted battle with Tiny Lund aboard Bud Moore's Mercury. "The starter finally gave Tiny the flag to move over, and I got around him. I was at the point that if he hadn't moved over soon, I was gonna move him over myself."

Pearson became only the second driver to sweep both Bristol races in a single season. Yarborough finished 2nd, with rookie Swede Savage 3rd, points leader Bobby Isaac 4th, and home-state racer Friday Hassler 5th.

No Three-Peat for Pearson

Pearson appeared headed toward a third-straight Bristol win in the 1969 Southeastern 500 after assuming the lead from Bobby Isaac with just over 50 laps remaining. Unfortunately, Pearson's Ford began smoking noticeably, and he pitted with 15 laps to go. His crew raised and slammed the hood, and Pearson returned to the track still leading, but his engine fell silent five laps from the finish, handing the victory to Bobby Allison in Mario Rossi's Dodge.

Pearson Masters the High Banks

The July encore played out on a completely reconfigured Bristol oval. In May, the day after Bristol hosted its final Automobile Racing Club of America (ARCA) race, construction crews began raising the Bristol banking to superspeedway-like proportions advertised as 35-degree-banked turns and nearly 20-degree-banked straightaways.

David Pearson's Ford (No. 17) shows the scars of battle as he races with Cale Yarborough (No. 21) in the Wood Brothers Mercury. Pearson swept both of Bristol's 1968 races and the July 1969 affair. Yarborough finished 2nd in 1968. (John Beach Photo)

David Pearson (No. 17) starts on the outside of row one as the field for the 1968 Southeastern 500 rolls off. Pearson had to battle pole sitter Richard Petty (No. 43) and Cale Yarborough to claim his first Bristol win in a Ford. (John Beach Photo)

"This should be the fastest and best half-mile track in the world, and that's what we're going to make it," co-owner Larry Carrier said, in announcing the changes. "The Goodyear people feel that we should not make the track any higher, but we feel that this is what the public wants. We will have three fast grooves in this track and no slow lanes. The drivers will run the fastest groove right up next to the guardrail."

Carrier's prediction of a 100-mph lap speed materialized during Volunteer 500 qualifying, as the eight fastest qualifiers all topped the century mark, with Cale Yarborough snagging the pole at 103.432 mph. Richard Petty, who posted the second-quickest time, was hardly enthusiastic, saying that they had "ruined" a good racetrack. "It's a lot different," Petty said of the changes. "I don't see how anybody can pass anybody."

Hall of Fame driver David Pearson made five visits to Bristol's Victory Lane during a stellar 105-win NASCAR career. Here he celebrates winning the 1968 Southeastern 500 with Miss Bristol Speedway. Pearson posted 10 top-10 finishes in 20 Bristol starts. (John Beach Photo)

The race turned into a survival test, with numerous crashes and only 10 of 32 starters running at the finish. Petty fell out with engine failure in his Ford after just 60 laps and then provided relief help for Pearson, who grew fatigued by the dizzying pace and 90-degree temperatures. "It seemed a little hairy out there at first, and I just missed the big wreck," Pearson said. "We had some trouble with the slower cars, and cars running side by side in the turns rubbed a little, but it was a two-groove track."

Turbulent, Tumultuous AHRA

On the surface, the 1967 NHRA Springnationals appeared to be the most successful of three major events contested at Bristol International Dragway. More than 500 cars from across the United States jammed every inch of available pit space, with another 100 reportedly turned away. Promoters claimed that a crowd of more than 50,000 came through the turnstiles despite afternoon temperatures between 90 and 100 degrees.

NHRA Sanctioned No More

Yet for all its success, the NHRA Springnationals also experienced controversy. Some post-race media accounts hinted at a confrontation between Bristol cofounder Larry Carrier and NHRA president Wally Parks, although they speculated that any differences would be resolved. They weren't.

"For some reason, we just didn't draw the people we thought we would," Carrier told *Super Stock* magazine's Woody Hatten years later. "After three years of losing money, the NHRA put a list of improvements on us that we just couldn't afford at that time. The cost of what they wanted was over $100,000, of which they wouldn't put up a nickel."

Carrier had unsuccessfully lobbied for a second national event, an unheard-of concept at a time when the NHRA had but three other major races in California, Indiana, and Oklahoma. Carrier was also dissatisfied with his financial split, because the NHRA received half of the proceeds for bringing its workers, attracting the racers, and conducting the event. "That tower will stand as a monument to your failure," an angry Parks reportedly told Carrier.

"We really didn't know what we were going to do," Carrier recalled. "The NHRA's demands were too great, and the AHRA didn't have that much to offer. They were still growing, and most of their tracks were in the Midwest and West. We thought about it for a while, and I called [AHRA president] Jim Tice and we eventually signed with him."

Dragway founders Larry Carrier and Carl Moore (standing left to right) switched Thunder Valley's allegiance to the AHRA and its president, Jim Tice (seated), for the 1968, 1969, and 1970 drag racing seasons. (Photo Courtesy Carl Moore)

1968 Spring Nationals

Carrier and Moore opened Bristol's gates for the 1968 AHRA Spring Nationals (written as two words to help distinguish it from the NHRA race), with more than a little trepidation unrelated to their sanctioning switch. The nation was reeling that week from the assassination of U.S. attorney general and presidential hopeful Robert Kennedy and nationwide protests from a country weary of the war in Vietnam. Fans apparently needed to tune out the turmoil, because the grandstands were full for three days, and the on-track action proved to be more than dramatic.

Eliminations and Fireworks

In the final pair of Top Fuel's opening round of eliminations, starting-line officials disqualified R. L. "Wildman" Peyton for taking too long to stage his car against opponent Gene Mooneyham. Peyton was furious, jumping out of the car, which was still sitting at the starting line in the lane nearest the grandstands, yelling to the crowd, and demanding to rerun the race. After officials refused his pleas, Peyton sprinted to the team's Buick push car, positioned it to block the right lane, and removed the keys. No sooner had public-address announcer Jon Lundberg declared that Peyton was disqualified than the crowd began throwing bottles and cans, and sheriff's deputies tried to tackle Peyton.

"Within 2 minutes, the full quarter-mile was covered on both sides with broken beer bottles, smashed beer cans, and a little bit of everything else with which the fans could arm themselves," John Raffa wrote in *Car Craft*. "Fortunately, and almost miraculously, there were no reports of injuries connected with the incident."

Tice banned Peyton forever from AHRA events as authorities took him to jail, where a magistrate took pity, fined him $38 for inciting the riot, and ordered him not to do it again.

Score One for "The Greek"

Track cleanup signaled the beginning of more bizarre circumstances for the Top Fuel class. In the semifinals, the engine in Chris Karamesines's car lost power while staging, and opponent Leroy Goldstein suffered mechanical breakage on his single run. Vic Brown was then disqualified for leaving before the green light appeared in his race, but opponent Don Cook's car drifted across the centerline under power, so he, too, was disqualified. Tice decided to bring Karamesines, long an AHRA favorite, back to face Goldstein for the finals, citing the Greek's low ET of the previous round. In the final, Goldstein's clutch failed as he staged, causing him to shut off the engine and allowing Karamesines a single for the victory in what *Car Craft* described as "one of the most different Top Fuel eliminator runs in history."

"There were 48,000 racing fans in the stands, and I thought they deserved to see something besides a bye run by Goldstein," Tice told reporters after the race was completed. All that drama nearly overshadowed the performance of Californian John Mulligan, who established world-record ET and speed marks of 6.87/226.00 in qualifying and then improved with a 6.85 in round one, a pass that came up short against the holeshot win by Karamesines.

The Mercury Cougar Funny Car of Ohio's "Fast Eddie" Schartman is towed into position on the Bristol track prior to running during the 1969 AHRA Spring Nationals. (Photo Courtesy Tennessee State Library and Archives)

The AHRA implemented a full Funny Car eliminator program, and the Bristol field featured heavy-hitter southern team Candies & Hughes (the quickest qualifier), Huston Platt's *Dixie Twister*, and midwesterners Bob Sullivan and fan favorite Dick "Mr. Chevrolet" Harrell. Sullivan singled for the victory aboard his unique roofless Camaro after Harrell's Camaro broke a transmission.

Among the weekend's other winners were Ronnie Sox, whose two triumphs in Super Stock and Grand Stock marked the first time the team captured multiple titles at a single major event, and Herb McCandless, who drove a Plymouth owned by Tennessean John Livingston. Sox ran a string of 10.60 ETs at the class-legal weight in SS/B to claim Super Stock, then removed the extra weight and rolled to the Grand Stock win aboard his 1968 Hemi Barracuda.

The 1968 AHRA Spring Nationals marked the first time that Bristol ran portions of a major event under the lights both Friday and Saturday, a move necessitated in part by 15 eliminator categories, three of which were completed Saturday night to make way for the remaining dozen on Sunday. The weekend also marked the first Bristol appearance of jet-powered cars, banned by the NHRA at the time, as Art Arfons provided the show.

The weekend's worst mishap occurred Friday night, when exhibition wheelie truck driver Fran Monaghan's *Gemini Cricket* Dodge tumbled down a 15-foot embankment past the finish line after performing a quarter-mile wheelstand. The Pennsylvania driver suffered a broken back and remained hospitalized in nearby Johnson City for weeks after the crash.

A subsequent *Hot Rod* story termed the 1968 Spring Nationals the "best meet ever staged by AHRA." Playing on those superlatives, the cover headline of the June 21, 1968, edition of AHRA's *Drag World* news weekly read, "Karamesines and Sullivan Win; 82,216 Drag Fans Watch AHRA Spring Nationals." Local newspapers reported a record crowd of 60,000 people at a time when the oval track was attracting crowds of about 23,000 to its premier NASCAR races.

1969 Spring Nationals

Another riot marred the 1969 Spring Nationals, as fans expressed their alcohol-fueled displeasure after perceiving popular Chevrolet Funny Car racer and top qualifier Dick Harrell was wronged. Harrell lost the Funny Car semifinals when the Christmas tree displayed a red light on Harrell's side of the track, handing the victory to Danny Ongais and Mickey Thompson's all-conquering Mustang. Fans jeered and yelled but likely weren't any more disgruntled than Harrell.

Fan favorite Dick Harrell poses with his Chevrolet-powered Camaro Funny Car in advance of the 1969 AHRA Spring Nationals. Fans rioted that weekend after perceiving that Harrell received a raw deal from race officials. (Photo Courtesy David McGee)

Bristol Bias?

"The red light turned on after only two yellow lights; obviously a malfunction," Harrell steamed to reporters. "I have been waiting six months to race Thompson, and there was no way he could have beaten me today. I think it would only be fair if we could have split the prize money. . . . If you really want to know who would have won, just ask the fans."

Those fans threw whatever was handy onto the track when Ongais pulled the blue Mach 1 Mustang into Bristol's water box for the final. Strapped into his idling car, opponent Leonard Hughes surveyed the scene and rolled through the light beam when the tree's second of five amber lights came on, triggering another red foul light. He idled down the track rather than risk running over debris already starting to litter his lane. Ongais recorded a winning 7.78 ET around the debris. Fueling the drama, Ongais lost in the second round via a redlight, but officials reinstated him after his opponent's machine broke and was unable to race in the semifinals against Harrell.

"It was just a bad way to end the day of racing, and I hated to see it end that way, especially for the large crowd," Thompson said afterward. "We always try to act like gentlemen on the track, and today we ended up looking like bad guys."

Danny Ongais wheeled Mickey Thompson's potent Mach I Mustang to a controversial Funny Car victory at the 1969 AHRA Spring Nationals. The Ongais-Thompson team was nearly unbeatable during the 1969 season. (Photo Courtesy Bristol Motor Speedway)

Hughes became Bristol's first Funny Car driver north of 200 mph, recording a 201.78-mph blast on Friday aboard *Cajun Cuda*. Gene Snow upped that ante on a Saturday qualifying run of 202.24 mph; Harrell, Snow, Ongais, and Hughes were the top four in a 16-car field that began with more than 40 teams trying to qualify. Hughes finally set top speed among the floppers at 202.70 mph.

Leroy Goldstein pushed his *Ramchargers* Dodge Hemi dragster to the Top Fuel title over Don Prudhomme, who burned a piston in the final. Goldstein clocked low ET and top speed with a winning 6.80/217.38.

Door Slammers

Camaro-driving Bill Jenkins defeated Dave Lyall's aptly named *Going Thing* Boss 429-powered Custom Speed Enterprises Mustang in the heads-up Super Stock final. Lyall, a Ford employee, turned the class on its collective ear on Friday with a 9.96-second qualifying pass that was the first sub-10-second run by a factory hot rod. However, the run was .4 second better than both the 10.35 national record and the 10.38 turned in by second-best qualifier Ronnie Sox. *Car Craft* branded Lyall's run a "popcorn" time; other publications chose not to report it, in part because he never approached that pace for the rest of the weekend. Local papers reported that it was "not designated as a record run."

On race day, Jenkins waded through the Fords of Ed Terry and Don Nicholson before stopping Sox & Martin in the semifinals. Jenkins dispatched Lyall's Ford in the finals with a winning 10.23 that many publications credited as low ET of the race for the class.

Jet Power

Art Arfons had the weekend's overall fastest runs, at 237 mph. His vaunted *Green Monster* was making only its second dragstrip appearance since establishing a land speed record of 278 mph at the Bonneville Salt Flats. Promoter Larry Carrier said he was afraid to have the car make a full-throttle run.

"No one ever had a crowd like this on a single day," AHRA's Jim Tice told the news media, claiming 50,000 people showed up for Sunday's final eliminations and 100,000 attended the three-day event. "Thunder Valley is the finest racing facility in the country. I've seen them all, and there is nothing in comparison with this."

1970 Spring Nationals

The AHRA transformed during the 1970 season, partially shedding its circus-sideshow persona to become a more serious national drag racing series by offering the sport's first season-championship program with the Grand American Series. Bristol played a significant role as one of two tracks hosting two races, the Spring Nationals in June and the All-American World Championships.

A "Rambunctious" 1970 for Gene Snow

Texan Gene Snow captured the Spring Nationals Funny Car title over Fritz Callier en route to sweeping dual NHRA and AHRA world championships. Callier's partner, J. E. Kristek, tuned him to the top qualifying spot in Funny Car at 7.40/224, but the orange Chevrolet-powered Nova came up lame in the final round, losing to Snow's all-conquering *Rambunctious* Dodge 7.35 to 7.77.

Sox and Tharp Take Their Classes

Ronnie Sox turned back Dick Landy in AHRA's professional Super Stock final after Landy out-qualified Sox by .03 second. Both drivers clocked identical 10.25-second ETs in semifinal wins before Sox defeated the quicker Landy on a holeshot 10.23/136.45 to Landy's 10.21/135.13.

Top Fuel honors went to Richard Tharp, who wheeled the Creitz & Donovan machine past upset-minded Eddie Carrecia in the final with a winning 6.76/222.22. Carrecia lost in round one, got back in on the break rule, and then advanced past Jimmy King and Jim Nicoll.

CHAPTER 2

"Big Daddy" Don Garlits won the 1972 and 1975 Bristol Spring Nationals Top Fuel titles with his string of **Wynn's Charger** *dragsters. (John Beach Photo)*

RACING INTO THE 1970S

American motorsports evolved from homegrown to more professional during the 1970s, thanks in large part to the investment of corporate backer R.J. Reynolds. Competition increased from NASCAR to NHRA and the fledgling International Hot Rod Association (IHRA), a new drag race sanctioning group established prior to the 1971 season and based on the grounds of Bristol's speedway and dragway.

Don Garlits: Big Daddy's Comeback

Overflow crowds at Bristol's 1970 Spring Nationals likely thought their eyes were deceiving them as they wandered through the Top Fuel pit area, for there was "Big

Daddy" Don Garlits, just 13 weeks removed from suffering a violent transmission explosion at California's Lions Dragstrip that claimed half of his right foot, broke his left foot, and left him hospitalized for six weeks.

Garlits, driver Connie Swingle, and crew chief T. C. Lemons came to Bristol with a rebuilt, shorter-wheelbase version of *Swamp Rat 13*, part of the same front-engine dragster that was cut in half at Lions. They joined Marvin Schwartz, who was already in Bristol aboard the primary Garlits car.

"After much persuading, [wife] Pat agreed I could go along with the boys, provided I wouldn't attempt driving. Swingle had been out of the cockpit for four years and failed to qualify in his first two attempts," Garlits wrote in his autobiography *Big Daddy*. "The temptation was too great; even though my foot was still in bandages and quite painful, and I had promised not to drive, I donned Swingle's firesuit and proceeded to make a run," Garlits wrote. "Richard Tharp came over as I dressed, looked at my foot, and passed out."

Through the first two days, New Englander Jimmy King was the quickest car in qualifying at 6.809 seconds aboard the King & Marshall slingshot. Schwartz was second quickest with a solid 6.88 in the other Garlits car. The Bristol crowd caught a glimpse of Garlits, wearing his firesuit pants, on the starting line to observe Swingle's 7-second qualifying attempt. That same crowd nearly lost its collective mind when Don climbed into the cockpit on Saturday evening to make that pass and promptly laid down the weekend's quickest and fastest run at 6.805/224.42, a run *Drag News* described as "strong, straight, and true."

"Needless to say, I was plenty scared, but as the powerful blown, nitro-burning Dodge Hemi fired to life, all fear and anxiety disappeared, and I felt confident I would be okay," Garlits wrote. "Words can't describe the joy and sense of fulfillment that

"Big Daddy" Don Garlits surprised fans at Bristol's 1970 AHRA Spring Nationals just three months after a catastrophic transmission explosion in California took half of his right foot. He further surprised them by storming to top-qualifying honors. (Chris Haverly Photo)

came over me when the crew came down the strip after the run to tell me I had just set top time and low ET of the event."

Drag News advertising director Don Rackemann recalled the incident: "About one o'clock [Saturday], Don Garlits and Connie Swingle pulled into the pits with an open trailer with the car Don had crashed at Lions last March. It was completely rebuilt but had the roll cage that helped save Don's life. They unloaded the car and the pits were buzzing. Connie Swingle, who has been associated with Garlits for many years and [was] an all-around competent guy, drug out his old silver firesuit.

"Connie made his first run about four o'clock. He went up in smoke and turned in the low 7s and 190 mph. Not bad, considering. After the run, Don told Connie, 'Swingle, I'm going to make a pass. You just watch me and how the car leaves.'

"At approximately 6 p.m., Don was strapped in the car. They pushed down to fire. Everyone was on their feet, and Top Fuel and Funny Car owners went to the fences to watch. Garlits left the line in an all-out pass. Yes, you guessed it, he set low ET at 6.80 and top speed at 224 mph.

"I feel that I have seen everything drag racing has offered, but I can't put into words how I felt. I can only say, 'Don Garlits, you are the greatest of the great.'"

With the largest crowd in Bristol history looking on, Garlits let Swingle slide behind the butterfly wheel for a first-round single run, in which Swingle carded a solid 6.92/212. Garlits returned to the seat for round two, but the storybook weekend ended when the engine spun a bearing in a loss to John Wiebe.

Returning to the driver's seat that weekend in Bristol "set the hook," and Garlits did race slingshots again, including at Bristol's 1970 All-American race, all while developing a safer design for 1971 that relocated the engine and clutch assembly behind the driver, which remains the standard of the sport today.

Decades after his miraculous comeback, the innovative Garlits remained active in the sport. After he was forced from the cockpit due to health reasons, Garlits tuned driver Bruce Larson to the 1992 Fall Nationals Top Fuel title. (David McGee Photo)

Second Event, No Second Fiddle

Silent racetracks generate no income, and Bristol's owners spent years trying to establish a significant second race in Thunder Valley. After hosting a pair of NHRA Southeast Division races headlined by Top Fuel dragsters, their efforts finally bore fruit under the AHRA.

The odyssey began in 1965 when the NHRA awarded Bristol one of its Southeast Division races originally scheduled for Atlanta Speed Shop Dragstrip. However, rain on Bristol's August weekend washed out the race until October 9–10. To spice up the weekend, Carrier announced that the Bristol oval track would host a 200-lap NASCAR Late Model Sportsman race on Saturday evening.

Bristol Blowover

In that era, NHRA divisional races featured Top Fuel and Top Gas dragsters, and this event attracted Springnationals champion Maynard Rupp and Julius Hughes among the nitro-burners, national champion Gordon Collett, and Atlanta's John Reed in Top Gas, along with Super Stock star Arlen Vanke. In true Bristol groundbreaking fashion, the event included drag racing's first documented dragster blowover. Hoyt "Granddaddy" Grimes sprinted across the finish line on a 160-mph Top Fuel qualifying pass on Saturday when strong winds caught the car's front end and suddenly snapped it skyward. Grimes went along for the ride as the car flipped a half-dozen times, and he was hospitalized with two broken hands and other injuries.

"I have always stressed safety in my cars, and I know darn well that is what saved my life," Grimes told a newspaper reporter from his bed at Bristol Memorial Hospital. "My car did a wheelstand just as I was going through the traps, and a gust of wind or something caused it to flip."

Collett nearly suffered a top-end tragedy while filming a TV commercial for Pure Oil. His car blasted across the finish line at 170 mph, but his braking parachute couldn't deploy due to the force of a tailwind. Collett used his brakes to finally stop the car just before it struck the chain safety net at the end of the asphalt surface.

In calmer eliminations, Hughes defeated Bill Mullins in the Top Fuel finale, and Reed captured Top Gas; other winners included Joe Lunati of Memphis and Californian Mike Schmitt. News accounts estimated that about 4,000 people witnessed Sunday's eliminations, about the same number who saw LeeRoy Yarbrough qualify on the pole and lead all 200 laps of the Saturday night oval-track race.

In 1966, Bristol's divisional race was branded the Dixie Drag Championships and again featured Top Fuel. After eliminations were rained out on the original September date, officials opened the fields to new entries the following weekend. Vic Brown of Tulsa, Oklahoma, set and then reset the NHRA national ET record, lowering the mark to 7.36 seconds to become the meet's top qualifier.

Wheeling the Bob Creitz and Ed Greer entry, Brown ran 7.22 to defeat Pete Robinson in the second round and 7.30 to top Bill Mullins in the Top Fuel final. NHRA officials allowed Brown to return and make another run, where he posted a new record time of 7.26 seconds.

Bristol's split with the NHRA preempted a third divisional race in 1967, but in 1968 Tice agreed to sanction the All-American World Championships. It was carefully scheduled for September 7–8, the weekend after Labor Day where the AHRA and NHRA went head to head, with Tice staging his Championship in Texas opposite NHRA's Nationals in Indianapolis. Although not part of AHRA's eight-race national-event schedule, the Bristol event boasted a substantial $60,000 payout and "speed carnival atmosphere," with a star-studded field of nitro Funny Cars, a jet car eliminator, and sportsman classes.

Ray Alley registered Sunday's Funny Car final-round win over Don Biggers and a field rivaling any national event, including Dick Harrell, Bob Sullivan, Gene Snow, Shirl Greer, Kelly Chadwick, Mike Burkhart, Della Woods, Don Nicholson, Al Vanderwoude, Bobby Wood, and Ronnie Runyon. Fans on Saturday also witnessed a separate 16-car Funny Car program, with Tennessean Bob Coleman of Memphis earning the final-round upset of Chadwick's Texas Chevy. Coleman lost in round one but was reinserted after posting the quickest time among all losers after Bob Sullivan's car suffered mechanical problems.

Jet racing pioneer Art Arfons became a regular when Bristol added a second national event under AHRA sanction. Bristol's initial All-American race featured a Jet Eliminator won by Ted Austin over Fred Sibley. (John Beach Photo)

Jet Car Eliminator

Much of the prerace hype surrounded a planned eight-car Jet Eliminator. And although only six were on the property, fans witnessed plenty of sizzle. Ted Austin wheeled the Walt Arfons *Green Monster* jet dragster to an undefeated weekend, turning back Fred Sibley in Sunday's final round. Arfons brothers Art and Walt provided all six cars in competition, including young Bob Motz aboard the Art Arfons *Hugger* Camaro jet-powered Funny Car and Bob Tatroe, who wheeled the *Exodus* jet to top speed at 252.11 mph.

"The cars will run faster at Bristol than any other dragstrip in the country due to the good shutdown area," Tatroe told the local news media. "That's what we look for at a track, to see how much shutdown area is available. You can't go very fast unless you have a place to slow down."

None of the jets were forced to test the experimental netting fitted with coiled cables that was installed should one of them fail to stop. It was designed to stop any car going up to 150 mph and installed after Art Arfons initially announced plans to bring his jet that ran more than 500 mph on the salt flats of Bonneville, Utah.

Adding to the "carnival," E. J. Potter rode his 500-hp motorcycle, *Bloody Mary*, down the quarter-mile at a jaw-dropping 160 mph. The bike featured a transverse-mounted 327-ci fuel-injected Chevrolet engine on nitromethane fuel. Its prerace ritual was to heat the rear slick in an aluminum paint tray of flaming gasoline before engulfing the track in tire smoke.

Ronnie Sox remained perfect at Bristol for the 1968 season, driving the Sox & Martin Barracuda past Dave Lyall's Ford Mustang with low ET for the class at 10.70 seconds and top speed of 131.19 mph in the Super Stock final. Among the Sportsman winners was Hubert Platt in Top Stock.

Official counts reported attendance at about 20,000 for each of the two days. Convinced that the All-American would be a worthy addition, Tice agreed to give Bristol two spots on the 1969 AHRA national-event schedule and later named Larry Carrier an AHRA vice president after he helped secure the new Rockingham, North Carolina, dragstrip for the AHRA.

1969 All-American

The 1969 All-American Championships featured the fastest run in drag racing history to that point as jet jockey Art Arfons clocked 275.35 mph in his *Cyclops* machine and then won Jet Eliminator. Magazine coverage of the event claimed that 50,000 fans attended the two-day program that included Terry Hedrick winning Funny Car.

Hedrick called the victory one of the "greatest thrills" of his life, and he celebrated by spinning around and driving back up the track. His *Super Shaker* Nova bested Jim Maybeck's red, white, and blue Corvair in the final.

Ongais versus Harrell: Take Two

Fans also got to witness a Sunday rematch between the pair that prompted the Spring Nationals riot months before: Danny Ongais aboard Mickey Thompson's mighty Mach 1 Ford Mustang against the Camaro of Chevrolet darling Dick Harrell. Ongais emerged with the win at 7.59/196.

The race also featured elimination of the rule that allowed promoters to reinsert losing drivers into the field. "Last time, this was agreed upon by the drivers so that it would make a better show for the spectators, with two cars in the final run. However, it didn't work out too well. And, in my opinion, it was an unpopular decision to have a backup car. If a car redlights, it's through," Carrier said.

As in 1968, the event's 16 Funny Cars also ran a separate Saturday program, with Ronnie Runyon claiming the final-round win after Fritz Callier's engine fell silent at the starting line.

Organizers added Top Fuel to the 1969 All-American lineup, and Californian Jim Nicoll set low ET and top speed of the meet (6.78/213.78) before downing former Spring Nationals champion Chris Karamesines in the final round. AHRA's heads-up Super Stock class went to Missouri's Larry Kimball, whose Chevy Camaro defeated Bill Tanner's Dodge in the finals.

1970 All-American

The AHRA Grand American tour returned to Bristol on the last weekend in August for the All-American World Championships, with Pete Robinson piloting the field's lone Ford-powered Fueler to low ET of 6.78 seconds in qualifying. Robinson ran 6.83/211.76 to slip past Jimmy King in the Top Fuel final, when King's engine throttle linkage broke at the 1,000-foot mark. The race's most memorable moment happened in round one when former AHRA world champions Casto & Boggs stood their dragster straight up in the air off the starting line after losing to John Wiebe. Don Garlits temporarily returned to the cockpit of a slingshot Top Fueler but lost to Robinson in the second round.

Gene Snow, who proved to be nearly unbeatable in both the NHRA and AHRA that season, qualified first, setting low ET and top speed of the category at 7.04/205.46 in the finals. Snow's *Rambunctious* Dodge Challenger edged out Don Prudhomme's

Don "The Snake" Prudhomme (near lane) struggles for traction in his race with Kenny Bernstein and Ray Alley's Engine Masters Cougar. *A former Bristol Top Fuel winner, Prudhomme reached the Funny Car finals at Bristol's final AHRA race, the 1970 All-American Championships. (John Beach Photo)*

yellow *Hot Wheels* Barracuda for Funny Car honors. Prudhomme's car smoked the tires at the starting line, forcing "The Snake" to pedal the throttle and ultimately lose at 7.83/185.

Top qualifier "Dyno Don" Nicholson's Cammer Ford Maverick appeared to be the class of the Super Stock field, running 10.11 seconds in a first-round win. He slowed to 10.24 in round two but still beat Don Carlton's 10.35. Herb McCandless posted low ET of round two with 10.19, his Sox & Martin–prepared Plymouth Duster edging out Dave Lyall's Ford. McCandless ran 10.15 to best Ed Miller in the semis and Dyno Don eased by Dick Humbert aboard Billy Stepp's Dodge, 10.16 to 10.26. Nicholson carded low ET of the weekend with a final-round 10.07 to best McCandless, who ran 10.17.

The event also featured the Bristol return of Art Arfons's *Green Monster* jet dragster, E. J. Potter's Chevy-powered *Bloody Mary* motorcycle, and the Turbonique turbine-powered *Odyssey* dragster owned by Wayne Knuth and driven by Larry Kisha.

Bristol, the IHRA Flagship

An August 1970 newspaper photograph portrayed AHRA president Jim Tice and Bristol promoter Larry Carrier smiling as they gazed across a sea of spectators jammed into Thunder Valley for the All-American World Championships. Just a month later, a dispute over money and sanctioning agreements washed away any smiles and ultimately touched off a split between Bristol and the AHRA.

It happened at the Rockingham, North Carolina, dragstrip where Carrier held an advisory relationship with track owners and longtime friends W. L. "Bill" Land and L. G. DeWitt. AHRA officials refused to allow track employees to collect money from racers entering the track's pit gate during the AHRA U.S. Open Nationals.

The incident, later documented in a lawsuit filed in U.S. District Court in North Carolina, was the last straw in an irreparable rift between Tice and Carrier. In the court filing, Carrier and Rockingham claimed that the AHRA failed to fulfill its promise to attract certain drivers to events, described the dispute over money, and stated that, in November 1970, they learned that the AHRA planned to promote major events within a 150-mile radius of Rockingham, which was prohibited under the terms of the Rockingham track's AHRA sanction agreement.

More than a decade later, all Carrier would say was, "We were happy with our deal with Tice at first, but later on he had some people we couldn't get along with, so we split with him."

The story goes that Carrier's partner, Carl Moore, famously asked him one day, "Now what do we do?"

IHRA Formation

That answer arrived on November 9, 1970, when Carrier and Moore ushered reporters into their Bristol Speedway offices to announce the formation of the International Hot Rod Association (IHRA). They held up artwork of the original red, white, and blue logo, which featured the outline of a globe surrounded by the organization's name and draped with a ribbon featuring "IHRA" in capitalized block letters.

"We feel there is an urgent need for a new drag racing sanctioning body," Carrier said during the announcement. "Unrest has developed among manufacturers, accessory companies, track owners, car owners, drivers, and fans throughout the country, and we feel we have the answer to the majority of the problems. It's our opinion that the big bite taken by other sanctioning bodies from the host tracks has endangered the sport, limited the purse for the car owners and drivers, and cut down on the quality of entertainment the fans deserve. [The] IHRA will work strenuously to revive the sport and offer first-class competition in all phases of the popular sport."

Carrier would run the daily operations as president; Moore would serve as chairman of its close-knit board of directors. In the pair's long line of gambles, this one might have been the most daring. During the announcement, Carrier pledged that the new association would buck the status quo and charge less than others for tracks hosting its major races, allow automotive-accessory companies to pay only winning drivers who used their products, and provide greater recognition for the sport's hobby racers who comprised the overwhelming majority of entries.

"We are aware of the problems and humbly accept the challenge of building a sanctioning body that will be respected and widely accepted by all in this growing sport," Carrier said. These were bold words for an organization that, at that time, claimed only the Bristol and Rockingham dragstrips, had no schedule or rulebook, and would initially rely on Bristol's speedway staff to carry out its operations.

Claiming "International" as part of its name and using the globe was clearly a stretch, but Carrier and Moore rarely dreamed on a small scale. The initial five-race IHRA national-event schedule was released a few weeks later, opening with an April race at Rockingham, followed by the Bristol Spring Nationals in late June, the All-American Nationals at Bristol in late August, a fall Rockingham event, and ending with the World Finals at a track in Lakeland, Florida.

The program would blend elements of the NHRA and AHRA, including three professional classes, Top Fuel, Funny Car, and Super Stock, initially borrowing AHRA nomenclature rather than NHRA's preferred Pro Stock for modified Detroit muscle cars. They also adopted AHRA's philosophy of paying some of the most recognizable professional drivers to guarantee their participation.

1971 Spring Nationals

From clicks at turnstiles and butts in bleachers to star power on the track, auto racing success is measured in multiple ways. Did an event run smoothly and reasonably on schedule? Was it an aesthetic success? Did performance barriers fall? Did it generate substantial buzz? With the eyes of the sport sharply focused on Bristol and wobbly kneed colt IHRA, the 1971 Spring Nationals boasted big names aplenty, the wild exhibition vehicles Bristol had become well known for, and a new thin layer of asphalt atop the racing surface, in hopes of exuding that new-racetrack smell. Those last two factors combined to nearly spoil the party.

Several days of rain prevented Bristol's new skim coat of asphalt from properly bonding with the existing asphalt and, once serious horsepower was applied, the

Drag racing's stars turned out in force at Bristol's first IHRA Spring Nationals. Here, Richard Tharp warms up the hides on Harry Schmidt's Blue Max *Mustang Funny Car. Tharp marched to the final round before losing to Don Schumacher. (John Beach Photo)*

Jet racer Art Arfons (left) explains the workings of his **Super Cyclops** *jet dragster to football star Johnny Unitas, who was the grand marshal of the 1971 Spring Nationals. In addition to running drag racing's first 280-mph pass that weekend, Arfons destroyed the starting line, blowing chunks of asphalt through windows in the control tower. (John Beach Photo)*

surface came apart. Track crews spent considerable time sweeping up bits of asphalt that flaked, chipped, and chunked throughout opening day. After rains mercifully ended Friday's qualifying at about 7 p.m., track workers blended blacktop with concrete dust to hastily patch the surface, but that, too, failed.

"Jet"isoning the Track

Shortly before noon on Saturday, Art Arfons brought his *Super Cyclops* jet to the starting line and uncorked drag racing's first 5-second run, an eye-opening 5.96/280.12. A few hours later, he returned to the right lane and thrust from the J-79 jet engine's afterburner peeled an 8-foot section of asphalt from the starting line and sent it flying in every direction, shattering a window in the base of the tower. Teammate Bob Motz carved out a 4-foot slab in the left lane with his jet, forcing officials to stop the race and relocate the starting and finish lines.

The change produced dramatically improved times, but qualifying sessions weren't completed until 2 a.m. Sunday. Among the highlights, Gary Dyer pushed the Mr. Norm's Dodge Challenger to a new IHRA Funny Car ET record at 6.70 seconds, even quicker than the 6.80 recorded on Friday by Top Fuel leader Jim Nicoll's new rear-engine dragster.

After race officials relocated the starting and finish lines and employed a concrete mix to solve a temperamental track surface, Mike Martini (near lane) drove Gene Mooneyham's slingshot to the 1971 IHRA Spring Nationals Top Fuel victory. (John Beach Photo)

Eliminations

When the smoke cleared on Sunday afternoon, Mike Martini wheeled Gene Mooneyham's Louisiana-based slingshot dragster to Top Fuel honors over Tennesseans Preston Davis and Ray Godman after their engine expired at mid-track. Don Schumacher's *Stardust* Barracuda topped a stellar Funny Car field, besting Richard Tharp in Harry Schmidt's *Blue Max* Mustang in the finals. Veteran Ronnie Sox remained unbeaten in the IHRA, sweeping Super [Pro] Stock from rival Don Carlton, who was quicker but fouled in Ted Spehar's *Motown Missile* Dodge Challenger.

Media reports claimed that 55,000 fans turned out for Sunday's final eliminations, despite Saturday's late finish. Reports put Bristol's three-day Spring Nationals attendance at 92,000, and although that number may be optimistic, it can't be disputed because crowds filled the stands and provided a financial grand slam for the new organization.

Ronnie Sox (far lane) took the Spring Nationals Pro Stock (originally called Super Stock) title aboard the mighty Sox & Martin Barracuda over runner-up Don Carlton, who triggered a redlight in the Motown Missile *Dodge Challenger. (John Beach Photo)*

Despite some significant weather challenges and a reputation for rain, the IHRA Spring Nationals continued to attract enormous crowds to Thunder Valley, including a record turnout for the 1974 event. (Photo Courtesy Bristol Motor Speedway)

From Soggy to Spectacular

The IHRA survived its opening season, but success and cash flow remained directly linked to Thunder Valley, where rain played havoc with the 1972 and 1973 Spring Nationals. Rains washed out most of the first two days of the 1972 event, pushing qualifying to Sunday morning, followed by the full elimination program, which stretched late into the evening. Don Garlits, Don Schumacher, and Bill Jenkins claimed the pro hardware at the end of an incredibly long day, with Big Daddy and the Grump running low ET and top speed of the day in their respective finals.

With fans filling the hillsides, John Paxon piloted the intimidating Courage of Australia *rocket-powered dragster to some 5-second clockings at nearly 290 mph at Thunder Valley during the 1972 Spring Nationals. (Photo Courtesy Curt Smith)*

Don Carlton won the 1973 Spring Nationals Pro Stock title in Ted Spehar's vaunted Mopar Missile Plymouth Duster. The victory was part of an amazing five-race IHRA win streak for the team. A Models Products Corporation (MPC) model kit of the car pictured it at Bristol. (John Beach Photo)

Dale Funk (right) and partner Bill Frakes rushed to complete their Bill Stebbins–built dragster in time to compete at the 1974 Spring Nationals. Running with a borrowed engine, Funk stormed to the Top Fuel title and reset the national records for elapsed time (ET) and speed. (Photo Courtesy Dave Huber)

The 1972 Spring Nationals showcased two remarkable rocket-powered machines. The first was the tiny hydrogen peroxide rocket–powered go-kart piloted by "Captain Jack" McClure. Weighing just 400 pounds with 2,000 hp and 1,000 pounds of thrust, McClure's kart ran 7.43/190.62.

That same weekend, John Paxson cracked 287 mph aboard Bill Fredrick's *Courage of Australia*, a needle-thin, land speed, record–styled, rocket-powered dragster that weighed 1,100 pounds and made 12,000 hp at 6,100 pounds of thrust.

1973 Spring Nationals

The next year, rain forced the finals to Monday afternoon, where Marvin Schwartz, Bill Leavitt, and Don Carlton claimed pro victories. All that rain contributed to a different kind of riot. After showers played havoc with Saturday qualifying, officials scheduled a Sunday-morning session, only to see it rain again. During the delay, some fans decided to take off all their clothes and participate in the national fad of streaking. As deputies hauled the offenders away, other fans threw bottles and cans onto the track, quickly covering the racing surface.

1974 Spring Nationals

Following those incredibly soggy Spring Nationals, three days of sunshine greeted the 1974 event, and fans responded in record numbers. A cover headline on the June 27, 1974, issue of the IHRA in-house *Drag Review* newspaper claimed, "Bristol Spring Go Packs 104,500 to Remain Granddaddy of Them All." It seems that the biggest story wasn't Dale Funk resetting the national record en route to capturing the Top Fuel title, Texas teenager Billy Meyer becoming the sport's youngest winner in a Funny Car sweep, or Atlanta plumbing contractor Reid Whisnant pulling the Pro Stock upset, but rather that so many folks had witnessed them.

National and regional newspapers dutifully recited the 104,500 figure, claiming 57,500 people attended Sunday's final eliminations. Inflated? Perhaps. Photographs of the event prove that attendance was significant, especially in the midst of a national energy crisis, when gasoline was often in short supply. By comparison, that season's Daytona 500 reported 85,000 attendees, Charlotte's World 600 reported 84,000, and Bristol's two NASCAR races combined attracted 38,000 people.

More than four decades later, Funk remembers the massive crowd when reliving that victory, "It was probably my biggest win and my biggest thrill. I've got all the newspaper clippings where they said 104,000 people were there. I think it was the largest crowd they'd ever had at Bristol Dragway. That was back in the beer-drinking days, and they let the spectators bring beer in, so it was wild."

Bristol was Funk's second win of that season but his first in the brand-new *Kentucky Moonshiner* entry he fielded with crew chief and partner Robert Frakes and sponsor Bill English. Funk won Top Fuel at an eighth-mile IHRA national event held on pit road at Charlotte Motor Speedway driving a car owned by Richard Holcomb because his own car wasn't done.

Even when the new Bill Stebbins–built car was complete, Funk still didn't plan to run Bristol until friend John "Tarzan" Austin offered to loan the team an engine. One major thrash later, the Kentuckians buttoned up the car and rushed to Bristol, arriving late on Saturday with just enough time to make a single qualifying run.

On its maiden voyage, the new machine (with its unpainted and unlettered aluminum body panels) ran 6.404 seconds to qualify 13th in a 16-car field that was the quickest in Bristol's 10-year history. On race day, Funk stormed to the finals, besting the higher-qualified machines of Sam Miller, Marvin Graham, and Tim Beebe with successively quicker laps of 6.25, 6.24, and 6.13 seconds. The Bristol final was memorable despite opponent Sarge Arciero being shut off on the starting line after his engine developed an oil leak.

"I was supposed to run *Jade Grenade* in the final run; in the semifinals we ran 6.13, and we needed a backup for the record," Funk recalled. In that era, a run within 2 percent was required to back up a new record. "We could have idled through, but I looked at Robert, shrugged my shoulders, and asked 'What do you want to do?' Robert said, 'Run the hell out of it.'

"So we ran low ET, top speed, and new national records on a single run. The crowd loved it," Funk said. He nabbed records previously owned by Don Garlits, who got into the rugged field on his final qualifying pass but then lost in the first round, and Tommy Ivo, who failed to qualify.

The win helped propel the Radcliff, Kentucky–based team to IHRA's first Top Fuel world championship title.

"I have never seen a happier man than Dale Funk. I believe he was more pleased about the 6.04/238.72 record than he was with winning. The team of English-Frakes-Funk just doesn't believe anyone should hold this record except them," Carrier said after the celebration.

Junior Johnson: Dominance Defined

Ford executives announced in December 1970 that they would abandon NASCAR racing, prompting standout team owner Robert Glenn "Junior" Johnson to put his Ford inventory up for sale and start searching for options. The news came right after Johnson selflessly directed potential sponsor R.J. Reynolds Tobacco to NASCAR after hearing of their immense marketing budget. That didn't solve his dilemma.

A solution arrived in an April phone call from Richard Howard, then the general manager of Charlotte Motor Speedway, who fretted that attendance for his World 600 might decline with some of the sport's biggest names either out of action or driving mediocre equipment. Howard reasoned that a competitive Chevrolet with Junior Johnson driving would spark interest and sell tickets. In the span of a few weeks, Johnson built a white No. 3 Chevrolet adorned much like the sport's last competitive Chevy, his iconic 1963 "mystery motor" Impala. Johnson declined the invitation to drive, instead hiring Indiana standout "Chargin' Charlie" Glotzbach.

Junior Johnson enjoys the fruits of victory after clinching Bristol's 1965 Southeastern 500 as crew chief Herb Nab (left) looks on. As a driver, Johnson won 50 NASCAR premier series races. (Photo Courtesy Bristol Motor Speedway)

"It was real fast," Glotzbach recalled years later of the Monte Carlo. "But it had a lot of valvetrain problems. Once they got that worked out, it ran good." What an understatement. In their first outing, Glotzbach put the Chevrolet on the pole for the World 600 and led four times for 87 laps before crashing.

Johnson put the Monte Carlo back together and decided that the team would only race where promoters guaranteed them $10,000 to compete, at a time when most race winners would be happy to earn that much. Bristol's Larry Carrier was among the first to ante up, saying, "I was really happy for Charlie Glotzbach, and I'm sure that Chevrolet fans are, too, that Junior Johnson, the old racing master, has prepared such a competitive car."

It was Bristol's second attempt to promote a competitive Chevy, which appeared to involve Johnson. In 1966, another white Chevrolet, a 1965 Impala sporting a similar white paint job, with red and gold stripes down the center, but a large, red "No. 1," made headlines at the 1966 Volunteer 500 with Curtis "Pops" Turner behind the wheel. After Turner qualified on the pole, Johnson told writer Jim Hunter of *Stock Car Racing* magazine that he didn't know whom the car belonged to, although longtime Johnson crewmember Fencil "Turkey" Minton seemed to be in charge of it.

"They don't believe Curtis won the pole in that car. They ought to have seen it runnin' earlier this week with a real strong engine in it," Johnson knowingly said. "The good engine blew before he could qualify." Turner dominated that race's first 68 laps before being sidelined by a broken rocker arm. The speedway's Larry Carrier later declared that getting the wildly popular Turner into that Chevrolet was his "greatest promotion" and that people "lined up to buy tickets."

Junior Johnson, who brought Chevrolet back into NASCAR in 1971 with a Monte Carlo owned by Charlotte promoter Richard Howard, confers with driver Charlie Glotzbach prior to earning their first victory in that season's Volunteer 500. (John Beach Photo)

Johnson-Equipped Chevrolets Dominate

Fast-forward to the 1971 Volunteer 500, where Glotzbach set a blistering pace and established an average speed of 101.024 mph for 500 laps, a record that still stands today. A crowd of 20,500 witnessed the only 500-lap Bristol race run caution free, and Johnson's white Chevy led 411 of them. Glotzbach exited after 255 laps, and relief driver Friday Hassler brought it home. The Glotzbach-Hassler tandem finished three laps ahead of James Hylton, who was subbing for Bobby Allison.

Allison took over the seat of Johnson's Chevrolet in 1972 after bringing sponsorship from Coca-Cola and a number change to "12." That combination generated 10 wins, 10 poles, and more than 4,300 laps led. It included winning both Bristol races from the pole, leading 445 of 500 laps in the spring, and finishing four laps ahead of Bobby Isaac, who took 2nd place. That summer's Volunteer 500 was a near repeat, as Allison snagged the pole and again led 445 laps at the Bristol oval, finishing three laps ahead of Richard Petty, who came in 2nd.

Bobby Allison (No. 12) races with Richard Petty (No. 43) during the 1972 Southeastern 500. Allison dominated both of that year's Bristol races, winning both poles and leading nearly 90 percent of the laps in each during his lone season of driving for Junior Johnson. (John Beach Photo)

When Allison, Johnson, and Howard split, Cale Yarborough moved into the seat for the 1973 season, and the team won four times. Johnson bought out Howard the following year, and over the next seven seasons the tandem of Junior and Cale combined to win three-straight NASCAR championships and 45 races.

Their initial visit to Victory Lane, and a prime indication of how dominant the team would become, happened during Bristol's 1973 Southeastern 500. After smashing the track qualifying record with a lap of 107.608 mph, Yarborough set a blistering race pace and put all but the top five cars a lap down after only 39 circuits as raindrops began falling. The race was red flagged and its conclusion scheduled for two weeks later. When they returned, Yarborough never missed a beat, leading every lap and putting the entire field a lap down after just 100 circuits. Richard Petty finished 2nd, two laps down.

"This [is] the longest I've ever led a race," Yarborough joked after celebrating. "I held the lead in this one for two weeks."

In four consecutive Bristol races, Johnson's three drivers combined to lead 1,801 of 2,000 possible laps, claiming all four victories and three poles. Glotzbach had the worst starting position, rolling off 2nd in the 1971 race. In addition to Johnson, the common element was master mechanic Herb Nab.

"You can bet I'm not gonna let out my secret," Nab said after Yarborough's first victory. "Handling is the most important thing on this track, but it does take a good driver to come home a winner. You'll recall Bobby [Allison] ran pretty good at this track while he was driving for us. You can bet he would like to know what I was doing, now that he's driving his own car, but that's one secret I'll never tell."

Their winning streak was interrupted when Yarborough and Bobby Allison crashed while battling for the lead of the 1973 Volunteer 500. Cale, Junior, and Herb

Cale Yarborough dominated his first Bristol start for Junior Johnson, leading all 500 laps to win the 1973 Southeastern 500. The team won eight more Bristol races over the next seven seasons, including the first night race. (John Beach Photo)

returned to the Bristol payout window by dominating the 1974 Southeastern 400, a race shortened by 100 laps due to a national energy crisis. It was no contest as Yarborough powered past Bobby Allison and led the final 310 laps. Bobby Isaac finished 2nd, one lap down; Benny Parsons was 3rd; Allison came in 4th.

Johnson's success inspired a wave of Chevrolet entries. In the 1974 Southeastern 500, Chevrolet claimed every top-10 spot, led by Yarborough, the first time in NASCAR history for a single manufacturer. Yarborough didn't dominate the 1974 Volunteer 500, but he still emerged with the win amid a shower of sparks with Buddy Baker. It was the first official win for Junior Johnson as the team's sole owner, after buying out Richard Howard.

Baker appeared to be headed for certain victory before J. D. McDuffie grenaded his Chevrolet's engine with 10 laps remaining, erasing Baker's big lead over 2nd-place Yarborough. After the cleanup, the field lined up single file for the restart with just two laps remaining. Yarborough caught Baker on the white-flag lap and pulled even as they exited Turn 2. They slammed together in Turns 3 and 4 with Yarborough's red and black Chevrolet emerging with a three-car-length victory. Afterward, each accused the other of causing the contact. "Buddy drove his car into the side of mine," Yarborough claimed; Baker countered, "He just put me out."

Mechanical failure snapped the Yarborough-Johnson streak in 1975 and allowed Richard Petty to sweep both Bristol races, the only time in the King's illustrious career. Yarborough and Johnson promptly began another streak during the following spring that included four-straight Bristol victories and winning five of the next six races. Cale led more than half of the 1976 Southeastern 400, beating young Darrell Waltrip by one lap and Benny Parsons by two.

"Junior's got this team together now, and we're going to win a bunch," the clairvoyant Yarborough said after the first of what became nine 1976 victories. The fifth came in that season's Volunteer 500, and it was no contest. Waltrip led the first 27 laps, but Yarborough led the rest. Cale bested Petty and Waltrip by two laps and went on to claim the first of three consecutive Winston Cup championships.

The 1977 Southeastern 500 was shifted to mid-April to escape cold weather, and Yarborough responded by qualifying on the pole and leading 495 of 500 laps. His seven-lap winning margin over 2nd-place Dick Brooks equaled the track record set by Benny Parsons and relief driver John A. Utsman in 1973. With few cautions, Yarborough's average speed of 100.989 mph also nearly matched the track's race record. The affable Brooks quipped after the race that the only way he could have won was to "have someone shoot out Cale's tires."

A late rainstorm sealed Yarborough's win in the 1977 Volunteer 500 because the final 34 laps ran under caution. It was Yarborough's eighth victory of that season. Afterward, the winner admitted part of his advantage was mental, saying, "I like the racetrack, and that's a plus on my side because everybody else comes here hating it."

Relief Is Where You Find It

In the *Stock Car Racing* July 1972 issue, Bob Myers wrote of Bristol, "The increased speeds on the oval track combined with the short distance and crowded traffic conditions make 500 laps of racing the most demanding on driver and equipment of any ribbon of asphalt on the elite Grand National circuit. Seldom does the winner make the 500 laps without relief. And in July, when the valley is turned into an oven by the relentless sun and when the second race is usually held, even the toughest drivers succumb to the elements."

From its very first race and throughout much of its first two decades, Bristol regularly chewed up and spit out the sport's biggest stars, who were doing more than just racing 500 laps around a tight oval. Bristol's banked corners, both the original configuration and the imposing cliffs installed in 1969, exerted significant g-forces on the necks, arms, and shoulders of men wrestling 2-ton stock cars in the era before power steering.

Please Relief Me!

And then there was the heat. Although Bristol's spring race typically occurred in March or April, you could fry eggs on the frontstretch during July Sunday afternoons as race cars became saunas.

"What you had at Bristol was part race and part fight," longtime crew chief and Fox TV analyst Jeff Hammond wrote in his autobiography *A Life in NASCAR: Real Men Work in the Pits*, "You fought the car and the track and other drivers, and your endurance and your stamina counted for as much as your equipment. There are more relief drivers used at Bristol, by far, than at any other track. Drivers just get worn down by the g-forces and the hard racing. You can't ever let up and you can't ever relax. There aren't any long straightaways where you can just let it go. You've got to be on top of the car, driving it, all the time."

That characteristic emerged with Bristol's first race, the 1961 Volunteer 500, when winner Jack Smith's feet were burned by heat coming through his Pontiac's floorboard. He was the first to call for relief, getting Johnny Allen to help capture the trophy in a race that lasted almost 3 hours and 40 minutes.

Racers also gave up their seats after suffering nausea from exhaust fumes. Among the earliest example was when Lee Petty substituted for Petty Engineering driver Jim Paschal during the 1963 Volunteer 500 after one of Paschal's exhaust pipes fell off. Collectively, they finished 3rd in Petty's lone documented Bristol driving appearance.

Fred Lorenzen required relief from fellow Ford driver Ned Jarrett to win the 1964 Volunteer 500, and 1969 Volunteer winner David Pearson received relief from rival Richard Petty in the first race contested on Bristol's steeper banking.

Bristol's two other celebrated winning relief roles belonged to a pair of Tennesseans. Chattanooga's Friday Hassler came on in relief of Charlie Glotzbach to spirit Junior Johnson's Chevrolet to victory in the 1971 Volunteer 500, Bristol's only caution-free race, and one that established the 101.074-mph race-record speed. In addition to the winners, 2nd-place Bobby Allison received relief from James Hylton, and 3rd-place Richard Petty received aid from teammate Buddy Baker, due to both the heat and exhaust fumes coming into the cockpit of his Plymouth. Hylton's Ford finished 5th with G. C. Spencer behind the wheel.

The other notable reliever was John A. Utsman, a local Late Model Sportsman standout from nearby Bluff City, Tennessee, who helped Benny Parsons win the 1973 Volunteer 500, the sole victory in Parsons's NASCAR championship season. Future Late Model Sportsman national champion Gene Glover spelled longtime rival L. D. Ottinger, who took home 2nd place. Utsman's performance led to other relief offers as he assembled a series of great runs at his hometown track, all in relief.

"I relieved Benny four other times at Bristol and finished 2nd, 3rd, and 4th, [and] then we crashed one other time," Utsman recalled. "Then I relieved Bobby Allison in 1976 after Allison injured his ribs in a crash

Charlie Glotzbach (left) is credited with winning the caution-free 1971 Volunteer 500, but he received relief help from Friday Hassler (right), who wheeled Junior Johnson's Chevy for the final 245 circuits. Their average speed remains the Bristol race record. (John Beach Photo)

Local driver John A. Utsman (right) relieved Benny Parsons during Bristol's 1973 Volunteer 500 and helped Parsons capture the lone victory during his NASCAR championship-winning season. Utsman had a well-earned reputation as a relief specialist at Bristol. (Photo Courtesy John A. Utsman)

Bobby Allison (left) shared Victory Lane with relief driver Dave Marcis after they teamed up to win Bristol's 1970 Volunteer 500. Allison took the lead for good on lap 222 and then handed off to Marcis, who led the final 130 laps. (Photo Courtesy Bristol Motor Speedway)

at Rockingham, and we finished 5th. In 1977, I ran Janet Guthrie's car. When I got in the car it was 12th, 13 laps down. We finished 6th, 13 laps down. That was her best career finish." Although official records reflect none of those runs, Utsman played a role in six top-five finishes at his hometown track, plus the sixth with Guthrie.

Parsons once received help from G. C. Spencer, who brought Parsons's Ford to a 5th-place run in the 1971 Southeastern 500.

Among the best examples of widespread relief-driver demand was the 10th annual Volunteer 500 in July 1970, the second summer race with the taller banking, where the first 16 drivers qualified above 100 mph on a 120-degree track surface. Cale Yarborough put the Wood Brothers Mercury on the pole at a track record speed of 107.375 mph. The race began with 49 cars, but only 30 made Sunday's starting field.

Bobby Allison gets credit for his first Bristol win, but it was Dave Marcis who wheeled Allison's Mario Rossi–prepared blue and gold No. 22 Dodge beneath the checkered flag. Marcis slid into the seat during a lap-370 pit stop after engine failure sidelined his Dodge.

"LeeRoy [Yarbrough] and Donnie [Allison] were putting the hurt on me. I knew Dave was standing by, and I never had any second thoughts," Allison told reporters afterward. "The heat was a real killer." At the finish, Allison/Marcis bested Yarbrough/Allison by two laps. Bobby Isaac ran 3rd without relief and G. C. Spencer received help from fellow independent Dick Brooks to finish 4th. Richard Petty took home 5th place, but that came with relief from teammate Pete Hamilton. Yarbrough tied rags to the bottom of his cowboy boots, saying the temperature inside the car "had to be 150 degrees."

In the 1972 Southeastern 500, winner Bobby Allison became only the second winner in six races since the track was reconfigured not to have a relief driver. Seven others who finished behind him, including 4th-place LeeRoy Yarbrough, switched drivers at least once. That race also marked the first time anyone, in this case Richard Petty, employed power steering at Bristol. Parsons chided him before the race, claiming, "Richard must be getting old." Asked about it after the race, Allison said, "Personally, I don't need it."

Results credit J. D. McDuffie with a 5th-place finish in the 1972 Volunteer 500, but that is only a tiny part of the story. John A. Utsman originally qualified the 1970 Dodge owned by Dr. Don Tarr 21st in the 30-car field, with plans that he and Tarr would split the driving duties. After McDuffie failed to qualify his own Chevrolet, he asked Tarr about starting the race in Tarr's car, since points are awarded to the starting driver, and McDuffie ranked 14th at that moment. They struck a deal and hastily renumbered Tarr's Dodge with McDuffie's No. 70.

Tarr and Utsman then agreed to relieve either McDuffie or G. C. Spencer, who qualified his Plymouth 16th on tires hastily removed from Tarr's car! When Spencer's engine expired after just 33 laps, the veteran independent joined the other three in taking turns wheeling the McDuffie entry that afternoon.

In the 1974 Volunteer 400, Buddy Baker began begging car owner Bud Moore to find a relief driver by the race's midway point, but Moore, a World War II veteran, convinced Baker that only 60 laps remained and he should hang on until the finish. Baker began backing off on corner entry and got faster, taking the race lead on lap 212.

Baker appeared to be headed for victory until Cale Yarborough bumped him out of the way as they exited Turn 4 on the final lap. After his 2nd-place finish, Baker quizzed Moore about the longest 60 laps of his life, and Moore confessed that it was closer to 200.

Financial Struggles

After several successful seasons, stock car racing in the 1970s was struggling amid a malaise that included a stagnant national economy and widespread gas shortages that prompted Detroit to turn its back on racing. Assembly lines that once produced Hemi Chargers and big-block Chevelles were churning out 4-cylinder Pintos and Vegas. New sponsor R.J. Reynolds attempted to rev up the sport, but established drivers Petty, Allison, Yarborough, and Baker won nearly all the races that mattered.

Driver Cale Yarborough and car owner Junior Johnson reeled off three consecutive titles and nowhere were they more dominant than at Bristol. The diminished competition kept fans away in droves. In 1976 and 1977, Bristol's attendance sank to its lowest levels, and Carl Moore finally convinced his partner to sell. "I told Larry, 'We just can't keep doing this.' We had notes at banks all over town and just kept losing money," Moore said.

On December 1, 1977, Carrier and Moore signed papers transferring the track they'd created and nurtured to Nashville businessmen Gary Baker and Lanny Hester. The deal was completed over the telephone before the new owners even inspected the facility. They wasted no time making changes, installing a new electronic scoreboard, raising the race purse to $100,000, returning the race to a 500-lap contest, and initiating a painting program to spruce things up.

"We will actually never finish improving our facility," raceway president Hester said in the 1978 Southeastern 500 souvenir program. "As long as we can see some way to make our track a better place for the fans who come to our races, we will continue to work toward making Bristol International Raceway the perfect place for them."

Night Racing Arrives in 1978

The new owners made one other significant change: They followed the path of Baker's Nashville track and switched the August race from Sunday afternoon to Saturday night.

"Basically everybody we talked to said we were crazy," Baker said at that time. "They told us not to even think about running a Cup race at night, because you can't do it. We talked it over and said, 'What do we have to lose?' We couldn't give away tickets as it was. Lights were a big experiment, but we saw instant success."

They weren't crazy. Attendance jumped from 12,000 to an estimated 30,000 that first season, and Cale Yarborough and Junior Johnson proved that, even in relative darkness, they could still find the fastest line around the high-banked oval.

The Hester-Baker duo remained in place for three seasons, signing Valleydale (meat packers) and Busch (beer brewery) as the track's first race sponsors and constructing a new building with seating for 140 members of the news media overlooking Turn 1, both in 1980.

"Never have I heard so many fans talk of their favorite track like they do Bristol," Baker said. "Something about the place is magical, and it simply turns the fans on."

Dale Earnhardt Sr.: The Breakthrough

Seven weeks after network television delivered the epic 1979 Daytona 500 live into millions of American homes, NASCAR's tour returned to Bristol and produced another finish for the record books. On April 1, 1979, young Dale Earnhardt became the first premier series rookie to win at Bristol, only the fourth time since NASCAR's founding that a rookie driver visited Victory Lane.

Although he was a hard charger with a winning pedigree, the son of 1956 NASCAR national Sportsman champion Ralph Earnhardt, his ascent to the sport's top level suffered its share of false starts. After dropping out of school and walking away from a mill job to drive race cars, he spent years beating around short tracks in the Southeast.

Earnhardt's break came in November 1978 when California millionaire Rod Osterlund put him in a second car to primary driver Dave Marcis, and he responded with a 4th-place finish, just behind his teammate. In that season's final race, Earnhardt came on in relief of Marcis and earned a 10th-place run. Marcis quit a few days later.

1979 Southeastern 500

The Southeastern 500 buzz centered around pole winner Buddy Baker in Harry Ranier's black and silver Chevrolet after he established a new track qualifying record of 111.099 mph, thanks to some handling magic from co-crew chief Herb Nab. "Herb really knows how to set a car up for this track. We travel together to and from every race, and he told me I would be sitting on the pole," Baker said.

First-day qualifying established just the top 10 starting spots, which included Darrell Waltrip, Donnie and Bobby Allison, Benny Parsons, J. D. McDuffie, Dave Marcis, Earnhardt, and fellow rookie Terry Labonte.

"It comes down to which drivers survive the best. Here, you're counting the laps down from the time they drop the green flag. You're just praying for it to end," Baker told reporters, after claiming the pole. "I'll just have to go 500 laps and not make any mistakes."

Trouble found Baker on lap 212 when he and rival Cale Yarborough got together. "Cale must have lost it momentarily. He came down on me. I spun out and parked my car, because the rear housing was bent," Baker said. Yarborough claimed otherwise, saying, "Buddy came up on me." With Yarborough also parked for the day, only three cars remained on the lead lap: Earnhardt, Waltrip, and Bobby Allison in the Bud Moore–prepared Ford.

Dale Earnhardt's First Win

The 28-year-old Earnhardt led three times for 164 laps in the early going. He surrendered the top spot to Waltrip on a restart and then watched Waltrip lead from lap 389 to 473. Earnhardt retook the lead thanks to quick service by his crew, led by Jake "Suitcase" Elder, after Mike Potter spun to bring out the race's sixth and final caution.

"We won it in the pits," Earnhardt admitted afterward. "Darrell was running good before that last pit stop; I'm not sure I could have passed him. I kept pulling away from Darrell in the final laps. I couldn't understand what was happening, but I didn't look in the mirror. I was just looking for the checkered flag." It was Earnhardt's first Bristol Cup start, but his third trip there after running a couple of Sportsman races, including one where he hit the wall.

Earnhardt's rivals offered nothing but praise for a driver who was making only his 16th series start. "Dale ran good, really good," said Waltrip, who wound up 3rd after being passed by Bobby Allison with five laps remaining.

"Dale did a super job. He ran hard all day," 4th-place finisher Richard Petty said. "It didn't surprise me he won here. It's a survival deal more than a racetrack."

After the race, Earnhardt was still coming to grips that he'd won at the sport's top level.

"This one came in the major leagues, against the best in the business. I still can't believe it," Earnhardt told the media. "This is what I wanted to do. I pulled a Sportsman car from Savannah [Georgia] to Coeburn [Virginia] and everywhere else on the weekends. It was hard, but it was what I wanted. I felt someday I could be a Grand National driver just like my father. After today, I think he would be proud of me."

Once the trophy was presented and the photographs taken, crew chief Elder and the crew dismantled the Chevrolet in Victory Lane for NASCAR's post-race inspection.

In addition to the fans in the grandstands, many others tuned in to the race via radio for the debut broadcast of the new Performance Racing Network (PRN).

Dale Earnhardt waves to a packed Bristol grandstand after claiming his first NASCAR premier series victory in the 1979 Southeastern 500. He was the first rookie to reach Bristol's Victory Lane. (Photo Courtesy Bristol Motor Speedway)

Anchor announcer Ken Squier, who weeks prior had succinctly called the landmark 1979 Daytona 500 for CBS TV, established PRN in conjunction with Bristol owner Lanny Hester and signed on to carry races from both Bristol and Nashville. NASCAR champion driver David Pearson provided color commentary that day. PRN replaced Universal Racing Network, which had previously broadcast every Bristol race since its formation.

1980 Southeastern 500

Some 364 days later, the newspaper headline read, "Earnhardt Does It Again."

Amid a startling array of similarities, Dale Earnhardt drove the blue and yellow No. 2 Osterlund-owned Monte Carlo to his second consecutive Bristol victory at the 1980 Valleydale Southeastern 500, thanks in large part to superior late-race pit work by crew chief Doug Richert and his team. Race leader Darrell Waltrip made a green-flag stop on lap 361 to temporarily cede the lead to Earnhardt, who pitted two laps later. When Cale Yarborough pitted next, it was Earnhardt, thanks to a quicker pit stop, who took the lead for good. Waltrip held on for a solid 2nd; Bobby Allison unlapped himself on the final circuit and finished 3rd. Earnhardt's mother, Martha, joined the winner in Victory Lane.

"Give my crew the credit. They sort of get in a hurry when we have to pit on green," a jubilant Earnhardt said afterward. "I had stomach cramps when I got out of the car. It was my fault for not eating, and I got hungry with about 50 laps to go."

The cover of the 1980 Southeastern 500 program celebrated Dale Earnhardt's first win and foretold the outcome, as he returned to Victory Lane that year. (Photo Courtesy Author Collection)

Earnhardt extended his championship points lead over Allison with the win and prophesized, "I don't see why we can't go on and win the points championship." That day, points rival Yarborough finished two laps down in 5th place, a 15-point swing that nearly equaled the 19-point margin by which Earnhardt ultimately claimed his first of seven NASCAR titles.

One difference was visible. After being devoid of sponsorship in 1979, the blue and yellow Chevrolet's sheet metal featured support from two other prominent Californians about to make major impacts in the sport. Mike Curb (California's lieutenant governor and co-chairman of Ronald Reagan's presidential campaign, as well as a record producer) had his name on the rear quarter panels. The hood carried the name of millionaire businessman Warner Hodgdon, who subsequently owned race teams and racetracks, including Bristol.

Car owner Rod Osterlund (seated next to Earnhardt) and his team celebrate after Dale Earnhardt took them back to Bristol's Victory Lane in the 1980 Southeastern 500. The team won five times during the 1980 season as Earnhardt earned his first of seven premier series championships. (Photo Courtesy Bristol Motor Speedway)

CHAPTER 3

Capturing a then-record $20,000 payday at Bristol's 1980 Spring Nationals meant that eventual winner Billy Meyer (near lane) had to get by 1979 IHRA world champion Kenny Bernstein. Meyer was up to the task, posting a 6.44-second ET at a slowing 196 mph while Bernstein hazed the tires on **Budweiser King** *but recovered to run a game-but-losing 6.57 at 230 mph. (Photo by John Beach)*

TAKING CENTER STAGE IN THE 1980S

Bristol's speedway and dragway gained greater prominence and underwent substantial changes during the 1980s. At the oval, multiple ownership shifts early in the decade temporarily threatened its spot on the NASCAR schedule. Yet, by decade's end, Bristol's wildly popular brand of action was leading a new wave of growth. Things were a bit reversed at the dragway as a decade that included hosting some of the era's most significant, dramatic drag racing events featured uncertainty amid dramatic changes tied to its sanctioning body, which moved away and then returned to Bristol.

Bristol Has the Buck$

Precipitation played no role in either the 1978 or 1979 Spring Nationals, but it returned with a vengeance in 1980, nearly spoiling one of the most anticipated events in Bristol history. IHRA-series sponsor Winston (cigarettes) replaced Sun Drop (soft drink) as title-rights backer of the Spring Nationals, and the agreement included unprecedented funding for eventual winners in the top professional categories. Top Fuel and Funny Car each paid $20,000 to win over the 8-car field, doubling 1979 payouts; Pro Stock offered $10,000 to win over a 16-car field, up from $3,000 the year before. The totals were roughly twice what major NHRA races paid to win over larger 16-car fields in the nitro categories.

A January 1980 *Drag Review* headline championed, "Winston Spring Nationals Drag Racing's Highest Purse." In the accompanying story, IHRA president Larry Carrier claimed, "The Winston Spring Nationals is expected to attract the best field of professional racers in IHRA history with the increase of the purse to record levels. The professional racers have been very important to us, and we want to reward them with one big race for top money."

The $300,000 total advertised payout was billed as Tennessee's largest sporting event. The promotion, known as "Bristol Has the Buck$," included scads of bright-red Winston T-shirts festooned with dollar signs. A subsequent story compared the $20,000 top prize to the $20,000 earned by the 1980 Southeastern 500 winner. "The money [Dale] Earnhardt won in the Southeastern 500 was probably the hardest money he'll ever earn," Carrier said. "At the Winston Spring Nationals, a driver could earn the same money for only driving a mile."

Unfortunately, unrelenting rains washed away weeks of advertising buildup for the original May date, allowing only the first day to be completed. Incessant showers canceled Saturday's program and continued on Sunday, forcing a one-week postponement. Rain even returned the following weekend.

"The rains came again for the rained-out, rained-on Spring Nationals. It didn't dampen the spectators or the racers, however, and after drying the track eight times, we got it in," a relieved Carrier told the media, once the marathon was complete. "The rain hurt the crowd somewhat but not enough to lose any money, even with the big purse. I doubt we could have done this anywhere else but Bristol, as the spectators at Bristol aren't fair-weather people. They came on, and I sure am grateful for this."

Young Bobby Hilton burns out in Jim and Alison Lee's Virginia-based Top Fuel dragster en route to the team's richest payday. They took home more than $20,000 by winning Bristol's 1980 Spring Nationals. (John Beach Photo)

Upset City

Challenging weather conditions often breed upsets, and that was the case in Top Fuel where 22-year-old Ohioan Bobby Hilton piloted Jim and Alison Lee's Virginia-based dragster to the $20,000 payday. Hilton made a final-round single as opponent Richard Tharp sat motionless on the starting line after the differential of his Candies & Hughes dragster failed.

"It'll take some time for me to realize what's happened," Hilton told reporters afterward. "I'll take 20 grand any way I can get it. The most difficult part was qualifying. We were here half the night Saturday and ended up on the bump spot twice before we finally made the finals." Tharp qualified on the pole with a 5.82/247 blast in Saturday night's final session. Fellow Texans Walt Barbin and Raymond Beadle qualified 2nd and 3rd, respectively, followed by reigning IHRA champion Connie Kalitta, Jeb Allen, Bill Selley, Mark Oswald, and Hilton.

Hilton tiptoed past Kalitta in round one 6.08 to 6.14, Tharp downed Allen 5.91 to 5.95, Beadle struck the tires in a loss to Oswald, and Selley slipped past a slowing

Funny Car racer Billy Meyer cashed in at the 1980 Spring Nationals, collecting a $20,000 payday for his win in Funny Car, his second Bristol victory. (Chris Haverly Photo)

Archrivals Warren Johnson (left) and Rickie Smith met in the Pro Stock final, with Johnson claiming the $10,000 top prize driving Jerome Bradford's Camaro past Smith's **The Oak Ridge Boys** *Mustang. (David McGee Photo)*

Barbin. Tharp remained the favorite with another 5.95 that dispatched Oswald in the semifinals; Selley fouled against Hilton to set up the final-round matchup.

Billy Meyer Cashes In

Funny Car top qualifier Raymond Beadle smoked the tires on his *Blue Max* and watched helplessly as Billy Meyer galloped to a solid 6.13/239 opening-round victory. Meyer advanced past Kenny Bernstein in the semifinals before besting Roy Harris to claim the cash. "This track is unbelievable," a jubilant Meyer said post-race. "It got better after every rain shower." Meyer especially appreciated the week's rain delay because his gleaming-yellow Chevy Citation–bodied Funny Car had been outside the field after the first day of qualifying on the original weekend.

WJ Wins

In Pro Stock, Minnesota native Warren "WJ" Johnson wheeled Jerome Bradford's Georgia-based Camaro to the top prize and half-jokingly announced his retirement. "Now I'm $10,000 further away from poverty," Johnson told reporters. "I'm going to concentrate on other business ventures this year, and maybe I'll be back on the track next year."

The odds-on favorite, Johnson set low ET of the weekend at 8.09/167, to take the top qualifying spot. The top six also included Rickie Smith, Ronnie Sox, Pat Musi, Roy Hill, and Bob Glidden, who was making his first IHRA appearance since winning the 1976 series championship. More than 30 cars attempted to qualify for the 16-car field. Smith knocked off Musi's Chevrolet in the first semifinal; Johnson soloed after Sox broke his Dodge's transmission. After a final-round staging duel, Johnson erased Smith 8.13/166 to 8.32/164 and took home the large purse.

Darrell Waltrip: Seven, Here Comes Eleven

Darrell Waltrip's seven-race Bristol win streak could have ended in August 1982 when he appeared to pass the pace car under the final caution period of the Busch 500, but he escaped with a narrow victory over Bobby Allison. It should have ended in August 1983 before a lightning-fast pit stop on a night cut short by a summer thunderstorm gave Waltrip the top spot over Dale Earnhardt just as rain began falling. And it would have ended in April 1984 had Bobby Allison's dominant Buick not suffered differential failure with around 50 laps remaining, allowing Waltrip to unlap himself and charge to his record-matching victory on the demanding Tennessee short track.

Waltrip tied Richard Petty that day in April as the only drivers to score seven consecutive victories at a single track, a mark that remains unchallenged at this writing.

1981 Valleydale 500

The streak began in March 1981, coinciding with Waltrip's switch from teaming with DiGard Racing to driving for Junior Johnson. The sport was in transition as NASCAR teams switched to downsized cars, and the Johnson-Waltrip pairing reeled off consecutive wins at Richmond, Virginia, and Rockingham, North Carolina. They unloaded at Bristol and promptly claimed the Valleydale 500 pole with a track record speed.

"Driving for Junior is the ultimate step in my career so far. The mark of my success now is to take the best piece of equipment on the racetrack and win the race," Waltrip pronounced before the 1981 race. He led 323 laps, including the last 79, to collect the 3rd Bristol victory of his career and Johnson's 11th as owner and team manager.

1981 Busch 500

The duo proved to be equally dominant that August, winning the pole, leading 251 laps, and finishing a lap ahead of 2nd-place Ricky Rudd and Waltrip's former DiGard team. "We saved the car for the second half of the race, and it worked for us," Waltrip said afterward. "The surface is rough here, and everyone was having handling problems."

1982 Valleydale 500

After plowing to a dozen victories and Waltrip's first NASCAR championship in 1981, Waltrip and Johnson reprised their success the following season with another 12-win campaign and a second title. Not surprisingly, their first win came when the tour returned to Bristol on March 14, as Waltrip again claimed the pole and led the final 103 laps to best 2nd-place Dale Earnhardt by nearly a full lap.

Darrell Waltrip's Mountain Dew Buick (No. 11) edged out Dale Earnhardt in the Bud Moore Wrangler Ford (No. 15) to win the 1982 Southeastern 500. It was the team's third consecutive Bristol win. (Photo Courtesy Bristol Motor Speedway)

Darrell Waltrip (right) confers with new crew chief Jeff Hammond prior to the 1982 Southeastern 500. The team won its third-straight Bristol race that weekend, and Waltrip gave Hammond his first victory as a crew chief. (Chris Haverly Photo)

Earnhardt and his Bud Moore Ford appeared to be the day's best car, but getting tangled with Gary Balough's spinning Buick on lap 398 sent him into the infield mud. Afterward, Waltrip admitted that he stole one: "We had some problems with the chassis that couldn't be adjusted under green because we would have lost too much time in the pits. We got the caution and were able to adjust it. We got four new tires, and the car was perfect for the last 100 laps."

That victory marked Jeff Hammond's first NASCAR premier series victory as a crew chief after replacing Tim Brewer.

"It might have been one of the happiest moments of my life, standing there in Victory Lane," Hammond wrote in his autobiography *Real Men Work in the Pits*. "I know for sure that I'd never felt such a sense of relief. I hadn't realized how much pressure I was under to win until I won. With the pressure off, all of a sudden I could feel what a load I'd been carrying around."

Although Hammond and the driver known as "Jaws" didn't always see eye to eye, Hammond grew to respect Waltrip's skill behind the wheel.

"He was so smooth that you thought of him as purely a finesse driver. The truth is, Darrell was a complete driver," Hammond wrote in his autobiography. "And he was a smart driver. He knew that on a track where everyone is wrecking, the best way to win a race might be to find the holes and get through them without hitting anyone or getting hit. Darrell knew what Junior was always saying, that the car runs better when you don't wreck it."

1982 Busch 500

Waltrip won Bristol again that August in the most controversial finish of the streak. Race leader Terry Labonte brought out the race's final caution with 22 laps remaining when he got together with the lapped car of Dave Marcis. After the lead-lap cars pitted and returned to the track, NASCAR ran three extra laps under caution to sort out the field when they allowed Waltrip to pass the pace car. "The deal on the pace car is that it was slow coming out. They were supposed to pick up [Bobby] Allison but didn't, so we got out in front before it picked up the leader," a jubilant Waltrip explained afterward. Allison finished 2nd but declined to dive into the argument.

1983 Valleydale 500

For 1983, yellow and red Pepsi colors replaced the green and white of Mountain Dew as Waltrip and Johnson's primary sponsor, but the Bristol outcomes looked much the same. That spring's Valleydale 500 was shifted to mid-May and run as a night race, with Waltrip again battling Bobby Allison to the checkered flag. After qualifying a poor 13th, Waltrip led 288 laps and edged out Allison by more than 2 seconds. "It's phenomenal. It's unbelievable," Waltrip said of his new Bristol record-fifth-straight victory.

1983 Busch 500

The streak nearly ended that August, until Mother Nature intervened. Waltrip qualified 2nd and led 207 of the race's first 225 laps but yielded control of the race to Dale Earnhardt. During a yellow-flag pit stop on lap 412, Earnhardt's Bud Moore crew had trouble changing the driver-side front tire, allowing Waltrip to snag the lead, with Earnhardt emerging from the pits in 2nd and Bobby Allison in 3rd. Before the green flag waved again, a violent thunderstorm moved over the speedway, forcing NASCAR to call the race complete after 419 laps.

Junior Johnson's team changes tires on Darrell Waltrip's Chevrolet during the 1983 Valleydale 500. A quick pit stop during that summer's Busch 500 enabled Waltrip to extend his Bristol win streak to six consecutive races, edging out Dale Earnhardt after officials called the race complete due to a thunderstorm. (Photo Courtesy Bristol Motor Speedway)

"Dale and I were having a pretty good go of it," Waltrip recalled years later. "There was rain in the area, and you could see the lightning off the third turn, and a caution came out. Everybody dove onto pit road, and Dale had beaten us out of the pits all night long. I was able to get in and beat Dale out of the pits. As soon as we came out and got up on the back straightaway, it started raining."

1984 Valleydale 500

Waltrip returned to Bristol for the 1984 Valleydale 500 with more new colors, a new sponsor, a new co-owner, and a new teammate, but he left with a familiar outcome. Sporting the red and white of Budweiser on the No. 11 Monte Carlo of Johnson and new partner Warner Hodgdon, Darrell and wife Stevie ultimately held up seven fingers in Victory Lane for seven straight wins.

This one had seemed improbable because Waltrip found himself a lap down to race leader Bobby Allison with just over 50 laps remaining, until Allison's car retired to the pits with mechanical ills. "I thought I saw Bobby's car smoking, and I told myself I was seeing things," Waltrip recalled. "But then he went into the pits. I just said, 'Seven, here comes eleven.'"

The Streak Ends

Darrell's own mechanical misfortune ultimately ended his remarkable winning streak during the 1984 Busch 500. Waltrip led 144 laps that night, the most of any driver, but pulled his Monte Carlo behind the wall with differential failure on lap 278. He returned to salvage a 21st-place finish that saw him fall farther behind race winner Terry Labonte in the 1984 championship chase. Labonte led the final 124 circuits on a rugged night as the recently sealed Bristol asphalt

Darrell Waltrip charges down the front straightaway in the 1984 Valleydale 500, heading toward his seventh-straight Bristol victory for team owner Junior Johnson. (David McGee Photo)

surface proved to be slippery and unyielding, sparking wrecks that eliminated many contenders.

"It's a shame," Waltrip said afterward. "All good things have to come to an end, but tonight was a real shame. That was probably the best car I've ever had here at Bristol." Decades later, he still reflects on the enormity of the accomplishment and the sting of losing.

"Winning seven in a row, that's 3½ years. That's 3,500 laps at Bristol that you could, I guess to some degree, say were flawless," Waltrip said. "Anybody that's ever raced at Bristol knows having one race there without any problems is pretty amazing. To have seven in a row? I look back on that, and it's got to be one of my biggest accomplishments."

Midwest ASA Magic

The Bristol Speedway's frontstretch concrete bleachers were scarcely half-filled with fans willing to sample the visiting American Speed Association (ASA), a primarily Midwest circuit making only its third foray into the Southeast. That 1982 Volunteer 300 was run in conjunction with another late-model racing group known as the All Pro Series, a southern circuit founded in 1980 by promoter Bob Harmon. Little did that paltry crowd of 8,200 folks know that they were peering directly into the future of NASCAR's Cup Series. Much like a minor-league baseball team showcases a future fireballer, Bristol's lineup included many rising stars.

1982 ASA Volunteer 300

The prerace hype focused on known commodities Darrell Waltrip, already a Winston Cup champion riding a three-race Bristol win streak at that time, and David Pearson, the three-time NASCAR champion and former Bristol winner who was reaching the twilight of his spectacular career. Knowledgeable railbirds kept their eyes glued on Russ Wallace's bushy-haired kid, Rusty, from Missouri; Bobby Allison's eldest son, Davey, who was in just his third season of driving; a quiet, self-confident youngster from Wisconsin named Alan Kulwicki; and that state's most famous racer, Dick "White Knight" Trickle.

Wallace, who already had nine NASCAR Cup starts under his belt, was using ASA and similar short-track-series victories to finance his then-meager NASCAR efforts. After getting his first look at Bristol's daunting high banks, Wallace obliterated the track qualifying record with a 15.912/120.500, 8 mph faster than the Bristol record for the heavier Cup cars and widely trumpeted as a world record for a half-mile oval. It surpassed a lap turned by Mark Martin in 1980 at Salem, Indiana.

The top 12 positions were determined by qualifying, and a trio of heat races established the rest of the lineup. Kulwicki qualified second fastest; Trickle and Darrell Waltrip comprised the second row as the 16 fastest qualifiers broke the previous track record. Butch Miller, Rick Wilson, and Jack Drolema won heat races.

A star-laden American Speed Association (ASA) field lines up for the 1982 Volunteer 300. Rusty Wallace set a half-mile qualifying record to earn the pole. In line beside his No. 14 Camaro are the machines of Alan Kulwicki, Dick Trickle, and Darrell Waltrip. (Photo Courtesy Bristol Motor Speedway)

NASCAR regular Neil Bonnett started last in the Volunteer 300 field after failing to qualify his Warner Hodgdon-backed Mustang, but he charged to the lead before the race's midway point. (Photo Courtesy Bristol Motor Speedway)

"Bristol Raceway is the elite track to me because it is in the South and it's a Winston Cup track," Wallace said, after qualifying. "There is no other track we go to where you can run this fast. When you've got three of the greatest drivers in the world out there, it's unreal to win the pole."

When the green flew, Rusty rode his red No. 14 Camaro to the initial lead but was quickly engulfed by a torrid battle between Waltrip and Georgia veteran Jody Ridley that wound up putting all but the top six cars a lap down by the 100-lap mark. When the leaders pitted under caution, Neil Bonnett's Warner Hodgdon–owned Mustang assumed the point after blazing through the 36-car field from his last-place starting spot. Then it was Trickle's turn at the lead, but he soon gave way to Wallace.

Series champion Mike Eddy took the lead on lap 165 and appeared to be cruising because a grinding crash eliminated Ridley's new Camaro, and Wallace fell five laps down due to a green-flag pit stop. Eddy earned the checkered flag after withstanding a late, furious charge from Trickle, who finished on his back bumper. Michigan's Bob Senneker finished 3rd, followed by Kulwicki and Wallace. Young Davey Allison registered a disappointing 21st-place finish, two spots ahead of Waltrip, who suffered a broken suspension. Pearson was unable to start the race due to an issue with his Camaro.

1983 ASA Volunteer 300

Local news accounts called the 1982 contest "one of the most competitive races ever run on Bristol's high banks," so despite that race losing $36,000, the ASA and the All Pro group returned to Bristol the following year, this time over the Fourth of July weekend. Eddy appeared poised for another victory until engine problems slowed his fleet Firebird, opening the door for Butch Miller.

Miller came from two laps down and took advantage of a late-race caution and a unique ASA rule to catch and pass Eddy's Firebird twice in the last three laps. Under

Legendary Midwest star Dick Trickle (No. 99) came up just short to eventual winner Mike Eddy in the 1982 Volunteer 300 and finished 2nd. Trickle crashed out of the 1983 installment after winning the pole and shattering the track qualifying record. (Photo Courtesy Bristol Motor Speedway)

ASA procedures, caution laps didn't count during the final 10 laps of the race, assuring fans of a sprint to the checkers. Eddy led 273 of the race's 300 laps, but Miller passed him for the lead on the white-flag circuit as Randy Couch pushed the series champion's car to the stripe.

"I didn't know Mike was having trouble until I closed on him for the second time," an elated Miller told reporters. "I didn't feel like I could have caught him without the last caution."

For the win, Miller's red and white Camaro appeared on the cover of *Circle Track*. Not bad, considering he was once four laps down after sustaining sheet-metal damage in an early-race five-car crash and a penalty for passing the pace car.

Dick Trickle was one of three drivers to better Wallace's year-old qualifying record, winning the pole at 120.842 mph, but he complained about the pace. "All of us like speed, but common sense tells you 120 is too fast here. You're just too busy. Lose your concentration for a second and you're done," Trickle told Bob Myers of *Circle Track*. Trickle led 14 early laps and was battling Jim Sauter for 2nd place when they collided.

"I was disappointed we lost the world record," 5th-place finisher Wallace admitted. "We used the record as a credential and would like to have kept it."

Alan Kulwicki started 4th and was running 3rd at lap 200 before encountering mechanical trouble and finishing 17th. That season's Winston Cup champion, Bobby Allison, saw his day end early after getting spun out exiting Turn 4.

The 1983 installment again attracted about 8,000 spectators willing to pay the $20 admission price for a show with an $85,000 payout, including $10,000 to win. Speedway promoter Larry Carrier had the final word, noting, "We can't charge $20 for a 300-lap race," adding that both ASA shows produced "big losses," ending the experiment after two tries.

All-American Challenge Series

Although the ASA didn't return, the retitled NASCAR All American Challenge Series was back at Bristol in August 1986, showcasing primarily southern late-model stars. Alabama's Dave Mader III won the 200-lap feature, but spectator turnout was again sparse. The following season, another midwestern organization, ARTGO, joined hands with NASCAR to bring many of the Midwest's brightest stars to Bristol. Dick Trickle didn't win the pole this time, but he outlasted fellow Wisconsin ace Rich Bickle and NASCAR's Bobby Allison for the win, one of eight that season that counted toward his seventh and final ARTGO series championship. A year later Trickle became NASCAR's oldest Rookie of the Year while subbing for an injured Bobby Allison in the Stavola Brothers Buick.

Larry Flickinger: Fastest Ever

The quickest and fastest run down Thunder Valley's quarter-mile dragstrip, either the original or today's improved, modern version, didn't occur at a national event or before a packed house. It wasn't run by a nitromethane-fueled dragster or a jet-powered beast, and, sadly, it wasn't even accurately recorded for the better part of four decades.

On a sunny Sunday afternoon, October 11, 1981, Larry "Flash" Flickinger made a single run down the left lane and into the record books at 4.30/344.82. It came during a lightly attended, one-off event called the IHRA World Jet Championships, featuring Flickinger and eight jet-powered dragsters.

Although modern drag racing fans are accustomed to quicker runs on the shorter 1,000-foot distance, even today's 10,000-hp Top Fuel Dragsters and Funny Cars have yet to attain (and may never reach) that speed. Tony Schumacher established Bristol's modern quarter-mile record of 4.477 seconds in 2004, and Doug Kalitta set the speed mark of 331.53 mph in 2006. The all-time NHRA quarter-mile speed record is Schumacher's 336.15 mph. Such speeds were nearly inconceivable in 1981.

What kind of vehicle ran 344 mph in 1981? A Chevy Vega–bodied Funny Car weighing about 1,000 pounds and powered by a solid rocket engine fueled by 90-percent hydrogen peroxide and compressed air. Branded *Natural High*, it generated about 5,000 pounds of thrust, or the equivalent of 10,000 hp, and Maryland native Flickinger established a track ET record on a half-power test run, running a 5.024/196.

The prerace drumbeat claimed that the car would run 400 mph, so Thunder Valley added 380 tons of sand at the end of its shutdown area in case of trouble

A look beneath the fiberglass Vega body reveals the fuel system, which fed hydrogen peroxide and compressed air to a rocket engine that generated 5,000 pounds of thrust, the equivalent of 10,000 hp. (Photo Courtesy Larry Flickinger)

for the much-anticipated run. Following his test pass, Flickinger predicted the car would run at least 380 mph. He was disappointed after clocking, what remains at this writing, the oldest record in organized drag racing after his survival instincts kicked in.

"It makes me mad because [if] I had held out just an instant longer before hitting the chutes, I would have had it," he said after his run at history. "The front body support broke and was rubbing a front tire. It's a wonder the tire didn't go flat. When you travel 600 feet per second and have a limited amount of stopping room, it's better to pull the chutes too early than too late. That's why I'm here now."

The car carried only enough fuel to travel 1,000 feet, so Flickinger estimated that if he momentarily delayed pulling the parachutes and shutting off the fuel to the engine, the car might have run in the 3-second range at 400.

Flickinger also exceeded his own IHRA unlimited records, surpassing the 4.72/342 marks established at Rockingham, North Carolina, in 1980, a run that earned him that season's IHRA Showman of the Year award. Flickinger, who operated an auto-body business in Maryland at that time, created the car with partner Roy "Speedy" Clark in hopes of eventually challenging for the world land speed record.

The website DragList.com ranks Flickinger's as the second-fastest rocket car to complete a run down an American dragstrip; the Bristol pass was his second-best effort, since the car ran 401 mph three years later at Blaney, South Carolina. The IHRA still maintains Flickinger's run as the rocket record.

Bristol fans have always held a special spot in their hearts for thrust-powered vehicles, jets, rockets, and the like: Jets for their flame shows and resounding burner pops, and rockets for their unimaginable speed. Flickinger's car was far from the first such creation to scoot down the Bristol quarter-mile, but it was the fastest.

In 1980, Ronnie Poole steered *Vulcan Shuttle*, a nearly stock-appearing Volkswagen embedded with a solid-propellant rocket for power, to a 9-second run during the 1980 Spring Nationals, making it one of the sport's slowest rocket cars. *Super Stock* credited the ill-fated *Shuttle* as drag racing's wildest exhibition vehicle of all time. The websites BangShift.com and Dragzine.com were less polite, calling it "one of the 11 most ill-fated drag cars ever" and one of the top-ranked "drag racing ideas that didn't work," respectively.

Candies & Hughes: Cajun-Spiced Nitro

One of drag racing's premier nitro teams, the Houma, Louisiana–based tandem of Paul Candies and Leonard Hughes, endured bitter disappointment in three consecutive Bristol Spring Nationals final rounds before changing drivers and categories to try to improve their luck.

1980 Spring Nationals

Candies & Hughes team driver Richard Tharp appeared to have the 1980 Spring Nationals field covered, qualifying 1st and running the best times of the first two rounds to defeat Jeb Allen and Mark Oswald en route to the finals. The car's differential seized up as he prepared to stage for the final, forcing him to sit helplessly as Bobby Hilton steered Jim and Alison Lee's car to Bristol's first $20,000 Top Fuel payday. A disgusted Tharp climbed out and stormed away.

The team's luck seemed to turn three months later. Tharp, Candies, and Hughes returned to Bristol as prohibitive favorites to win a new event on the Bristol schedule, the Summer Nationals. It was there that the enigmatic Tharp brashly proclaimed that he would take home the trophy after pacing qualifying with low ET of 5.878 seconds.

"I'm planning on winning this thing tomorrow, or, let me say, we are going to win it tomorrow," Tharp said on Saturday night. "I really can't see too much which would cause me trouble. The only thing that could give me trouble at all would probably be tire shake. That has given us some trouble in the past, but I'm not anticipating it happening on Sunday."

True to his word, Tharp dispatched Hilton in the semifinals with a new IHRA record speed of 247.93 mph and then knocked off Jeb Allen in the finals. The winner wasted no time reminding writers of his predictions. "I said I would run a 5.8 in qualifying, that I would set an IHRA speed record, and that I would win the race."

Richard Tharp burns out aboard the Candies & Hughes Top Fuel dragster at the 1980 Spring Nationals. He wheeled the team's car to two straight Bristol Spring Nationals final rounds, but breakage in 1980 and smoking the tires in 1981 dashed any hopes of victory. (David McGee Photo)

Leonard Hughes (left) installs pistons in the engine of the team's Top Fuel dragster during the 1980 Spring Nationals as team co-owner Paul Candies looks on. The car thundered all the way to the final round, but the team's bid to win the $20,000 top prize ended with mechanical failure. (David McGee Photo)

1981 Spring Nationals

That race wasn't the more prestigious, more lucrative Spring Nationals, and frustration developed again when the tour cycled back to Bristol in the spring of 1981. A whopping 23 Top Fuel dragsters were there to vie for a spot in the 8-car field and a shot at the $20,000 payday. After striking the tires on his first qualifier, Tharp's car stuck to the tune of 5.859 seconds, the weekend's third-quickest run behind pole winner Marvin Graham's 5.773 and rookie Mark Oswald's 5.850. At that time, the field was the quickest dragster field in Thunder Valley history, anchored by opening-day leader Jody Smart at 5.904.

Race-day misfortune again struck the Candies & Hughes team in the day's biggest contest. After losing lane choice in the semifinals, Tharp smoked the tires down the left lane against Jeb Allen, the 1980 IHRA champion. His shutoff 11.91 provided a frustrating view of Allen roaring to his second Spring Nationals title with a winning 5.99.

1982 Spring Nationals

Tharp and the team shook off that disappointment to wrest the 1981 IHRA Top Fuel crown from Mark Oswald by a scant 41 points. Tharp abruptly "retired" at season's end, opening the door for privateer Oswald to slide behind the butterfly steering wheel of the blue Candies & Hughes machine. That 1982 pairing appeared to gel at Bristol, where Oswald thundered to the Spring Nationals top-qualifying spot at 5.829/247.25 on Thunder Valley's new concrete starting pad.

"We've got more power, but the track won't hold it," Oswald said, before doing his best Richard Tharp imitation. "If we run three times tomorrow like that last run, we'll have $20,000." They didn't. After setting an IHRA speed record of 250.69 mph and marching into the finals, Oswald earned the team's third consecutive Spring Nationals runner-up at 6.02/247.93 to winner Jerry Ruth's quicker 5.96/241.93.

After also coming up short in that season's Top Fuel World Championship battle with Connie Kalitta, Candies and Hughes made the significant decision to return to the nitro Funny Car category for 1983 and pursue both the NHRA and IHRA world championships.

1983 Spring Nationals

The team arrived in Bristol that spring fresh off back-to-back final rounds, including a win in Oswald's native Ohio. The two-tone blue and white Candies & Hughes Pontiac Trans Am–bodied machine was second quickest behind Tom McEwen on opening day, and Oswald's 245.90-mph charge equaled Kenny Bernstein's track speed record. Oswald jumped to the top slot on Saturday night with a quicker 5.937/238.72 that set up a first-round matchup with McEwen, who ran 5.986 but fell out of the top half of the quickest eight-car field then assembled at Thunder Valley.

Oswald called the field "stout," given that it also included Raymond Beadle, Don Prudhomme, Kenny Bernstein, Billy Meyer, Dale Pulde, Al Segrini, and Rick Johnson in Roland Leong's *Hawaiian Punch* Charger.

Candies & Hughes shattered its Spring Nationals final-round jinx by switching to Funny Car and inserting Ohio native Mark Oswald behind the wheel. (John Beach Photo)

Mark Oswald (near lane) used a holeshot to earn the 1983 Spring Nationals Funny Car victory for Candies & Hughes over the quicker and faster machine of Don "The Snake" Prudhomme. (John Beach Photo)

Oswald turned away Beadle's *Blue Max* in the semifinals despite smoking the tires, but it cost him lane choice to Prudhomme's stellar 5.81/246.57 blast that took out Dale Pulde. For the win, underdog Oswald needed a massive holeshot and nailed it, outrunning Prudhomme's favored Pontiac Trans Am 6.00/236.22 to Prudhomme's substantially quicker and faster 5.86/245.90.

"Our car was capable of running the times he was running, but we were heading the wrong way," Oswald told reporters afterward. "We knew his car was running good, but we had to just make sure we could get ours down the track and hopefully beat him at the starting line."

The victory was worth $20,000, which matched their winnings for claiming the IHRA Funny Car Championship.

"We were definitely at a disadvantage," Oswald said. "His car was running extremely well, but anything can happen at this track. It makes me feel good to win this way. When the cars are running this close, it's critical at the line. I'm glad I was on time." Oswald admitted that they loaded up the clutch for the final round to make the car leave harder.

Prudhomme, who set a track ET record of 5.87 seconds in an opening-round triumph over two-time defending champion Billy Meyer, was matter-of-fact about the loss. "I was trying to run a conservative race, and he just took a chance on the start," Prudhomme admitted. "He gambled and won. What else can I say?"

While Candies and Hughes celebrated ending their Spring Nationals drought, their bad luck hitched a ride with former driver Richard Tharp. In a veritable replay of the 1980 final, Tharp's Top Fuel dragster sat motionless at the Thunder Valley starting line while he watched in disbelief as Gary Beck streaked to the $20,000 payday. "The rear end broke. It broke when I left the line. That's all I've got to say," a disbelieving Tharp said afterward. "It's the same story as three years ago. Three straight times I've watched somebody else win! I don't want to talk about this stuff anymore."

Dale Pulde: War Eagle to Warrior

Dale Pulde and crew chief/partner Mike Hamby faced a pleasant quandary as they prepared for Bristol's 1985 Spring Nationals. Should they continue to race their proven, year-old Firebird Funny Car or assemble their gleaming new Buick Somerset?

Tough Choices

The team's familiar orange transporter arrived in Bristol carrying the Firebird that was fresh off a victory at an IHRA race in North Carolina and the top qualifying spot at NHRA's Louisiana event. Parked nearby in the Bristol pits was a rental truck containing the new car's swoopy Buick Somerset body, resplendent in a gleaming yellow-gold scheme designed by artist John Pugh to suggest the color of primary sponsor Miller Brewing's product. Spread out like a giant model-car kit on Tuesday afternoon, the engine, driveline, tires, and other parts were bolted to the new Jim Hume chassis ahead of Friday afternoon's initial qualifying session.

Although Pulde and Hamby gained their fame and funded some of their efforts through T-shirt sales promoting a colorful series of *War Eagle* machines, the Buick, like its predecessor, was aptly rebranded *Warrior*.

"Even though Miller was the first beer company to put an eagle on its can, the eagle had to go because another company is using it as a trademark," Pulde explained at the time. "We still got to keep the [eagle] logo and an arrow down the side of the car."

1985 Spring Nationals

The plan was to test the new car in Friday qualifying and, if there were problems, unload the proven Pontiac for the Saturday sessions. A first-round 5.91 left Pulde 4th on the qualifying chart. "We're extremely happy with the new car, and we'll go with it," Pulde said afterward. "We're 4th, and that's not bad on the car's third run ever."

When the qualifying dust settled Saturday night, Pulde and Don Prudhomme used their quickest runs of the weekend to qualify 1st and 2nd at 5.694 and 5.705 seconds, respectively.

That knocked previous pole sitter John Force down to the 3rd spot. Kenny Bernstein, Jody Smart, Tom McEwen, Billy Meyer, and John Collins rounded out the top eight; the balance of IHRA's then-quickest Funny Car field (third quickest to that time among all associations) included Ed McCulloch, Rick Johnson, Joe Amato, Mark Oswald, Paul Smith, John Lombardo, John Pott, and Jim Head, who anchored the show at 5.989 seconds. Alternates Tim Grose and Jerry Caminito also brandished 5-second time slips.

On race day, Pulde opened his march to the finals with a stunning 5.710/260.11 blast to load Head's machine, but Prudhomme upped the ante on the oppose side of the ladder. He backed up a 263-mph qualifying run with a stellar 5.699/266.27 to dispose of John Pott, faster than any Funny Car or Top Fuel dragster had run at that time.

Dale Pulde enjoyed some of his greatest success when he teamed with Mike Hamby to field a series of War Eagle and Warrior Funny Cars. Between 1977 and 1985, they captured five Bristol national-event wins and three IHRA Funny Car championships. (David McGee Photo)

Californian Dale Pulde and teammate Mike Hamby finished their gleaming new Buick Somerset–bodied Funny Car in the Bristol pits in the days before the 1985 Spring Nationals. From there, they qualified atop the stellar 16-car field and won the Funny Car eliminator. (David McGee Photo)

Bristol was hardly a two-car shootout. Kenny Bernstein clocked low ET of round one at 5.673/260.11. He was also quickest in the second frame, using a 5.682 to down Texan Jody Smart, whose engine kicked the rods out at the finish line and whose parachute didn't deploy, sending the car into the trees near the shutdown area. Pulde, meanwhile, unleashed a 5.686/260.86 effort to best John Collins, and Prudhomme slipped to a 5.737/263.15 shot that was good enough to beat Billy Meyer.

Three of four semifinalists ran in the 5.60s; Pulde needed a holeshot to withstand Bernstein's Dale Armstrong–tuned *Budweiser King* 5.691/257.14 to a quicker and faster 5.667/258.62. Prudhomme then ran low ET of the eliminations. His fourth consecutive 260-mph pass earned him lane choice in the finals by acing out longtime rival Tom McEwen 5.662/263.15 to 5.867/242.58.

Both had trouble in the finals. Pulde clocked a winning 5.829/199.11; Prudhomme lifted off the throttle after an O-ring failed, spraying fuel onto his windshield.

"We never did get the car shifted out of first gear. I ran it as far as it could go in low gear. I expected Don to come roaring past at any time," Pulde said, after claiming $40,000, the team's richest payday ever. "The way it ran this weekend shocked us as much as anyone. We talked about running both cars during qualifying and seeing which [car] ran better. I think we made the right decision."

Prudhomme said that lifting was a split-second decision. "If I hadn't pulled out of it, it might have blown the supercharger into the stands," Prudhomme said. "Maybe if I had stayed on it, we might have been all right. I don't know."

1985 Fall Nationals

The Pulde-Hamby team ripped off two more IHRA victories that summer to take a commanding lead in that season's championship battle and then virtually sealed the deal when the tour returned to Bristol for the Fall Nationals. The

Dale Pulde returned to Bristol for the 1985 Fall Nationals and duplicated his spring performance by winning the Funny Car eliminator and virtually locking up his third IHRA Funny Car World Championship. (David McGee Photo)

gleaming, golden *Warrior*, one of the last holdouts to switch to dual fuel pumps and use an onboard computer, wasn't the weekend's top qualifier. That honor belonged to Kenny Bernstein, a rival in the title chase, who sailed to the top spot with a stunning 5.559/265.46 that covered the field by more than .10 second. Defending series champion Mark Oswald qualified 2nd, John Pott was 3rd, and John Lombardo was 4th in Raymond Beadle's *Blue Max* Mustang. He was followed by Pulde, Jim Head, Australian Graeme Cowin, and Billy Meyer, all separated by just .04 second.

On race day, Pulde was quickest of the first-round winners, as his 5.615/258.62 loaded Al Segrini; Bernstein clocked a 5.673/259.36 single and Lombardo went 5.698/253.52 to best Ed McCulloch and set up a titanic second-round race with Pulde. In the day's best contest, Pulde's Bill Schultz–tuned juggernaut got past the *Max* 5.672/250.69 to 5.685/249.30. Bernstein clocked a 5.622/257.14 bye run, but his hopes evaporated in the semifinals as Pulde's slowest pass of the day, 5.83/238.72, was enough to slip past Bernstein's tire-smoking 6.502/228.42 run in the right lane.

Oswald's day ended with a tremendous engine explosion against Cowin's *Aussie Raider*. The Candies & Hughes machine was leading when the supercharger let go. Oswald's car crossed from the right to left lane, slammed the guardrail, and caught fire, destroying the fiberglass body and seriously damaging the chassis, not to mention the 2nd-place team's bid for a second-straight championship.

"The explosion knocked my shield off my helmet and I couldn't see," Oswald said afterward. "I knew I was going to hit something, but I was trying to keep it straight. I got a burn around my eye and hurt my ankle, but I'm okay."

Pulde equaled Raymond Beadle's then-IHRA record of 18 Funny Car victories with a final-round single after opponent John Pott lost oil pressure and shut off. Pulde's 5.734/250.00 earned the victory and virtually clinched the team's third and final IHRA championship.

"We had some tough rounds to run. We kind of got a break against Kenny [Bernstein], and it was what we needed," Pulde said. "He smoked the tires, and we had changed engines in the car. The engine we put in had a bad coil, and the car slowed down. That's the first time all year we've changed the engine in the car. This is the win we needed."

Speedway Ownership Shuffle

The 1980s brought a flurry of changes in the ownership of Bristol's speedway, changes that brought the speedway to the brink of bankruptcy.

Owners Lanny Hester and Gary Baker split up in 1981, with Baker purchasing Hester's interest, ascending to the track presidency, and hiring a young Eddie Gossage to replace former public relations director Ed Clark. By that November, Baker partnered with millionaire California industrialist Warner Hodgdon on both the Bristol and Nashville tracks, despite Hodgdon never having seen Bristol. Their 1982 season began with plans for $2.5 million in new grandstands, restrooms, parking, and other improvements.

"Bristol is one of the finest tracks on the Winston Cup circuit and has long enjoyed being an important stop for competitors," Baker said at the time. "We plan to expand on that and make it much bigger. I don't think you are going to see the track sit still. We have still more plans for it, and by the time we are finished, Bristol will be a monument to the sport."

Many of those plans never came to fruition. Hodgdon became Bristol's sole owner in July 1983, buying out Baker's shares, naming Larry Carrier president and general manager, and publicly pledging to continue improvements. "We've had fantastic spectator support, and we'd like for it to continue. We're smart enough to know that if it wasn't for the spectators, none of us would be here," Hodgdon said.

A Black Cloud's Silver Lining

Just over a year later, in late 1984, Bristol's future hung perilously in the balance. Hodgdon was preparing to file Chapter 11 bankruptcy in California, and both the Bristol and Nashville tracks would be included. As word spread, names of potential buyers began to surface, prompting Carrier to play his cards. First, he secured an affidavit from NASCAR stating that, regardless of who owned Bristol, the race dates belonged to Carrier. He then filed his own action against Hodgdon, who owed him money through Hodgdon's purchase of Bristol Dragway and interest in Carrier's IHRA drag race sanctioning group.

The California bankruptcy court appointed Carrier as a debtor in possession and selected him to run the track. That allowed him to purchase Speedway stock, pay off the banks, and continue operations in the 1985 season, the same year that Nashville disappeared forever from the premier series schedule.

The sellout streak began in the 1980s, and then Carrier poured gasoline on a fire that could be seen from coast to coast. Through his relationship with a new cable-television entity (the Entertainment and Sports Programming Network, ESPN), Carrier prevailed on them to televise the August night race in addition to the spring show. With temporary lighting towers filling in the shadows, a primetime audience got to witness Dale

Earnhardt, Tim Richmond, and Darrell Waltrip slug it out for the win, with many of the fireworks Bristol had become known for. On Monday morning, the ticket-office telephones didn't stop ringing as fans clamored for tickets to 1986 races.

Rusty Wallace: My Favorite Track

Rusty Wallace felt right at home the first time he surveyed Bristol's speedway. Its high-banked corners closely resembled the midwestern cliffs of Salem and Winchester, Indiana, and Odessa, Missouri, where he regularly plied his trade with ASA and other short-track series. It was during his first venture south to Bristol in 1982 that Wallace established a single-lap qualifying record for a half-mile oval that surpassed Bristol's Cup record by a whopping 8 mph.

Determined to race in NASCAR's premier division, Wallace moved to North Carolina in 1984 to compete full time in the Cup Series, securing a deal with car owner Cliff Stewart and received Rookie of the Year honors.

Wallace led his first competitive laps at Bristol in 1985 and posted a top-five finish in that season's Valleydale 500. That owner/driver relationship soured, and Wallace departed Stewart's team at season's end, taking sponsor Alugard Anti-Freeze to Blue Max Racing, where he replaced Tim Richmond in Pontiacs prepared by crew chief Barry Dodson. Raymond Beadle, the three-time national drag racing champion, added a NASCAR team to his holdings in 1983 but, despite a few wins, hadn't contended for championships.

Wallace and Beadle sprayed champagne in Victory Lane the first time they ventured to Bristol together, but it wasn't easy.

Rusty Wallace captured his first NASCAR premier series victory at Bristol in the 1986 Valleydale 500. Driving for car owner Raymond Beadle, a world-champion drag racer, Wallace led the race's final 101 laps. He credited his crew with a fast pit stop that helped with track position. (Photo Courtesy John Beach)

1986 Valleydale 500

Wallace found himself 2 mph off the pace of Geoff Bodine's pole-winning Chevrolet when qualifying was over for the 1986 Valleydale 500. Bodine's Hendrick Motorsports entry shattered the old track record with a lap of 114.859 mph; all Wallace could muster was a lap of 112.447. His 14th starting position would be nearly halfway back in the 32-car field, meaning the driver who ranked 5th in NASCAR points entering the race would have to charge to the front.

The Valleydale 500 finally took the green flag following an hour-long rain delay, with pole sitter Bodine quickly surrendering the lead to Neil Bonnett, who led until lap 74 when the accelerator stuck and his Chevrolet slammed into the outside wall. After pit stops, Dale Earnhardt took the point and led until another caution on lap 160. In all, Earnhardt led three times for 105 laps during the first half of the contest. Wallace worked his way to the front for the first time on lap 240 and led 68 circuits before another caution.

Wallace paced the field back to green but soon gave way to Bristol master Darrell Waltrip, who took his first lead on lap 315 and began pulling away. A four-tire change on the next pit stop righted Wallace's handling issues, and he soon tracked down Waltrip's Chevrolet. "I had a hard time getting by him because Darrell's a doggone good driver. He was running a high line, and I was running good down low, but I couldn't get around him," Wallace told reporters after the race.

Wallace passed Waltrip to lead lap 400 and extended his margin to more than half a lap over the race's final 100 caution-free circuits.

"It's a dream come true. It was just something I didn't think would ever happen," Wallace said afterward. "Those last 20 laps seemed like 200. I think I started losing my lead at one point because I was too busy watching the scoreboard change every lap." The winner admitted that he refused to believe he'd won until the checkered flag flew. "I knew I had a shot at winning, but I never thought I had it. Even when they showed the white flag, I stayed cautious until I tiptoed across the finish line."

Wallace collected $34,780 for the victory and moved to 4th in points. Ricky Rudd never led a lap in Bud Moore's Ford but posted a 2nd-place finish, 10.6 seconds behind the winner. Waltrip finished 3rd and was the only other driver on the lead lap. Bodine suffered engine failure and finished 24th. The victory was the first of 35 in Wallace's Hall of Fame career.

However, the Bristol track that Wallace regularly called his favorite nearly claimed the Missouri native in a vicious 1988 practice crash. Wallace was exiting Turn 4 when a blown right-side front tire sent his car into the outside wall before barrel rolling down the front straightaway and contacting the inside frontstretch wall. Dr. Jerry Punch, an ESPN broadcaster and emergency room physician, rushed to the car and revived an unconscious Wallace, who was transported to the Bristol hospital.

1989 Valleydale 500

Although Wallace returned to compete that weekend, he was in pain, and the accident damaged his championship bid. When he and his Kodiak-backed team returned to Bristol the next spring, it was with a chip on their shoulders: Bristol owed them, and they were intent on collecting.

"I woke up sick on Friday, and when I got in the car everything was spinning," Wallace confessed. "At Bristol, it's so small and so fast you feel like you're spinning in a salad bowl anyway, and it's a real problem. I went to Bristol Memorial Hospital, and Jerry Punch gave me some stuff to knock it out. I woke up in the middle of the night, and the vertigo was gone."

Wallace ultimately emerged victorious from a wild 1989 Valleydale 500 that saw 16 drivers swap the lead a Bristol-record 34 times in a race slowed by a record 20 cautions, many for blown tires. At that time, NASCAR was in the midst of a tire war between Goodyear and upstart Hoosier, and Wallace and crew chief Barry Dodson tried both brands in their quest for victory. The team started the race on Goodyears, tried one set of Hoosiers, and then returned to Goodyear during the race's latter stages.

"We're a never-say-die team," Wallace said afterward. "We got a lap down when we had a tire problem, but we were able to get it back, thanks to the crew."

The victory was Wallace's third in the season's first six races, as he beat rival Darrell Waltrip back to the stripe by .26 second. Geoff Bodine, who had been running 2nd before his passenger-side front tire went down in the final 10 laps, finished 3rd, followed by Davey Allison, rookie Dick Trickle, and pole sitter Mark Martin, who finished 6th.

Rusty Wallace won Bristol's 1989 spring race, which served as a stepping stone toward clinching that season's NASCAR premier series title for car owner Raymond Beadle and crew chief Barry Dodson. (David McGee Photo)

Rusty Wallace celebrates his 50th NASCAR premier series victory after winning the 2000 Food City 500 at Bristol Motor Speedway. Wallace later swept that season's August night race at a track he long described as his favorite. (Photo Courtesy Bristol Motor Speedway)

Dale Earnhardt had a different kind of tire problem. After leading 74 laps, Earnhardt pitted and hit a tire left on pit road by a crewman for Michael Waltrip. His Richard Childress team replaced the damaged tie-rod, but Earnhardt returned to the track 13 laps down. He made up 5 of those laps but still finished 16th.

That 1989 victory helped catapult Wallace to that season's championship. Before hanging up his helmet, Wallace brought his Bristol victory total to 9, the most of any of the 26 tracks he ran on NASCAR's premier circuit. It included his 49th and landmark 50th victories in 1999 and 2000, the wins exactly one year apart. Those nine wins tie him with Cale Yarborough and Earnhardt for second-most victories of all time at Bristol, behind only Darrell Waltrip. Ask Wallace about it, and he'll likely recount the ones that got away, especially a pair of bump-and-run finishes with Jeff Gordon.

Top Sportsman Takes Over

Much like the Funny Car phenomenon of the 1960s, the Top Sportsman eliminator revolutionized drag racing during the second half of the 1980s, and its overwhelming popularity ultimately led to establishing Pro Modified. Top Sportsman, the outrageous class with the innocuous-sounding name, evolved from an IHRA quick-ET eliminator to attract massive amounts of media and fan attention. Many of its outrageous machines resembled classic 1950s and 1960s Detroit iron, packing headline-grabbing performance and piloted by some larger-than-life characters.

The Top Sportsman brand name arrived in 1985, at a time when the number of competitive Top Fuel cars was rapidly dwindling and the nitro Funny Car class was dominated by a few heavily supported teams fielding wind-tunnel-influenced bodies bearing scant resemblance to production cars. Top Sportsman gave the sport a much-needed breath of fresh air, offering a visually varied mix of entrants that regularly appeared on the covers of enthusiast magazines. The full-bodied cars generally lacked "corporate correctness," were colorful and imaginative in appearance, in some cases ran quicker and faster than Pro Stock, and could be as unpredictable to drive as a Fuel Altered.

It's little wonder that handlers Charles Carpenter, Rob Vandergriff, Bill Kuhlmann, Gordy Hmiel, Scotty Cannon, Blake Wiggins, and others quickly became household names and that Revell Models immortalized many of the machines as plastic model-car kits.

Carpenter, a Charlotte, North Carolina, racer with a penchant for 1955 Chevrolets, became the Daniel Boone of outrageous door slammers. After coaxing his mostly steel, 2,700-pound behemoth to run in the low-8-second range, *Super Stock* labeled it the "Beast From the East."

Just three races into the 1985 season, Carpenter burst out of the pack at Bristol's Spring Nationals to qualify 13th in a 32-car field, with an 8.21/165. On race day, Carpenter earned more exposure than race winner Don Young by guiding the classic shoebox into the final round but losing to the eventual world champion's rear-engine dragster. The car was featured in magazines and aptly dubbed the "world's fastest '55 Chevy."

It wasn't long before other trendsetting cars appeared. Tennesseans Jim Bryant and Rob Vandergriff prepared a 1957 Chevy Bel Air replica with a fiberglass body and Pro Stock–style chassis. The team qualified atop the 1986 Spring Nationals field. Soon, similar 1950s-era Fords and Chryslers and 1963 Corvettes were entering the fray. Bill Kuhlmann's Camaro was the first to break through the 200-mph barrier in 1987, but it was October 1988 before a Top Sportsman car blasted into the 6-second zone, and that run occurred at Bristol.

The Knoxville, Tennessee–based team of driver Rob Vandergriff and owner Jim Bryant captivated the sport of drag racing in the 1980s with their series of radical 1957 Chevrolet entries in the wildly popular Top Sportsman eliminator category. (David McGee Photo)

6-Second Rocket

Driver Gordy Hmiel and engine builder Scott Shafiroff made the 1988 Fall Nationals crowd erupt when a 6.99-second ET appeared on the scoreboard. Hmiel won over Ronnie Hood, but the run still could have been quicker.

"I left, and when I pulled second gear, the tires broke loose and the car started to skate around," Hmiel told *Super Stock*. "Farther down the track, I activated the second stage of nitrous [oxide], and it kept spinning. At 1,100 feet it stabilized and smoothed

The pioneer of the "shoebox" revolution was Charles Carpenter, whose series of radical 1955 Chevrolets earned a huge fan following from coast to coast. Engines packing more than 600 ci and copious amounts of nitrous oxide spawned low-7-second performances in the 1980s. (David McGee Photo)

A swoopy later iteration of the Vandergriff and Bryant 1957 Chevrolet earned the No. 1 designation for winning the Super Chevy Series title. After Top Sportsman evolved into Pro Modified, Vandergriff qualified quickest at the 1991 Spring Nationals and was class runner-up. (David McGee Photo)

The first Top Sportsman team to record a 6-second run was the **Not Quite Over The Hill Gang** *Pontiac* of New York driver Gordy Hmiel and car owner Scott Shafiroff. The historic pass occurred at Bristol Dragway during the 1988 Fall Nationals. (David McGee Photo)

Chapter 3: Taking Center Stage in the 1980s 129

Among the fan favorites in the new Pro Modified class was Ronnie "The BOSS" Sox. The veteran captured a victory at the 1990 Fall Nationals and remained a force for years with this throwback Mercury. That last victory gave Sox Bristol wins in four decades. (David McGee Photo)

out." Expecting to hear that the car had run yet another 7.0, Hmiel was relieved to learn that he'd run 6.99.

At the 1989 Spring Nationals, fans saw the sport's first side-by-side 200-mph race between full-bodied cars as Bill Kuhlmann defeated Blake Wiggins 6.97/201.81 to 7.04/200.01. After two years of lobbying, IHRA president and Thunder Valley owner Jim Ruth and executive vice president Ted Jones established Pro Modified as a professional category for 1990. Racers responded with 36 cars entering the Spring Nationals to try to qualify for the 16-car field. Kuhlmann qualified on the pole, but New Yorker Mike Ashley nabbed the victory. Legendary Ronnie Sox was runner-up aboard a Mercury Comet and returned later that year to capture that season's Fall Nationals title.

At the 1991 Spring Nationals, Rob Vandergriff's Pro Modified roared to the weekend's quickest ET at 6.97 seconds and then ran that number in successive wins over Pat Moore and Bill Kuhlmann. He narrowly escaped Sox in the semifinals, 7.03/198.62 to 7.03/198.53, before falling to Scotty Cannon's aerodynamically enhanced 1937 Chevrolet 7.01 to 7.06, Vandergriff's slowest lap of the day.

Mountain Motor Mastery

Selecting four names to fill a Mount Rushmore–like monument for Pro Stock drag racing would be a daunting task, but Bob Glidden, Warren Johnson, Don Nicholson, and Lee Shepherd all certainly deserve consideration. All rank among NHRA's most successful drivers, and each man also played a role in legitimizing IHRA's rowdy, down-south brand of "Mountain Motor" Pro Stock competition, a fact borne out every time the class raced at Thunder Valley in the 1980s.

After years of operating in the shadow of the NHRA and AHRA, IHRA's profile rose sharply during the first half of the 1980s with races that attracted large crowds, full fields of name-brand drivers and cars, national television coverage, and significant sponsorship. Although the unlimited-displacement concept took root in 1977, southeastern superstars Lee Edwards, Roy Hill, and Ronnie Sox primarily shared the victories in IHRA's earliest offerings.

The Professor's Office

Minnesota native Warren Johnson changed that, making a championship splash during the 1979 season by winning three national events, including Bristol's Spring Nationals. (The next year, the record $10,000 Spring Nationals winner's purse attracted Bob Glidden back to an IHRA race for the first time in four seasons.) Johnson, in a Camaro fielded by Georgian Jerome Bradford, bested rising star Rickie Smith for the cash. Johnson captured his third-straight Spring Nationals title in 1981, beating Harold Denton for the $10,000 payout with a swoopy Monte Carlo that resembled a NASCAR stocker but likely couldn't fit many stock-body templates.

"IHRA is the only organization in the business which is making an effort to improve the purses, and I realize they are doing what they can in terms of upgrading the Pro Stock money," Johnson said, after winning the 1981 race.

Nicholson and engine builder Jon Kaase ventured over to Bristol for the first time in years and reached the 1980 Summer Nationals finals before losing to Smith's

Bob Glidden returned to Thunder Valley for Bristol's 1980 Spring Nationals after a four-year absence to try his luck at unlimited Mountain Motor Pro Stock racing. The veteran went a couple of rounds in this Ford Fairmont and soon became a series regular. (Chris Haverly Photo)

Mustang, the first such machine to run in the 7-second range. Warren Johnson and Ronnie Sox largely owned the following season, with Sox abandoning his traditional red, white, and blue Mopars to wheel Dean Thompson's black and yellow Mustang to the championship.

1982 Spring Nationals

The floodgates cracked wider in 1982 when Lee Shepherd and engine-building partners David Reher and Buddy Morrison ventured east from Texas, putting together a powerplant larger than 500 ci and winning Bristol's Spring Nationals title over another NHRA stalwart, New Jersey's Frank Iaconio.

Iaconio was the early qualifying leader, followed by Rickie Smith, Ronnie Sox, and Lee Shepherd, all in the 7-second range. Shepherd served notice the following day with a track-record lap of 7.822/176.47 in his Camaro, telling reporters, "We have the car dialed in, and everything is right for racing." No kidding. The top six qualifiers were all in the 7s, and Bob Glidden was among those who didn't make the 16-car show. On race day, Shepherd punished the Pro Stock field, making four runs between 7.87 and 7.89 that turned back Jerome Bradford, Warren Johnson, Rickie Smith, and Iaconio to win the purse.

"We weren't sure of the engine's capabilities at first, [but] it sure responded well," the soft-spoken Shepherd said of the team's foray into Mountain Motor racing. "You always have to be on your toes when you're facing someone like Iaconio."

Shepherd Owns Bristol

Much to the competition's chagrin, Shepherd and his team committed to running the full 1983 season and promptly wrestled the championship title from Smith by reaching six final rounds in nine races. Those included a runner-up at the Spring Nationals and a victory at Bristol's new Fall Nationals. Shepherd was the favorite to reprise his Spring Nationals victory, qualifying number one and clocking low ET of each round of eliminations, but he fell victim to Rickie Smith's patented, quick reaction time in the final.

"I knew there wasn't but one way to win it, and that was to cut a good light," a relieved Smith told reporters. "He [Shepherd] had me covered." Shepherd ran 7.72 in the finals but still trailed Smith's holeshot 7.82 at the stripe. "He was exceptionally fast off the line. I must have been exceptionally late," Shepherd said.

The story was much the same in 1984 as Shepherd emerged from a season-long battle with Rickie Smith, Roy Hill, Billy Ewing, and Darrell Alderman to retain

Driver Lee Shepherd warms the Goodyears prior to winning the 1984 Spring Nationals. Shepherd and teammates David Reher and Buddy Morrison formed a virtually unbeatable combination when they ventured into IHRA Pro Stock racing in the 1980s. They won Bristol four times in five final rounds, along with a pair of championships. (David McGee Photo)

the world title. When Shepherd turned back Billy Ewing in the Spring Nationals finals, it marked his third-straight victory that season. To nobody's surprise, Shepherd also swept the Fall Nationals crown, downing Bob Glidden's Ford in the finals 7.556/186.33 to 7.603/183.67.

Shepherd's March 1985 death in a testing crash in Ardmore, Oklahoma, sent shockwaves through the sport. The Reher-Morison team regrouped and returned to the track at Bristol's Spring Nationals with Pro Stock rookie Bruce Allen in the driver's seat. In true Hollywood fashion, they won the race by beating points leader and engine customer Billy Ewing in the final round. Allen said his greatest challenge was learning to leave the starting line on a pro tree given the team's voluminous horsepower.

"We had driver training one day in Texas," Allen said after winning. "They have never put any kind of pressure on me. Any pressure that has been there has been put there by myself. But really, it's easy for me; all I do is drive."

Glidden's Turn

Indiana native Bob Glidden took ownership of the Fall Nationals in 1985 and 1986, becoming a factor in both world championship points chases. His 1985 victory came on a string of 7.4-second ETs that broke an eight-year Bristol drought and allowed him to pass Ford rival Rickie Smith for 2nd place in the title fight.

"We were really consistent today, something that's been missing much of the season in the IHRA races, and that's why we're behind in the points," Glidden said afterward. "We really hadn't put our full effort into IHRA races until this season. We spent a lot of time during the winter building our big engines for IHRA events."

After finishing 2nd in the 1985 points, Glidden was a player in the 1986 chase, the final season IHRA enjoyed corporate support from R.J. Reynolds. Although the man known as "Mad Dog" missed out on the title, his 1986 Fall Nationals was a performance for the ages.

Glidden parlayed his number-one qualifying status into a doubleheader victory, claiming both the $15,000 Hurst Pro Stock Shootout and the Fall Nationals titles. He defeated Jim Ruth's *Party Time* Pontiac in Saturday's Hurst final round and rebuffed Buddy Ingersoll's turbocharged V-6 Buick, which IHRA's *Drag Review* called "the world's most controversial race car," to win the event. Buick had successfully lobbied IHRA to allow the car to compete. Its science-project technology made it inconsistent until the Bristol showdown.

Ingersoll sent shockwaves through the pits by pacing the weekend's first qualifying session with his 268-ci Buick at 7.37/191.48 while the carbureted 600-plus-ci cars were stranded in the 7.40s. That changed on Saturday, when Glidden unloaded his Thunderbird and obliterated the track record on his first pass. Although Glidden's Ford had the field covered, it was Ingersoll, ultimately the weekend's second-quickest qualifier, who sent shivers through the field. The Buick shot to the finals, disposing of world champion Rickie Smith in the semifinals.

"I'd just as soon run Buddy as anybody," Glidden said after putting away the white Buick 7.282/193.96 to 7.371/189.07.

Bob Glidden (far lane) captured an epic win in Bristol's 1986 Fall Nationals Pro Stock final, turning back the upset bid of Buddy Ingersoll's radical twin-turbocharged 268-ci Buick V-6. Ingersoll's car sparked much concern among the Mountain Motor racers as he narrowly lost to Glidden's 700-ci Ford. (David McGee Photo)

CHAPTER 4

Front-row starter Dale Earnhardt needed lots of attention from his Richard Childress Racing crew after backing his Chevrolet into the outside wall early in the 1991 spring race. Although it was a forgettable day, with the team placing 20th, the crew eventually claimed the 1991 championship. (David McGee Photo)

RAISING THE BAR IN THE 1990S

Transformational change was the central theme of the 1990s as Bristol's growth during the first half of the decade paled in comparison to improvements delivered by new owner O. Bruton Smith. After acquiring both Bristol facilities in 1996, Smith's team raised the bar to once unimaginable levels. By decade's end, Bristol's speedway ranked among the world's largest, best appointed sports stadiums and the Smith empire's first dragstrip was transformed into a world-class showplace.

Home Cooking

The day before Bristol's 1990 Busch 500, a prophetic Ernie Irvan predicted he and his Morgan-McClure Motorsports team were "not far" from their first win. The transplanted Californian made good on his prediction, wheeling the team's bright-yellow Chevrolet to his first premier series victory and the first for the team from nearby Abingdon, Virginia.

Ernie Irvan wheeled the Morgan-McClure Motorsports Chevrolet to his and the team's first NASCAR victory at Bristol's 1990 Busch 500 night race. In his first season driving for the team, Irvan held off a furious charge from Rusty Wallace to take the checkers. (Photo Courtesy Bristol Motor Speedway)

"We've been saying a win would come. We just didn't know it would come tonight. But it couldn't have come at a better place," a jubilant Irvan said. Team co-owner Larry McClure called the moment "a dream come true."

Irvan started 6th and ran among the leaders all night. Pole sitter Dale Earnhardt appeared to be the class of the field, leading four times for 350 laps before getting together with the lapped car of Ricky Rudd on lap 411, allowing Irvan to shoot the gap and take the lead exiting Turn 4.

"We didn't have our car just perfect after Dale had his problem, [but] we felt we were good enough to win," Irvan said. From there he had to withstand challenges from former Bristol winner Rusty Wallace during the closing laps. Wallace made several runs at Irvan but never touched him. "All he had to do was tap me. He ran a hard, clean race, and my hat is off to him," Irvan said.

Mark Martin finished 3rd, followed by Terry Labonte, Sterling Marlin, and Alan Kulwicki, all on the lead lap.

"We beat the best with the best driver, the best crew chief, and the best sponsor," McClure said at the end of a landmark day that included announcing a three-year extension of their Kodak sponsorship.

The Morgan-McClure team formed in 1983 when auto dealer McClure and business partner Tim Morgan acquired the assets of longtime NASCAR journeyman G. C. Spencer. McClure's brothers Ed, Jerry, and Teddy, soon joined the effort. They first operated in a small garage near the landmark Moonlite Drive-in Theater, with the veteran Spencer serving as advisor and young Tony Glover, son of 1979 NASCAR National Late Model Sportsman champion Gene Glover, serving as crew chief.

The team earned its first premier series pole at Bristol's 1988 Valleydale 500 with driver Rick Wilson; by 1990, Irvan succeeded Wilson as the team's ninth driver. The

Morgan-McClure team ultimately found its greatest success on the superspeedways of Daytona and Talladega; its first victory-lane visit, after 161 starts, occurred surrounded by the home folks at Bristol. The team ultimately posted 14 premier series wins.

Unlike most NASCAR teams, Morgan-McClure chose to operate three hours north of the Charlotte metro area, which serves as the epicenter for nearly all other teams. It was a close-knit group, drawing most of its employees locally rather than from Charlotte, where crewmembers often switched teams with regularity, taking tools and trade secrets to their new employers.

A Heritage of Speed

A big reason for the Morgan-McClure team's success, despite operating in relative isolation, can be traced to its home region's vibrant racing history. East Tennessee and Southwest Virginia have produced generations of racers and an ample supply of capable mechanics and fabricators.

As far back as the 1950s and 1960s, pioneer drivers Bill Morton, Brownie King, Paul Lewis, Bill McMahan, Herman Beam, and George Green trekked down from the mountains to compete at Daytona, Darlington, and other far-flung speedways. Also during that time, Bristol auto dealer Ron Henard used his Ron's Ford business to field cars for Nelson Stacy and the Wood Brothers, often prompting other regional dealerships to sponsor race cars.

Paul Lewis, for example, scored back-to-back top-five Bristol finishes during the 1966 season. He ran 2nd behind Dick Hutcherson in the Southeastern 500 and finished 4th in that summer's Volunteer 500, sandwiched between David Pearson and Bobby Allison. Four nights later, Lewis held

Paul Lewis of Johnson City twice won Bristol poles in the NASCAR Late Model Sportsman class during the 1970s. Lewis was a premier series regular for nearly all of the 1960s, earning one victory and narrowly losing a couple of Bristol races. (John Beach Photo)

off Pearson and Allison to score his lone Grand National win at Smoky Mountain Raceway in nearby Maryville, Tennessee. In both cases, Allison drove a 1965 Chevelle, owned by East Tennessee car owner J. D. Bracken.

After leaving the Grand National ranks, Lewis enjoyed a successful second career in NASCAR's Late Model Sportsman ranks, often driving for the Bracken brothers. That combination later earned back-to-back Bristol poles for Late Model Sportsman races in 1971 and 1972 against packed fields that included Cup stars David Pearson, Cale Yarborough, Bobby Allison, and Benny Parsons.

"We sat on the pole twice at Bristol, [but] we never had any luck there," Lewis recounted years later. "I almost won that [1966] Grand National race, [but] I lost the brakes and had a bad vibration. They knew we were there."

During the 1970s and early 1980s, the region became a hotbed for NASCAR Late Model Sportsman racing, served as a forerunner of the Busch (now Xfinity) Series, and produced national champions L. D. Ottinger of Newport, Tennessee, and Gene Glover of Kingsport, Tennessee, as well as race winners Brad Teague and John A. Utsman and other notable car owners, including the Bracken brothers, Charlie Henderson, A. J. King, and Ed Whitaker.

Ottinger won the 1975 and 1976 NASCAR national championships and enjoyed success at Bristol. He won a 300-lap NASCAR Late Model Sportsman race at Bristol in 1973 and a week later finished 2nd in the premier series Volunteer 500 with relief help from Late Model Sportsman rival Gene Glover. Ottinger also collected a Bristol Busch Series race win in 1990.

Utsman made all six premier series starts for car owner Ed Whitaker, but Whitaker enjoyed his greatest success in the NASCAR Busch Series, where his machines, prepared in a compact garage in Bristol, Virginia, amassed 28 victories with standouts Harry Gant and Morgan Shepherd behind the wheel. Whitaker's last win came in 1994; his record stood for a decade before factory-supported, Cup-affiliated teams surpassed it. Not surprisingly, much of that success came at Bristol.

Between 1983 and 1986, Whitaker's cars captured two victories, a pole, and five top-five finishes in the five times he and driver Morgan Shepherd competed there. "The first time we went there, we sat on the pole with Morgan [Shepherd] and had Dale Earnhardt on the outside pole," Whitaker recalled years later. Shepherd wound up 3rd that afternoon, trailing Jack Ingram and Butch Lindley; Earnhardt was eliminated in a second-lap crash.

Shepherd and Whitaker returned to dominate Bristol Motor Speedway in May 1983, leading the final 115 circuits of the 150-lap race and finishing a lap ahead of 2nd-place driver Dale Jarrett. After a season of driving for someone else, Shepherd

Harry Gant races with Dale Earnhardt (No. 8) during the 1988 Budweiser 200, Earnhardt's lone series Bristol victory. Bristol car owner Ed Whitaker's No. 7 machines once made him one of the winningest owners in the former Busch Series, primarily with Gant behind the wheel. (David McGee Photo)

returned to the seat of Whitaker's Buick in 1986 and recorded back-to-back victories at Martinsville and Bristol. At Thunder Valley, Shepherd led 120 of 200 laps, holding off Earnhardt and Brad Teague.

Gant joined Whitaker in 1987, and the team put together a series of wins at larger tracks. However, bad luck haunted them at Bristol. "One night the alternator went dead. One night we had a pit stop, and the wheel fell off. One day he [Gant] ran over a tire on the track. It was just one thing and then another," Whitaker said.

They broke the jinx in March 1992 thanks to some strategy by crew chief Chris Carrier that rewarded Whitaker with his final Bristol victory. Early on, the team's chances appeared as dismal as the cold, rainy weather, with Gant mired near the back of the 29-car field. "Jeff Gordon was about to lap us, and they put the caution out, so we came in and changed tires. We went back out, and everybody else had stayed out," Whitaker said. Rain prompted NASCAR to stop the race and restart it hours later.

"When they started the race back, everybody else had to stop, and we were in front. He ran away and hid from them," Whitaker said of Gant, who led the final 134 laps and beat Davey Allison for the win.

Chris Carrier, who grew up within earshot of the Bristol Speedway, made a visit to Bristol's Victory Lane while working for Henderson Motorsports, also based in Abingdon, Virginia. Rick Wilson, who also drove for Morgan-McClure at that time, qualified the Henderson team's Oldsmobile on the Budweiser 200 pole and captured his first Busch Series victory. Rain pushed the race to Monday afternoon, where Wilson led four times for 161 laps.

Rick Wilson (center) captured the win in Bristol's 1989 Budweiser 200 for car owner Charlie Henderson (right) of Abingdon, Virginia, and crew chief Chris Carrier, who grew up a short distance from the Bristol track. (David McGee Photo)

That victory was the second of three for Henderson, who has fielded cars in NASCAR's top three series and other divisions. Second-generation driver Caleb Holman of Abingdon brought Henderson back to Bristol's Victory Lane in the track's final Hooters Pro Cup Series race, the 2008 Aaron's 150.

Carrier later served as crew chief for a number of teams and drivers at every level, including a stint at Morgan-McClure Motorsports. He returned to Bristol's Victory Lane in 2012, calling the shots for K&N East Series driver Nelson Piquet Jr., and again in 2016, with driver Chad Finchum and the Martin-McClure Motorsports team led by former driver Eric McClure, son of Morgan-McClure partner Jerry McClure.

Valleydale Meats 500

Race winner Rusty Wallace may have been the only happy driver after Bristol's 1991 Valleydale Meats 500. Most of the other 32 starters were upset, mostly about confusing new pit-road and restart rules that they blamed for numerous accidents. The guidelines, in place for the first time that weekend, propelled Wallace past six other cars under a late caution and into position to record his first win for new team owner Roger Penske.

The landmark race included a record 40 lead changes, including many under caution; a near-record 19 cautions; a feud of words and sheet metal between contenders Darrell Waltrip and Davey Allison; a vicious, fiery crash that hospitalized driver

Rusty Wallace waits on pit road prior to qualifying for Bristol's 1991 Valleydale Meats 500. Wallace went on to capture his first Bristol Cup Series pole and survived an incredible series of events to earn the weekend win. (David McGee Photo)

Sterling Marlin; a rain delay of more than an hour; and one of Bristol's closest-ever finishes, as Wallace edged out Ernie Irvan by 12 inches. The then-record crowd of 58,500 surely got its money's worth.

Odd, Even Pit Rule

One short-lived rule divided the field as even- or odd-numbered, based on each car's qualifying position. Under caution, odd-numbered cars were directed to pit first, followed by even-numbered cars on the next lap. Once back on the track, all cars lined up, with odd-numbered cars to the inside and even-numbered cars to the outside.

Bristol was also the first race of 1991 where teams were allowed to change tires under caution. During the previous five races, teams could only change tires under green-flag conditions, prompting widespread criticism from drivers and fans about the lack of competitive "racing."

Davey Allison, the defending race winner from 1990, prepares to climb into his Robert Yates Racing Ford prior to qualifying for the 1991 edition. Allison qualified 3rd quickest in the 33-car field and battled for the win but finished where he started, in 3rd. (David McGee Photo)

Rusty Wallace (No. 2), Davey Allison (No. 28), and Ernie Irvan (No. 4) staged a titanic battle for the top spot during the 1991 Valleydale Meats 500. Wallace came from two laps down to earn his first victory for car owner Roger Penske. Irvan narrowly missed his second-straight Bristol win, while Allison settled for 3rd. Trailing them is Alan Kulwicki (No. 7). (David McGee Photo)

This race was also NASCAR's first attempt at having lead-lap cars restart in double-file because, until then, leaders restarted in a single outside lane and cars one or more laps down restarted on the inside. NASCAR said the changes were designed to improve pit-road safety, which had been a point of emphasis after a crewmember was killed in the final race of the 1990 season.

Davey Allison was leading Ernie Irvan when rain began falling late in the race that Sunday afternoon. NASCAR displayed the caution at lap 449, and Wallace darted onto pit road for four fresh tires from his 7th spot, returning to the track before the red flag was displayed on lap 458. When the red flag was lifted and caution displayed, Allison pitted for tires and Wallace surged to the inside front row.

Irvan was an even-numbered starter, so he pitted a lap later and was forced to restart each time in the outside lane at a time when the inside was generally regarded as the only way to navigate Bristol.

When the race resumed, Wallace grabbed the lead from Irvan and then withstood a final restart on lap 478, following the race's 19th caution. Irvan closed up on Wallace's rear bumper several times, tapping him and moving him up the racetrack in Turn 3 of the final lap. Wallace held on, reversing the outcome from the previous August and keeping Irvan from winning two straight at his team's home track.

"Everybody in the field had the opportunity to do what I did and take advantage of the new rule. It just kept moving me up to the front," Wallace said afterward. "You can take the new pit rules and twist them into what you like. I won today, and that was the final decision by NASCAR. It was a good rule for me today. That's all I can say. If I were in somebody else's shoes, I probably wouldn't like them."

Wallace said he was surprised by how strong Irvan's car was on older tires.

Irvan said, "I gave him a real good lick down there in Turn 3, and I think our car was just a little bit better than his but not enough to really get in there and dig on him. I knew I was going to have to get in there and shove him a little bit. I could have knocked him a whole lot higher, [but] I thought we'd better race clean."

Larry McClure, the owner of Irvan's 2nd-place Chevrolet minced no words after seeing their chances for a second-straight Bristol victory evaporate. "It's a shame," McClure said. "We should have won that race. There wasn't an even-numbered car that made up a lap all day long, and Rusty was able to make up about six. You tell me, does that sound right?"

McClure and Allison's car owner, Robert Yates, protested the finish. NASCAR rechecked the scoring and declared Wallace the winner.

Wallace and then-points leader Ricky Rudd, who started 4th, officially swapped the lead 15 times in the race's first 100 laps, but 7 of those lead changes occurred during caution periods with the alternating-pit rules. Wallace pitted first as an odd-numbered starter, allowing Rudd to lead a lap and then surrender the spot when he pitted. A cut tire sent Wallace's Pontiac to pit road around lap 100, leaving him laps down to the leaders, and he never saw the front again until after the race went back under green in the final 40 laps.

Darrell and Davey's Dustup

Nine cars finished on the lead lap, with Allison winding up 3rd, Mark Martin 4th, and Rudd 5th. Darrell Waltrip worked his way back to 6th after a dustup with Allison. Waltrip passed Allison on lap 367, and Allison bumped the rear bumper of Waltrip's Chevrolet, sending him spinning down the frontstretch. During the ensuing caution period, NASCAR ordered Allison to the rear of the field. When the red flag appeared, Waltrip climbed out and walked to Allison's car, where the two exchanged words.

"I told him he better get control of his big old Ford. I got hit nine times today; only once did I get hit intentionally," Waltrip fumed, promising to have a "father-son" talk with him later.

Allison, not surprisingly, was also upset. "He came over here and started mouthing off about me spinning him out on the fourth turn. I didn't spin him intentionally. I guess it's okay for him to run all over the side of my car. When we hit and he spun out, somehow I'm in the wrong."

Drivers were skeptical of the rules before the race, but afterward they were downright livid. Ken Schrader, who won at Atlanta three weeks prior, said NASCAR had a "real mess" with its pit-road rules, adding, "To have these cars starting side by side like this isn't going to work. I think that's obvious from the number of caution flags today."

Crewmembers prepare the Ford Thunderbird of Alan Kulwicki. The Wisconsin native qualified 5th quickest but had a poor finish after being caught in one of the race's 19 cautions. This marked the second time he bannered sponsorship from the restaurant chain Hooters, a combination that won the following season's championship. (David McGee Photo)

Mark Martin, who lost the 1990 Valleydale 500 to Davey Allison by 6 inches, blamed drivers as much as the rules. "I thought we, as drivers, would be smarter than we were. It was pathetic what we did to our race cars those first 100 laps," Martin said. "I'm ashamed for all of us."

The day's scariest incident saw Sterling Marlin's Junior Johnson–prepared Ford slam into the outside wall in Turn 1 on lap 421 before bursting into flames, sliding down the track, and coming to rest on the apron. Marlin jumped out and rolled on the ground to extinguish the fire. He was transported to the Bristol hospital and treated for second- and third-degree burns on his face, thighs, and right shoulder. His car had been damaged around the fuel-filler neck in an earlier crash when Dale Earnhardt hit the Turn 2 wall and collected him.

Finishing 26th, one spot ahead of Marlin in the running order, was independent owner-driver Alan Kulwicki, whose Ford bannered sponsorship from Hooters for only the second time. Kulwicki won the pole at Atlanta three weeks before Bristol and picked up a one-race deal there. At Bristol, he qualified a solid 5th, but he was involved in a couple of incidents and was the last car running at the finish.

About the only thing drivers didn't complain about was the Bristol track surface. After being repaved the previous fall amid widespread criticism, it had been coated with a new sealer, and racers universally pronounced it excellent.

Jim Ruth: *Party Time*

Wherever Jim Ruth went, a party was sure to follow. The Kentucky millionaire was a Curtis Turner–like character who worked hard and played harder. After making his fortune in business, the lifelong hot rodder turned his attention to drag racing. A string of bracket cars led to his 1982 purchase of a William Parris Pro Stock Monza, which he enlisted longtime friend Darrell Alderman to drive. The car's name? *Party Time*.

Alderman failed to qualify at the first race, Bristol's 1982 Summer Nationals. The team soon improved, and Ruth commissioned a new black and silver Pontiac Trans Am that he would drive. Other black Pontiacs followed, each quicker and faster than its predecessor, as Ruth became a fixture in IHRA's Mountain Motor Pro Stock class. His involvement deepened in 1986 when he purchased Bristol Dragway from Larry Carrier, who was seeking capital to invest in the NASCAR oval after reassuming control following Warner Hodgdon's 1985 bankruptcy.

In 1988, Carrier sold IHRA to Billy Meyer, who moved the entire organization to Texas. Ruth and partner Ted Jones brought what remained back to Bristol in 1989, beginning a rebuilding process that relied heavily on Thunder Valley for cash flow. It wasn't easy, and it wasn't always pretty, but the organization began to flourish after giving the crowd-pleasing Pro Modifieds their own class and reinstituting Ruth's beloved unlimited-displacement engines in Pro Stock.

The party ended in December 1990 when Ruth lost his battle with cancer at the age of 50.

Ruth's sons, Rick and Duane, fulfilled their father's wishes, retaining Thunder Valley and the race team. Their efforts were quickly rewarded as team driver Harold Denton wheeled their immaculate black and silver Pontiac to the Pro Stock title at Bristol's 1991 Spring Nationals.

Just qualifying for the 16-car field was a challenge, as 37 cars answered the call. When the dust settled, rookie Steve Williford edged out world champion Rickie Smith

Driver Harold Denton performs a burnout in the Ruth family's **Party Time** *Pontiac Pro Stocker. Denton earned an emotional victory, the team's first, during the 1991 Spring Nationals. The win came six months after team owner and Bristol Dragway owner Jim Ruth succumbed to cancer. (David McGee Photo)*

In the years that the Party Time *team continued racing after Jim Ruth's untimely death, their black-and-silver machines always displayed this heartfelt tribute to the founder, a successful businessman from Kentucky. Ruth's sons, Rick and Duane, sold Thunder Valley to Bruton Smith in 1996. (David McGee Photo)*

for the pole. Denton barely made it in, qualifying 15th; a mere .11 second separated Williford from Ed Dixon's bump-spot 7.346.

Denton needed some breaks to reach the final round, and he received two in the early rounds. Terry Adams rattled the tires and shut off against the *Party Time* machine in the first round; Denton ran a clean 7.33/188.83. Opponent Tim Nabors gambled and lost, drawing a redlight start in round two and advancing Denton into the semifinals and a matchup with Smith's vaunted STP Pontiac. Denton needed a nearly perfect reaction time and got it, letting the clutch out well before Smith and nipping him at the stripe 7.376/188.17 to Smith's quicker and faster 7.332/189.17 losing run.

Awaiting him in the final was Williford's top-qualified Pontiac, the same car that Tommy Mauney guided to the 1990 world championship and a car that ran quicker than Denton in all three preliminary rounds. Denton's years of experience paid off as the 20-year-old rookie driver left too early; his redlight triggered a boisterous cheer from the crowd, who understood the implications. Denton dedicated the victory to his late friend and car owner.

"Jim Ruth was the greatest man that could have been involved in drag racing," an emotional Denton said afterward. "We couldn't make the final pass in qualifying because of an ignition problem. I wondered if I was still gonna be in the field. I know that even though Jim wasn't able to be here with us today, he was here with me, and he was in this car. His memory will always be with me. I couldn't have won a better race."

Alan Kulwicki: Special K

Alan Kulwicki grew up in the Milwaukee suburb of Greenfield, Wisconsin, 700 miles from Bristol Motor Speedway. The two are inexorably linked, with the high-banked, half-mile track nestled in the Appalachian Mountains providing so many of his career highlights. Tragically, the racer, nicknamed "Special K," perished a scant 5 miles from the speedway in 1993 while en route to compete there.

With its massive banking and high speeds, Bristol had much in common with the Midwestern half-miles that Kulwicki frequented during his ASA career. When that circuit visited Bristol years before, Kulwicki finished 4th in his first visit and ran 3rd in his encore trip until mechanical gremlins set in.

He claimed his first ASA pole and his first ASA victory a short distance from Bristol at Lonesome Pine International Raceway in Coeburn, Virginia, in August 1982.

After making the leap to NASCAR, Kulwicki showed solid improvements in his first three Bristol visits in the Cup Series, running 15th, 10th, and 5th. His first Bristol pole came at the 1988 night race, where he scored another 5th-place finish. The following year he grabbed another pole and raced Bristol master Darrell Waltrip for the victory but settled for 2nd place after nearly being overcome by carbon monoxide due to a broken exhaust pipe.

Kulwicki maintained a love-hate relationship with the Bristol track, the only NASCAR track where he scored multiple victories, because those wins included battling the track surface as well as the competition. As speeds rose in the early 1990s, the impact of 3,600-pound

Alan Kulwicki celebrates winning the 1991 Budweiser 500 premier series race with Miss Winston in Bristol's Victory Lane. Kulwicki passed Sterling Marlin's Ford on lap 364 and led Marlin to the checkers for his first of two Bristol triumphs. (Photo Courtesy Bristol Motor Speedway)

stock cars landing on Bristol's high-banked corners battered the surface, making it rough and nearly impossible to navigate. Kulwicki, grateful to accept the trophies of back-to-back victories in August 1991 and March 1992, was sharp in his criticism.

"We shouldn't have to race on this kind of surface. It's not up to par. It's not safe," a frustrated Kulwicki told reporters after winning the 1991 Budweiser 500. His Hooters Thunderbird was among a dozen cars to suffer flat tires attributed to the rough surface. "We got two laps down, [but] we battled back for a great victory. This is a great day for us."

Kulwicki's misfortune occurred early, allowing him to make up the deficit by lap 167. He passed Sterling Marlin for the lead on lap 364 and led the final 137 circuits to the checkers. Marlin wrestled a tight Junior Johnson Ford to a 2nd-place finish; Ken Schrader ran 3rd, the only other car on the lead lap. It was Kulwicki's third career victory, and his lone win during the 1991 season. The win prompted Hooters to sign a three-year sponsorship agreement characterized as "one of the best out there," which was a godsend for Kulwicki's small, struggling team.

Bristol's track underwent a $1-million repave prior the circuit's return for the April 1992 Food City 500, and Kulwicki immediately found the surface to his liking, grabbing the top qualifying position with a new track record of 122.474 mph. It was Kulwicki's third Bristol pole and a lap that shattered the nine-year-old record set by the lighter, quicker ASA cars in 1983.

"We were good when we unloaded. We just tuned the car up a little bit and, though it was good when we started, we made it just a little bit better," a jubilant Kulwicki said, prompting some optimism for the race. "We've had a top-five car everywhere we've been. I just hope to have another one Sunday and have all four wheels on the ground at the end. We should have a real good shot."

That proved to be an understatement. Kulwicki led the first 95 laps and 282 overall but still needed a bit of luck. He pitted under caution with 50 laps remaining but slid through his pit and had to back up. The delay allowed Dale Jarrett to beat him out of the pits. They battled for the lead before Kulwicki slid past him while exiting Turn 4 on lap 474, holding off Jarrett's Joe Gibbs–owned Chevrolet.

"Once or twice I almost got him, and the traffic worked against me. When we were side by side, I ran him clean like I try to run everybody else," Kulwicki said, saving some praise for the new surface. "Overall, it's the best it's ever been. . . . I commend them for putting forth a good effort repaving this place."

The Bristol surface changed again for the August 1992 Budweiser 500, this time to concrete, and competitors raced radial tires at Bristol for the first time. Despite the variables, Kulwicki again posted a solid 5th-place finish. Most important, he gained 10 points on championship leader Bill Elliott. That ultimately became the exact margin by which Kulwicki defeated Elliott to claim the 1992 Cup championship three months later at Hampton, Georgia, the closest margin in NASCAR history at that time.

He could scarcely enjoy it. Kulwicki made one more trip to Bristol in a race car, completing a two-day Ford test with Rusty Wallace in March 1993. Two weeks later, he left an autograph session at the Hooters restaurant in Knoxville, Tennessee, and boarded N500AK, a twin-engine Fairchild Merlin 300 at McGhee-Tyson Airport, bound for the Tri-Cities Regional Airport near Bristol. As the plane was making its final approach, eyewitnesses reported seeing it make a steep, rapid descent before crashing into a hillside along Island Road some 5 miles from the runway. All four men onboard, Kulwicki, pilot Charlie Campbell, and Hooters executives Mark Brooks and Dan Duncan, were killed.

The following morning in the packed track press box, an emotional Larry Carrier said, "It is difficult to put into words how we feel right now. Alan Kulwicki was a friend and a great champion. He and the others killed will be greatly missed."

A short time later, transporter driver Peter Jellen started the Kulwicki team's orange and white Ford hauler parked on the track's frontstretch, idled beneath the green flag at the start-finish line, and made a slow memorial lap around the oval before taking the checkered flag. Jellen then proceeded around the track again and headed out the Turn 3 gate.

Fans and competitors completed the weekend with heavy hearts. An inspired Rusty Wallace, Alan's longtime friend and mentor, claimed the pole and the race win, then circled the track clockwise, performing one of Kulwicki's traditional "Polish victory laps."

Alan Kulwicki's transporter exits the Bristol track the morning after the 1992 series champion and three others perished in a plane crash a few miles from the speedway. Transporter driver Peter Jellen made a somber lap around the track, took the checkered flag, and departed to return to Charlotte. The team was eventually sold. (David McGee Photo)

"We came from the Midwest together," an emotional Wallace told reporters. "We both came to NASCAR Winston Cup, we both won Rookie of the Year, and we both realized our dreams to be NASCAR Winston Cup champions. He was my buddy. I dedicate this race to him and his family, along with the others who were on the plane with him."

Mark Martin: The Stupidest Thing Ever

Mark Martin glanced to his left as competitor Tommy Houston pulled alongside, waving congratulations like a surrender flag. The two veterans had battled through the afternoon in Bristol's 1994 Goody's 250 NASCAR Busch Series race, but the contest was effectively over in the era before green-white-checker overtime finishes.

Half a lap after rolling beneath simultaneous white and caution flags for a late-race crash, the day's outcome seemed assured. Martin, following the Mustang pace car, had led 195 of the first 249 laps and was a few hundred feet from his second series win at the high-banked Tennessee half-mile. Behind him was David Green, who had dropped the veteran Houston from 2nd to 3rd place but was unable to challenge for the win as laps ran out.

Houston appeared headed for pit road, and Tracy Leslie pulled alongside Martin's black Ford Thunderbird to wave congratulations. As the field exited Turn 4 for the final time, Martin inexplicably turned the tires of his black and yellow Ford to the apron, dropped the window net, and made a sharp turn toward Bristol's Victory Lane. However, there would be no celebration: Martin forgot to take the checkered flag.

Mark Martin (No. 60) follows the Bristol pace car through Turn 3 on the final lap of the 1994 Goody's 250. Martin gave away certain victory by mistakenly pulling off the track in Turn 4 and heading for Victory Lane before taking the checkered flag. That handed the win to a nearly speechless David Green (No. 44). (David McGee Photo)

A stunned Green pulled his Chevrolet up behind the pace car and led the field to the stripe.

"That was the stupidest thing I've ever done," an embarrassed Martin said afterward. "I thought the race was over. Everybody was pulling up and waving, and I thought I saw [Tommy] Houston pulling into the back pits."

Car owner Jack Roush had been spotting for Martin all day but left his rooftop vantage point to return to the pits for the upcoming Cup practice session. Crewmembers tried yelling at Martin over the radio, but he'd already removed his helmet. When asked what Roush might say, Martin replied, "He won't say anything. Everybody feels sorry for somebody who does something that stupid."

Houston pulled his Ford onto the apron beside Martin as the field entered Turn 2. The drivers exchanged waves, and Martin flashed the okay sign. Houston's crew quickly alerted him, and he pulled back into line and finished 2nd.

Martin admitted that he'd been "pulling" for Green to get a victory, but not at his expense. Green had been cutting into Martin's lead, hoping that there wouldn't be a late-race caution.

"I kept saying the last 20 laps, 'Please, Lord, let there not be a caution.' Then the caution flew, and I knew we were gonna finish 2nd," an amazed Green said in Victory Lane. "I saw him pull off and said, 'I'm going to make another lap.' I even made an extra one."

Doug Herbert: DougZilla Reigns

At 6 feet, 5 inches tall, Doug Herbert casts an imposing shadow. Behind the wheel of a land-locked missile, he became only the second man in drag racing history to surpass 300 mph in a Top Fuel dragster. When he began competing at Thunder Valley in 1992, the California native assembled a remarkable string of six national-event wins over the track's final six seasons under the IHRA banner.

Possessing royal racing blood as the son of drag and Bonneville racer and cam grinder Chet Herbert and nephew of *Drag News* publisher Doris Herbert, Doug moved to the Charlotte, North Carolina, area to start his own high-performance auto parts business. Advancing from alcohol- to nitromethane-fueled dragsters, he became a quick study, running 301 mph at an NHRA race at the age of 24. Not surprisingly, there was plenty of buzz when his bright-red and white dragster unloaded a few months later during Bristol's 1992 Spring Nationals.

Herbert earned the nickname "DougZilla" due to his competitive spirit and take-no-prisoners attitude. Four of his Bristol victories directly translated into four

IHRA Top Fuel titles. He was the first driver to cover the Bristol quarter-mile at more than 300 mph and in less than 5 seconds. Since Herbert's first IHRA win at the 1992 Bristol Spring Nationals, he became the man to beat. Interestingly, much of his Bristol success involved defeating some of the sport's best female racers.

1992 Spring Nationals

That trend began during Herbert's initial Thunder Valley visit when he defeated two women to claim the trophy. Herbert took the top qualifying spot away from Kim LaHaie and her Larry Frazier–owned and –tuned machine by .004 second during Saturday's final qualifying session, 5.254 to LaHaie's 5.258. Also in the field, former NHRA national-event winner Lori Johns made just one qualifying run, but it was quick enough to place 5th in the eight-car field.

After dispatching Michael Smith, Herbert was paired with Lori Johns, who posted a stunning first-round 5.089 that sent Robert Reehl packing. "The crew told me that if I let the girls beat me, not to come back to the trailer," Herbert said half jokingly. "Seriously, that first-round 5.08 was pretty impressive, so we hopped it up just a little bit."

Herbert stormed to a 5.033/283.64 effort that loaded Johns' 5.156/267.69. "I think we did good for a new team," Johns said after her semifinal loss. "We burned the engine up on that 5.08, and we just really didn't have time to get it back together."

LaHaie also ran 5.08 in the opening round to defeat Randy Meyer, and she advanced to the finals with a slower 5.188/272.72 that loaded Michigan veteran Jack Ostrander, as both cars smoked the tires. Herbert and crew chief Jim Brissette turned up the wick for the finals. "We figured she would run at least another .08 or smoke the tires, so we added more wing and speeded the clutch timers up," Herbert said.

Smoke billows from the rear tires of Doug Herbert's Top Fuel dragster as he performs a burnout prior to scoring another Bristol victory. Between 1992 and 1997, Herbert won six Bristol national-event Top Fuel titles, including four Spring Nationals. (David McGee Photo)

Despite running a track record of 5.031/283.55 for the victory over LaHaie's 5.161/270.43, Herbert seemed a bit disappointed not to run in the 4s. "The air actually got better before the final. I expected it to go a little quicker than it did," he said.

1993 Spring Nationals

Herbert established a new standard the following year, becoming the first Top Fuel driver to claim back-to-back Spring Nationals titles, although he was never seriously challenged. He paced all three rounds of qualifying, set low ET of each elimination round, and easily handled Jack Ostrander in the finals by running low ET and top speed of the event at 5.112/278.98.

"We felt like we could run a .10 in the final, and we ran an .11," the winner said afterward. "We didn't want to take a chance on smoking the tires, but on the final, you have to go for it."

1994 Fall Nationals

Herbert's Spring Nationals win streak ended temporarily at the 1994 event, but he recovered when the tour returned to Bristol, claiming both the Fall Nationals trophy and the IHRA championship by outrunning 20-year-old Top Fuel rookie Rhonda Hartman. Herbert entered the event trailing in the title chase by 260 points, then struggled to qualify 5th in the rugged eight-car field; Hartman stole his track ET record with a 5.014 blast that topped qualifying.

Both won their opening-round battles, but Herbert gained lane choice with a marginal 5.42 after dropping two cylinders just off the starting line. He should have been easy pickings for lane choice, but Hartman faced her brother, who waited until she reached the finish line before launching to give her the win. Her car got crossed up off the starting line, forcing her to click it off early and surrender lane choice to Herbert.

Rain began falling before the semifinal pairings could be run, forcing the event to conclude on Monday. Herbert took the left lane where Hartman had clocked a barrage of qualifying 5.0s. To add another wrinkle, he rolled up and deep staged. Herbert had the advantage, and Hartman's blower belt came off just as she caught him.

"For a first year, we did a great job," a disappointed Hartman said. Her opponent agreed, saying, "She does a good job, and they ran pretty good out here this weekend."

In the final round, Herbert again faced off with Jack Ostrander, but victory nearly slipped away when his rear tires struggled for traction. Herbert won 5.220/283 to 5.328/167. "We figured it would run about a 5.10, but at about 300 feet it started smoking the tires. I yanked on the brake until I could feel it quit spinning," the victor said afterward, admitting that they were "lucky."

1995 Spring Nationals

Luck also played a prominent role in Herbert's subsequent 1995 Spring Nationals victory, the one he earned by knocking off former world champion Shirley Muldowney in the final round in yet another Monday showdown. In her return to drag racing, Muldowney out-qualified Herbert and ran low ET of eliminations in her semifinal win over Rhonda Hartman, 5.215/284.00 to 5.348/269.54; Herbert lost lane choice by clocking a 5.253 that defeated former champion Richard Langson.

With showers looming, the two teams hurriedly prepped for the finals and then pushed up into the water box. Race officials hit the pause button moments later when the skies opened, forcing the finals to Monday. A green racetrack yielded a tire-smoking pedal fest captured by Herbert, 5.65/192.02 over Muldowney's 6.874/129.34.

"I did everything wrong [that] I could to give the race to her," Herbert said afterward. "I smoked the tires off the line. Then at about 800 feet the blower belt came off. I kept waiting for her to come by me, and she never did. I went through the lights and thought, 'I'm lucky today.'" Muldowney said she pedaled once but couldn't recover.

1996 Fall Nationals

The two champions reprised their battle at the 1996 Fall Nationals as each took turns recording the track's initial 4-second runs, qualifying 1st and 2nd, and then squaring off in the finals with the IHRA championship again on the line. Herbert and Muldowney entered the event locked in a battle for the title along with Jim Bailey and his Frank Faifer–owned team. While Bailey struggled, Herbert and Muldowney

Doug Herbert, who received the nickname "DougZilla" for his intense, competitive demeanor behind the wheel of a Top Fuel dragster, flashes a thumbs-up prior to pushing the pedal on a few thousand nitromethane-fueled horsepower. (David McGee Photo)

took turns one-upping each other. Herbert and tuner Jim Brissette fired the first salvo, recording Bristol's first 4-run with a 4.935/298 that stood as the best lap of qualifying.

Muldowney wasted no time clawing into the 4s, running a 4.998 that wound up 2nd quickest. However, it was Rhonda Hartman who stole the first-round thunder with a stunning 4.972/299.90. Muldowney then singled at 5.214/279 when opponent Vicky Fanning shut off, and Herbert singled at 5.052/285 when Chris Karamesines also shut off. Muldowney carded a matching 5.214/279 semifinal run to advance past Bruce Litton. Rivals Herbert and Hartman met, with Hartman suffering mechanical trouble and Herbert moving on at 5.143/280.

Much like their previous Bristol showdown, Muldowney blazed the tires and shut off while Herbert carded a solid 5.11/287.63 for the victory. "We like Shirley, but we like to win even better," an enthused Herbert said afterward. "We changed engines every round. We threw the clutch out of it the last round; we had to change clutches, bellhousings."

The pair raced once more at Thunder Valley at the 33rd and final Spring Nationals. Muldowney and Rhonda Hartman-Smith clocked the track's first side-by-side 4-second runs during qualifying, but it was Herbert, on a Saturday-afternoon qualifier, who carded Bristol's first 300-mph run, at 300.06. A short time later, Muldowney wrestled the top speed away with a new IHRA record blast of 302.80 mph.

On race day, Herbert's car suffered clutch woes, but he escaped Hartman-Smith, who lifted after the car started a sudden wheelstand. Muldowney carded a superb 4.997/300.06. With lane choice, Shirley selected the right side; Herbert was elated to run the left. Herbert claimed the victory, 5.024/298.07 to 5.158/294.18.

"It shook the tires a little bit. I got on and off the gas, pulled on the brake a little bit and let off, and it cleaned up. I figured when I got on and off the gas [that] she would shoot by me, but it didn't happen," a relieved Herbert said.

Muldowney summed it up as "a hell of a drag race."

Johnson and Hill: Pro Stock's Professors

There have been some great nicknames in the annals of Pro Stock drag racing: "Dyno Don" Nicholson, "Dandy" Dick Landy, Ronnie "The Boss" Sox, Herb "Mr. Four Speed" McCandless, Bob "Mad Dog" Glidden. Two men, likely the most disparate pair to ever strap into Pro Stock machines, share the handle "Professor," and both sampled different levels of success at the track nicknamed "Thunder Valley." Warren Johnson was an engineer from Minnesota who spent most waking moments developing engines that produced copious amounts of horsepower and confounding the competition. Roy Hill, originally tagged "the Hillbilly," was a self-made Southeastern star whose early career was linked to his friends at Petty Engineering, who built his first Plymouth Duster with every aerodynamic trick learned in NASCAR in the era before body templates. What Hill lacked in formal education he more than made up for with street smarts. Hill earned his professorial stripes during the 1990s upon establishing a drag racing driving school and teaching many of the sport's best racers how to improve their techniques.

Warren Johnson

Johnson spread Bristol victories over four decades, winning with his aged *Hulk* Camaro in his initial trip through the Bristol gates at the 1979 Spring Nationals. He ultimately stormed to three consecutive spring race titles before devoting much of his attention to NHRA's brand of 500-ci Pro Stock. He returned to Bristol's Winner's Circle twice in 1988 and again in 1989, amid the experiment of blending engine combinations from the two sanctions.

In his signature above-and-beyond style, Johnson's approach surpassed brute horsepower.

"The cars just weren't built for the high-torque engines that were put in them," Johnson once told CompetitionPlus.com. "The cars were flexible, and they had the tendency to shake a lot. Knowing that, my primary objective in those days was to stay away from it. If you remained shake free and went from one end of the track to the other, you had about a 95-percent chance of winning the race. I concentrated more on clean runs than putting one of the bigger engines in it."

As the IHRA Pro Stock's displacement continued increasing from 600 toward 800 ci, Johnson wandered away again, resuming his barrage on NHRA racing by winning

Minnesota native Warren Johnson stages Jerome Bradford's revolutionary Monte Carlo Pro Stocker at the 1981 Spring Nationals, which he won. Before earning his "Professor" nickname, Johnson was known simply as "WJ." The W also likely stood for winner, given his remarkable career. (Chris Haverly Photo)

Even in the latter stages of his driving career, Warren Johnson remained one of the sport's most feared competitors, fielding a string of General Motors entries. Johnson accumulated a remarkable 8 Bristol victories in 11 Pro Stock final rounds. (David McGee Photo)

five world championship titles during the 1990s. Johnson returned to Bristol when NHRA again hung out its sanctioning shingle in 1999 and captured Thunder Valley Nationals trophies in 2002 and 2005.

Although not officially retired at this writing, Johnson has accrued 97 NHRA national-event wins.

Johnson's final Bristol victory was the 94th of his illustrious career, and the Professor was a backbreaker, running a new track ET record of 6.715 seconds in dispensing Jason Line. He turned back son Kurt 6.757 to 6.759 in the semifinals and ran 6.756 in the finals to take out Richie Stevens, who redlighted in a car fielded by Don Schumacher.

Roy Hill

Some nine years before, at Bristol's 1996 Spring Nationals, teenager Richie Stevens burst onto the drag racing scene by winning Pro Stock in a Ford Thunderbird owned and sponsored by Roy Hill's Drag Racing School. "This is just unbelievable. This is great," an excited Stevens said of the victory, which came on the heels of his high-school graduation. "I can't believe it. I was nervous as I could be."

The Stevens victory more than validated Hill's teaching skills, since it came in just Stevens' fourth race behind the wheel of the 1,500-hp machines.

"In the finals, he did what he was trained to do," an emotional Hill said. "He out-qualified Roy Hill, and I've been doing this 30 years. Whoever would believe a junior dragster driver could come out and, after four races, win? I was in tears down there."

Roy Hill's original nickname was "Hillbilly," which he bannered on a series of Mopar Pro Stock machines affiliated with his North Carolina friends and neighbors at Petty Enterprises. Hill's Hemi-powered cars, such as this 1980 Plymouth Horizon, were always tough outs. (Chris Haverly Photo)

Stevens's victory closed out a remarkable six-race stretch where Hill or Hill-owned cars advanced to five Bristol final rounds and captured four victories.

Mike Bell registered the most convincing victory of the Hill streak, sweeping top qualifier honors, the $20,000 Sunoco Pro Stock Shootout, the Pro Stock final, and the IHRA championship at Bristol's 1995 Fall Nationals. The title came down to the final round between Bell and points leader Doug Kirk, who edged out Hill in the semifinals.

"I couldn't help but think about the points, but I tried to concentrate on the race with Kirk," an elated Bell said. "Winning the shootout pumped everyone up and gave us more momentum. We got better and better with every round. It was really a great weekend, and it's been a great year."

Bell, who at the time worked as an instructor at Hill's drag racing school, previously constructed many of the *Blue Max* Funny Cars of Raymond Beadle and later relocated to Charlotte to work for Beadle's 1989 NASCAR championship team with driver Rusty Wallace.

"I've known Roy since the 1970s, and getting back together with him was great," Bell said. "I'm having fun teaching people how to drive at the school, and this deal also gives me an opportunity to drive."

Hill was equally effusive. "I can't tell you how proud I am of Mike," he said. "I let him drive a Top Sportsman car for me in 1991 and saw that he had a lot of potential."

The Hill team's Bristol streak began during Roy's heavily publicized 1993 comeback tour, where he dominated the Fall Nationals and registered his initial Bristol victory after being away from the sport for a few years.

"It's the first time I've won at Bristol, and it's the greatest of my wins," Hill said that day. "Being here at Jim Ruth's track and winning means an awful lot. There's

Roy Hill graduated to "professor" status after opening his incredibly successful drag racing school. His greatest Bristol success came in the 1990s, with a fleet of Fords promoting the school. Hill captured two Bristol Pro Stock victories himself; students Mike Bell and Richie Stevens also each scored wins. (David McGee Photo)

Roy Hill gives the thumbs-up from behind the wheel of a Pro Modified machine in the Bristol staging lanes. In a drag racing career spanning five decades, Hill has driven about everything except a Top Fueler and a modern Funny Car. (David McGee Photo)

a lot of love for the Ruth family in IHRA, and they sure put on a good show here. I hadn't raced since 1987. The ultimate goal this year was to win the shootout, and to do that and win here is like having a birthday cake with all the icing."

The cake arrived in Saturday's $20,000 shootout finals, as Hill outran Tim Nabors 6.96/198.50 to 7.03/196.93, and the icing was applied when Hill set down rookie Mark Thomas in the Pro Stock final. Hill also reset both ends of the Bristol track record, running 6.926/199.55 in a convincing semifinal triumph over rival Rickie

Smith. Earlier that weekend, Hill emerged from the 33-car pack to record Bristol's first 6-second Pro Stock time slip.

Hill's second and final Bristol win as a driver occurred at the marathon 1995 Spring Nationals, where he overcame a poor qualifying effort to reach the finals and down Carlton Phillips 6.99/198.36 to 7.02/198.19. The final was his lone test of the day and one of the few runs not interrupted by a downpour that forced much of the racing to Monday. Hill's previous opponents, Mark Thomas, John Konigshofer, and Robert Patrick, broke or encountered traction woes. "We were very lucky," Hill admitted. "Each round we just kept picking it up. That's what you have to do, and then it just went my way. As the track got slicker, we got quicker."

Jeff Gordon: Rainbow Warrior

Four-time NASCAR premier series champion Jeff Gordon relished the challenge of Bristol's high-banked brand of competition, where brightly painted cars hurtled around its tight confines in precarious proximity. During a four-year stretch in the 1990s, Gordon's Rainbow Warriors team, led by crew chief Ray Evernham, found an untouchable zone, capturing Bristol's monstrous trophy in four consecutive editions of the Food City 500.

1995

Disarmingly dubbed "Wonder Boy" by perennial championship rival Dale Earnhardt, Gordon's first visit to Bristol's Victory Lane was doubly remarkable because it was his first Bristol finish inside the top 15 after numerous run-ins with the track's unforgiving concrete walls in his first four starts.

Driver Jeff Gordon (left) and crew chief Ray Evernham talk during practice for Bristol's 1995 Goody's 500 night race, a contest where they qualified 4th and finished 6th. Together the tandem captured three of Gordon's four NASCAR titles and four consecutive wins in Bristol's Food City 500. (David McGee Photo)

Gordon elbowed his way into the exclusive club of Bristol winners on April 2, 1995, leading Bristol contenders Rusty Wallace and Darrell Waltrip to the checkers. He led 205 circuits, including the race's final 99 laps.

"This is awesome," Gordon said afterward. "I've always liked Bristol, and it seems like I've always run good here. Before, I'd always knock the rear end or the front end off this thing. That was our only goal today, to try and take a car out of here in one piece, and we did that and a whole lot more."

Pole sitter Mark Martin ran 2nd before a cut tire late in the going relegated him to an 8th-place finish. Gordon was patient throughout as Martin and Wallace led much of the race's second half. "The longer we ran, the better we got," Gordon said. "Rusty and Mark would jump out on new tires, but as the run got longer, it came back to me." The winner slowed late in the going when his passenger-side rear tire began to fail, but 2nd-place Wallace was too far back to take advantage.

1996

Gordon entered that spring's Food City 500 as one of the favorites after a respectable 6th-place finish in Bristol's 1995 night race (amid the final-lap fireworks between Terry Labonte and Dale Earnhardt) and two early wins in the 1996 season. Translating that into a second-straight victory involved one of the strangest Bristol races ever.

After rain showers delayed the start by more than 30 minutes, pole sitter Mark Martin jumped into an early lead. Gordon assumed the point on lap 108 and paced the next 100 circuits before pitting for tires. The race included a 258-lap stretch without a single caution until rain began falling, bringing out the yellow flag on lap 321.

The Rainbow Warriors pit crew services Jeff Gordon's Chevrolet during the weather-abbreviated 1996 Food City 500. Gordon returned to the track in the lead before rain began falling. NASCAR eventually called the race complete after 342 laps. (David McGee Photo)

Terry Labonte hustled onto pit road for new tires and fuel ahead of the leaders and believed NASCAR should have designated him the new leader, but the pace car picked up Gordon as the leader just before the red flag was displayed.

Gordon led once the rain stopped and the race restarted, but another caution soon flew when Darrell Waltrip smacked the wall, bursting his car's fuel cell and necessitating another red flag to clean up the track. After an 18-minute delay, the field was headed for a restart when the skies opened. With no letup in rain, NASCAR officials waited more than an hour before declaring the race official at lap 342, with Gordon the winner.

"I hated to see the race end the way it did. It's not nearly as exciting and not exactly the way you want to do it," Gordon said, following a soggy victory-lane celebration. "I've never won one quite like this ever before; to be in Victory Lane and absolutely not a soul in the grandstands and it pouring down rain; it was interesting."

Labonte was irate after posting a 2nd-place finish, saying he didn't understand NASCAR's decision. "We outsmarted them and should have come out leading the race. That's the bottom line," Labonte fumed.

1997

Gordon's victory the following year included a very different kind of controversy, as the driver of the multicolored Chevrolet bumped Rusty Wallace out of the way on the final circuit to extend his Food City 500 winning streak to three.

Jeff Gordon celebrates in Bristol's Victory Lane after winning the 1997 Food City 500. Gordon, who went on to earn four NASCAR premier series championships, won Bristol's spring race for four consecutive years, from 1995 to 1998. (David McGee Photo)

"I've never been part of a last-lap deal like that, and it was exciting," Gordon said in Victory Lane. "It was just typical, wide-open Bristol racing."

Wallace, the victim of the final-lap mugging, was less enthusiastic, saying, "I don't like anybody running into me to pass me."

Until that final lap, the weekend had a familiar Rusty look to it. On Friday, Wallace cruised to his third career Bristol pole as his Ford Thunderbird edged out Sterling Marlin and the Morgan-McClure team for the top spot. "This car is really flying," Wallace said. "It came off the truck great, and the crew did a helluva job." Gordon qualified three positions lower, starting fifth behind Ted Musgrave and Rusty's younger brother, Kenny Wallace.

Gordon led 124 laps in the early going but only 1 in the final 100, the one that mattered. "It came down to the last lap, and my car started pushing, but I could get a run off [Turn] 2. He [Wallace] shut the door a little bit, but that last time, I got a great run and kind of pushed him down the straightaway. When we got into [Turn] 3 and he got sideways, I jumped underneath in the hole he made. He got a little loose, and we kind of touched; the hole opened up, and I went for it."

Wallace led four times for 240 of the 500 laps but couldn't hang on at the end.

"I just can't believe I gave it away on the last damn corner," a frustrated Wallace lamented. "It's just unbelievable. I wasn't surprised he touched me; I would have probably done the same thing if I had gotten that close going for the checkered. Here at Bristol, you can touch a little bit and that will do it."

1998

Rusty Wallace opened the door the following spring for Jeff Gordon to match Darrell Waltrip's Bristol spring-race win streak. A lap down and outside the top 10 due to engine woes, Wallace's Ford blew a passenger-side front tire and clobbered the Turn 1 wall on lap 437 to bring out the day's 12th caution flag. Gordon's Rainbow Warriors over-the-wall crew responded with their best pit stop of the day. From there, Gordon held off teammate Terry Labonte for the top spot in the 1998 Food City 500.

Gordon secured his first lead of the day by beating Labonte and Dale Jarrett out of the pits on a caution-flag pit stop on lap 437 and then held off Labonte's Chevrolet by a half second. "All we needed was a good pit stop, and we got it," Gordon said. "What an awesome crew. They deserve all the credit for this win." Gordon said that he didn't think he could outrun either of his rivals.

Labonte's struggles to return to Bristol's Victory Lane continued, but he blamed himself. "I was kind of asleep there. I was looking in my mirror to see if I was going to beat Dale Jarrett, and I didn't go when they dropped the car," he said.

Bristol Motor Speedway awards its winners one of the largest trophies in motorsports, and Jeff Gordon likely had to expand his trophy case after capturing four consecutive Food City 500s from 1995 to 1998. (Photo Courtesy Bristol Motor Speedway)

Gordon said that Bristol is one of his favorite places to compete.

"You just have to get into a rhythm and be smooth out there. At times you need to be aggressive, and at times you need to be patient," Gordon said. "I love this place, and it's been really good to me. To win four races in a row here is pretty awesome."

His victory was met with a boisterous chorus of boos from a then-record crowd of 134,000, but he took the response in stride. "When I first came along, that's what they were doing to Dale Earnhardt. Now, I don't remember many fans booing him when he won at Daytona this year. When I hear people booing me, I consider it a good problem to have."

Building the New Bristol

Bristol Speedway was well into its second decade of sold-out NASCAR races when owner Larry Carrier's telephone rang in early 1996. "Larry, this is Bruton Smith. I want to buy your racetrack," came the voice on his phone.

Slightly taken aback, Carrier paused for a moment, then replied, "Really? That's funny, because it's not for sale."

Smith persisted. "Well, you think about how much you'd have to have, and I'll call you back in a few days."

Sell? Bristol was in the midst of an unbroken string of sold-out Cup races that began in the early 1980s. Carrier had more than doubled the seating capacity to approximately 67,000, with consideration for increasing it to 100,000. ESPN continually named Bristol its Track of the Year. Television ratings were exceptional, and during the previous August night race Dale Earnhardt had sent Terry Labonte into

The sight of construction equipment on the Bristol Motor Speedway track became a familiar one after Smith's crews undertook a series of projects to improve every aspect of the facility and make it more fan friendly. (David McGee Photo)

Bruton Smith (right) holds court during a press conference inside the Bristol office building that bears his name. To the left is former speedway president Jeff Byrd, who left a career at R.J. Reynolds to guide the "new" Bristol's fortunes to new heights. (Earl Neikirk Photo, Courtesy Bristol Herald Courier)

the wall at the start-finish as the checkers fell, the track's most iconic finish to date.

When Smith called back, Carrier was ready. "That's quite a figure," Smith replied to Carrier's asking price.

"It's quite a track," Carrier replied.

No argument there. They settled on a deal quickly and announced it on January 22, 1996, 35 years and five days after Carrier and Carl Moore originally announced plans to build the track. Carrier walked away with $25.5 million after Smith paid his taxes, and Speedway Motorsports began transforming the track that Warner Hodgdon's wife, Sharon, once termed a "jewel box" into one of the largest, most accessible sports stadiums in the world.

Smith was quick to tamp down unfounded speculation that he might strip Bristol of one or both of its NASCAR race dates and award them to another of his burgeoning list of tracks. Instead, he described plans for a massive overhaul of virtually every aspect of the facility, including increasing the seating capacity to once-inconceivable levels. Capacity eventually reached 160,000 seats, fully encircling the track and topped with a double-decker ring of luxury suites.

"A lot of the things we're doing is to make the Bristol Motor Speedway more fan friendly," Smith said at that time. "It's gonna be easier for them to park. It's going to be easier for them to get in, get out. We're just making it bigger and better."

What ensued during the spring and summer of 1997 was a race unlike any ever staged on Bristol's speedway; a race run not on the track itself, but on virtually every square inch of earth surrounding it. Hundreds of workers labored around the clock to finish a massive reconstruction project that included essentially doubling Bristol's seating capacity. The monotonous hum of diesel-powered earthmovers and the sparks from welding steel provided the backdrop as a new Bristol Motor Speedway took shape.

By midsummer, only weeks before the landmark August night race, virtually nothing had been completed. Around the property, 2.5 million cubic yards of earth and rock had been redistributed. A mountain behind the backstretch came down to make way for better access and infrastructure. A monumental increase in seating capacity required replacing virtually all of the old grandstands and establishing the foundation for thousands of new seats, as well as new concession and restroom facilities.

Smith and track manager Jeff Byrd intended to make good on their promised improvements before the fans arrived, but the heat, the hours, and the breakneck pace were taking a toll on the workers. To alleviate the stress, Smith and Byrd scheduled a midweek shindig to rejuvenate the workers and remind them how important the tasks were. After pitching tents and ordering barbecue, they invited a special guest to provide a little pep talk: seven-time NASCAR champion Dale Earnhardt.

NASCAR champion Dale Earnhardt (left) and track owner O. Bruton Smith unveil a T-shirt commemorating a massive reconstruction project to "build a new Bristol Motor Speedway." Smith completed the purchase in 1996, and improvements have been ongoing nearly ever since. (Photo Courtesy Bristol Motor Speedway)

In this aerial view from the 1980s, Bristol had changed very little from its original 1961 design, with the addition of only a couple of frontstretch grandstand sections to supplement the original concrete seating. (Photo Courtesy Bristol Motor Speedway)

This aerial view from around 2000 shows a much more modern view of Bristol Motor Speedway, with 160,000 grandstand seats surrounding the track, capped off by a double layer of luxury suites nearly encircling the bowl. (Photo Courtesy Bristol Motor Speedway)

"I just can't believe what you all are doing," a smiling Earnhardt told the masses. "From when we were here in April until today is just amazing. Bristol has always been special. I won my first race here, and I've won a lot here."

After Earnhardt and Smith posed for photos with a T-shirt emblazoned, "We're Building the New Bristol Motor Speedway," they handed out shirts by the armload. Then NASCAR's most revered driver spent the next 2 hours signing autographs, posing for photos, and saying thank you to everyone involved. Afterward, with their bellies full and darkness falling, many laborers went right back to work.

They were bolting the last of the aluminum grandstand seats into place when the gates opened on August 22 for Goody's 500 practice and qualifying.

John Force: Superman Wins Showdown

John Force and Kenny Bernstein made an explosive return to Thunder Valley in June 1998, not behind the wheel of nitromethane-fueled missiles but instead steering bulldozers tethered by heavy cables to Bristol Dragway's original four-story control tower. Amid a mammoth fireball from some well-placed gasoline bombs, the drag racing superstars pressed the throttles, forcing the heavy equipment to lurch forward and bringing more than three decades of memories tumbling to the Tennessee turf.

The remarkable moment signaled the official start of a mammoth $14 million rebuilding project as 600 workers moved about a million cubic yards of rock and earth, widening Thunder Valley and filling in about 23 feet of the old track to accommodate more seating, more pit area, more amenities, and improved drainage. A spacious, modern tower replaced the old landmark and the starting line was moved

Bruton Smith (left) welcomes fans to the all-new Bristol Dragway during opening ceremonies at the 1999 Winston Showdown event. Smith's company, Speedway Motorsports, finished a comprehensive, multimillion-dollar makeover of the legendary Thunder Valley. Shown at right is announcer Bob Frey. (David McGee Photo)

The Top Fuelers assembled at the 1999 Winston Showdown were no match for John Force and his alter ego, the "Man of Steel." Cloaked in Superman livery, drag racing's all-time winningest driver collected his biggest paycheck, a $200,000 prize, at Bristol. (David McGee Photo)

back 358 feet to create more shutdown area and eliminate the signature right-angle shutdown area that terrified more than one errant racer whose parachutes had failed.

The reconstruction project coincided with the announcement that Bruton Smith was bringing the NHRA back to Thunder Valley to host the Winston No Bull Showdown, in which a dozen Top Fuel dragsters would race against an equal number of Funny Cars, forcing racers used to leaving simultaneously to deal with Funny Cars getting a programmed head start, with the winner guaranteed a $200,000 payday. Just as when the original track was built, the clock was ticking, but all was complete when the NHRA rolled into town in 1999.

The unique format prompted sometimes-bitter rivals such as John Force, Cruz Pedregon, Al Hofmann, and Whit Bazemore to rally each other in a true battle of dragsters versus Funny Cars. Force was quickest among the floppers and Bob Vandergriff topped the dragster field. Rains ultimately pushed Saturday's first round to Sunday.

Racing with a .37-second head start over the traditionally quicker and faster fuelers, Force used a 5.063/292.33 opening-round blast to defeat 20-year-old Cristin Powell, who smoked the tires in Nick Boninfante's car. Force's second-round foe, Jim Head, also struggled for traction and failed to back up a first-round 4.74, slowing to 5.502/286.98; Force improved slightly at 5.019/287.44.

Besides Force, an eight-time Funny Car world champion at that juncture, the third round included mostly dragsters. Doug Kalitta was reinserted as the quickest losing Top Fueler of round two, along with Gary Scelzi, Cory McClenathan, Kenny Bernstein, and Bob Vandergriff. Also advancing were flopper pilots Chuck

Tommy Johnson Jr. launches his Firebird Funny Car alongside eventual runner-up Bob Vandergriff's Top Fuel dragster. The Showdown pitted Top Fuel dragsters versus Funny Cars, with a unique head start provided for the fuel coupes. Johnson Jr. and Vandergriff met in round two, with Vandergriff taking the win. (David McGee Photo)

Etchells and Tommy Johnson Jr., who went back into the program as the quickest second-round-losing Funny Car.

Vandergriff, the quickest qualified Top Fueler at 4.559 seconds, nearly matched that number with a come-from-behind 4.585/314.68 victory over Tommy Johnson's Joe Gibbs–owned flopper at 5.119/281.19. After downing the stout Funny Cars of Ron Capps and Whit Bazemore via better reaction times, Kenny Bernstein triggered a foul to advance Etchells, who ran 5.506/296.89. Cory McClenathan took the round's only all-dragster matchup via a holeshot over a quicker and faster Scelzi 4.633/306.33 to 4.603/313.22 aboard Alan Johnson's dragster. Funny Car top qualifier Force finally re-entered the 4-second zone, clocking 4.941/304.80 to down Doug Kalitta's dragster, which clocked a solid 4.623/310.27.

Force tuners Austin Coil and Bernie Fedderly dialed up their best run of the weekend for a semifinal showdown with McClenathan. Force's Mustang marched down the right lane at 4.879/306.88 to best the Joe Gibbs–owned Top Fuel dragster of Cory Mac, whose engine issues slowed him to 4.672/298.27. Etchells fouled away his chances against Vandergriff, who struggled for traction but posted a winning 4.938/281.19.

"The 4.87 against Cory Mac really helped us win the race," Force proclaimed afterward. "I think that pushed them." Vandergriff's tuners, Ray Alley and Johnny West, changed engines before the $200,000 round; Force's tuning team dialed up additional power to capitalize on cooler evening conditions. Each car strained for traction in the final round, with Force emerging first at 5.470/262.18 to Vandergriff's 5.876/243.90.

Mimicking the Superman persona bannered on his Mustang Funny Car and matching yellow, red, and blue firesuit, Force trailered Top Fuelers in all five rounds to claim the unique title. No cape required.

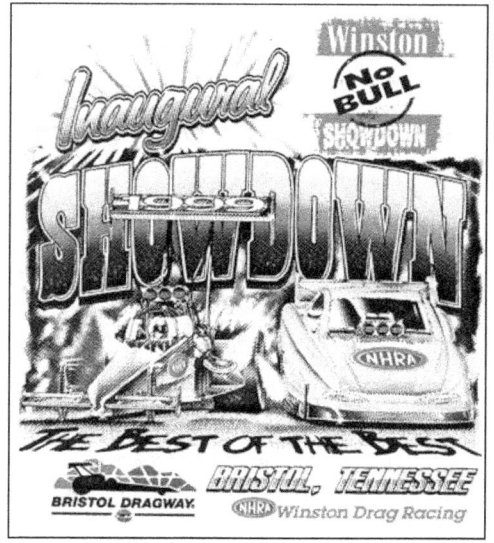

This decal marked the inaugural Winston Showdown, pitting Top Fuel versus Funny Car in a unique event at Bristol Dragway. (Photo Courtesy David McGee)

"This is the biggest deal of my career," an emotionally drained Force proclaimed afterward. "The dragsters are the kings of the sport and we aren't going to change that, but for this weekend Funny Cars rule."

More than 15 years after hoisting the inaugural Showdown trophy, Force still counts that Bristol victory (which isn't reflected in his sport-leading total of national-event wins because it was a non-points race) as one of his greatest achievements.

"Probably the biggest [thrill] was when we raced Top Fuel. I love to come here, love the town, love the people," Force said before being inducted into the Legends of Thunder Valley. "I went on to beat a great racer, Vandergriff, in the finals, but it was a pedal fest. Biggest paycheck in history, and we won it, just to show our big brother Top Fuel we could race with them." The oversize check he received in the Winner's Circle remains on display in his California facility.

"That Superman car was really special," Force recalled. "I just believed in the caped crusader, that he could do the unbelievable. It was quite a night."

Terry Labonte: Rattle His Cage

"I didn't mean to turn him; I only meant to rattle his cage."

These words defined a moment in time, a race outcome, and the intersection of two unforgettable stock-car racing legacies. Dale Earnhardt offered these words to explain the incident in which he mugged Terry Labonte en route to the checkered flag of Bristol's 1999 night race in front of 141,000 eyewitnesses, with millions more tuned in on television. Captured forever in video replays, Labonte's yellow and red Chevrolet sails into Turn 1 only to get a tap on the rear bumper from the Intimidator's ominous black and silver Chevrolet.

Terry Labonte (No. 5) races door to door with Dale Earnhardt (No. 3) during the 1999 Goody's 500. Labonte led the field beneath the white flag, but contact with Earnhardt's bumper was all "The Intimidator" needed to claim his ninth Bristol win. (Photo Courtesy Bristol Motor Speedway)

In one of Bristol's most memorable finishes, Terry Labonte (No. 5) spins in Turn 2 on the final lap of the 1999 Goody's 500 after Dale Earnhardt (No. 3) rattled his cage with a bump-and-run maneuver. Earnhardt raced to claim his final Bristol Motor Speedway victory. (Photo Courtesy Bristol Motor Speedway)

In the next frame, Labonte's car skids up the track sideways, smoke boiling from the rear tires like a drag racing burnout, clearing a path for Earnhardt to plow on and capture his ninth and final Bristol victory. Emerging from the car a few moments later, Earnhardt tries to conceal one of his patented grins beneath his mustache as he utters the sentence heard 'round the racing world: "I didn't mean to wreck him; I only meant to rattle his cage."

Fireworks couldn't hold a candle to what had just transpired on the racetrack. Any highlight reel of greatest NASCAR finishes or wildest Bristol moments is sure to include the final laps of that 1999 night race.

The hot August night grew even more intense as fans by the thousands rained a chorus of boos down from even the stadium's most remote corners. Those close enough threw items on the track. They weren't buying what Earnhardt was selling.

Dale Earnhardt displays his game face during prerace activities for the 1999 Goody's 500. The seven-time NASCAR champion earned his ninth Bristol win later that night with a controversial last-lap bump of Terry Labonte. (Chris Haverly Photo)

"Terry caught me coming to the white flag in [Turn] 3 and [Turn] 4, and we bumped a little," Earnhardt said later in the press box. "When we went back to [Turn] 1, I went back in there to get under him. Whether he checked up or I got in deeper or what, I bumped him too hard and turned him. It spun him. I didn't do it intentionally. I meant to get in there and race with him, but that happened, and I know he's not going to see it that way."

He was right. "I don't know what he was thinking. He never has any intention of taking anybody out. It just happens," Labonte curtly said afterward, adding that he had no plans to protest. "I won't even waste my time to go to the [NASCAR] trailer and talk about it. I've been there before." NASCAR officials reviewed the last lap for an hour after the race before ruling that the outcome would stand.

Dale Earnhardt and Terry Labonte previously got together off the final corner of the final lap of Bristol's 1995 night race. That time, Labonte held on to take his battered, steaming Chevrolet to Victory Lane. He was less fortunate in the rematch. (Photo Courtesy Bristol Motor Speedway)

Chapter 4: Raising the Bar in the 1990s   173

The finish conjured images of the last lap of a 1995 night race where Earnhardt tagged the back of Labonte's Chevrolet as they exited Turn 4 headed for the checkered flag. That shot sent Labonte careening into the frontstretch wall after crossing the line in a haze of smoke and steam. On that night, Labonte said from Victory Lane that he'd been watching Earnhardt's Chevrolet grow larger in his rearview mirror and just stood on the gas when the inevitable contact came.

All but lost in the encore 1999 skirmish were the remarkable comebacks by both combatants just to put themselves into position to win.

Earnhardt overcame a miserable qualifying effort, a backstretch pit stall, and used some pit-stop sequence strategy to finally pass Labonte for the lead on lap 380. In fact, the two series champions were the only drivers to lead the race's final 200 laps, exchanging the top spot six times during the last 100 circuits.

With just 10 laps remaining, Labonte appeared to be cruising toward his third Bristol victory when Jeremy Mayfield and Wally Dallenbach got together in oil dumped by Bobby Labonte and brought out the race's 10th and final caution flag. Labonte slowed, but Darrell Waltrip didn't and hit the race leader's Chevrolet. Terry Labonte headed for pit road for four new tires and a check of his wrinkled sheet metal, emerging in 5th place behind Earnhardt, rookie Tony Stewart, Jeff Gordon, who all stayed out on older tires, and Mark Martin, who pitted for two fresh tires.

That set up a five-lap shootout for the win, as Earnhardt took the green flag and held the top spot while Labonte blazed past the other three. Labonte passed Earnhardt for the lead between Turns 3 and 4 heading for the white flag, slightly bumping Earnhardt's Chevrolet as he went by. Earnhardt responded by charging deeper into Turn 1, then driving up and under Labonte as they raced through Turn 2.

Labonte's spin collected others and allowed Jimmy Spencer to slip through for a 2nd-place finish; Ricky Rudd recovered from contact with Labonte's car to finish 3rd. Rudd opined that Earnhardt "pretty much took him [Labonte] out." Spencer called Earnhardt "the fiercest competitor" to ever climb into a NASCAR stock car.

"Our car was awesome," Labonte said, after finishing 8th but leading for 155 circuits. "The [Waltrip] 66 wrecked me on the caution, and then I got wrecked again." Asked if he had a message for Earnhardt, the normally soft-spoken Labonte warned, "He'd better tighten his belts up," before turning and walking back into his team's transporter.

After pleading his case to the media, Earnhardt admitted, "I'm sure we'll hear about the race for a while." Ironman and Ironhead, re-rack the videotape.

CHAPTER 5

Bristol Motor Speedway has a well-deserved reputation for wild racing action where high speeds frequently spawn multi-car crashes like this melee from the 2008 night race involving Michael Waltrip (No. 55), Casey Mears (No. 5), Sam Hornish Jr. (No. 77), Kasey Kahne (No. 9), Robby Gordon (No. 7), and Reed Sorenson (No. 41) while Dale Earnhardt Jr. (No. 88) takes evasive action. (Photo by Earl Neikirk, Courtesy Bristol Herald Courier)

THE 2000s AND BEYOND

A new millennium delivered more growth, change, and some dynamic racing action on Bristol's oval, and Bristol's dragway secured a spot on the NHRA national event calendar after hosting the all-star race for two seasons. More than two decades after becoming part of the Speedway Motorsports family, Bristol remains the ultimate bucket list destination for race fans the world over.

Dirt Weeks

A new millennium brought an audacious experiment to Bristol Motor Speedway as crews hauled in 14,000 cubic yards of East Tennessee red clay, carefully covered the concrete racing surface, and invited the world's best sprint-car and late-model drivers to have at it for two unforgettable weekends, June 2–3 and 9–10. A pair of preliminary practice sessions proved that radical could become reality.

Red clay covered Bristol's concrete surface for a few weeks in 2000 and 2001 during one of the speedway's most memorable events. Known as Dirt Weeks, the unique promotion attracted the nation's best sprint and dirt late-model racers. (David McGee Photo)

"We had a lot of engineers come in here and tell us we couldn't do this," former track president and general manager Jeff Byrd said at that time. "Folks told us from a construction standpoint that it was impossible to put the dirt down, keep it down, and put it all the way to the top of the track. We figured out a way to do this and make it happen."

What they figured out was that the clay would cling to a layer of sawdust, transforming Bristol into a world-class dirt track. The largest crowd in sprint-car racing history, an estimated 50,000, was there to witness the blisteringly fast World of Outlaws sprinters dice and dig before home-state hero Sammy Swindell captured the Channellock Challenge A-Main feature.

"This place is awesome, and it's fast," Swindell said from the victory podium. "The cars are real fast here, and there was a lot of good racing."

Stevie Smith, Steve Kinser, Mark Kinser, and Dale Blaney rounded out the top five drivers in the 30-lap shootout. "This place compares to no [other] place," Mark Kinser said, after capturing the previous night's A-Main over Donny Schatz, Danny Wood, Steve Kinser, and Stevie Smith.

Swindell's normally calm demeanor barely masked a raging competitive fire exhibited when he set fast time of opening night, carding a lap of 13.860/138.441, 12 mph faster than the NASCAR track record at that time.

Swindell also set fast time the second night at 14.019/136.871. He became irate when series officials ruled that he jumped the start in his eight-lap heat race, but he overcame it and took the heat win via a deft, high-side pass. After arguing his point with series officials, he was penalized $10,000. "It doesn't matter if they penalized us; we're still the fastest car on the track," Swindell said.

Tennessee native Sammy Swindell (No. 1) works the low side against Dale Blaney (No. 10). Swindell captured both the 2000 and 2001 World of Outlaws A-Main feature victories during Bristol's Dirt Weeks events. (David Crigger Photo, Courtesy Bristol Herald Courier)

Dirt late-model stock cars actually christened the surface during the prior weekend's Living Air 100, which attracted 189 cars from 28 states, all attempting to qualify for history's largest-ever Hav-A-Tampa dirt-series race. Nearly seven hours after qualifying began, Wendell Wallace claimed the pole with a fast lap of 16.22/118, narrowly edging out Tennessean Skip Arp's 16.315-second lap as an estimated 12,000 spectators remained until the wee hours to see qualifying conclude.

"I told my guys that we would be good if I ever got up enough nerve to go out around here wide open. That second lap was do or die," an excited Wallace said. "This is probably one of the biggest things we've ever done, to come into a place like this and race on dirt."

The fastest 144 qualifiers advanced to a series of Saturday heat races that ultimately set the 30-car starting lineup. The winners included Freddy Smith, Chub

Steve Francis (No. 15) battles with race winner Dale McDowell (No. 17) and Earl Pearson Jr. (No. 1) for the top spot in the 2000 race. Dirt late models regularly raced three and four wide on Bristol's temporary dirt surface, providing an amazing show for the thousands of fans in attendance. (David McGee Photo)

Frank, Mike Balzano, Dale McDowell, Donnie Moran, and Shannon Babb. Heavy rains pushed the start time back nearly three hours to 12:45 a.m. A crowd originally estimated at 45,000 dwindled to about half that by the time McDowell led the parade to the checkered flag at 2:15 a.m.

"Man, this is awesome," McDowell said, after holding off pole sitter Wendell Wallace, Steve Shaver, Skip Arp, and Booper Bare. "You have to attack this place; you can't slow down."

Attrition, primarily due to tire and wheel failure on the high-banked high-speed course, was a problem for many. Luckily for McDowell, his crew found and replaced a cracked wheel during the race's midway fuel stop. "You enter the corners here at such a great speed, and everything lands on those right-side wheels. I felt all kinds of vibrations those last 10 laps," McDowell said.

Attendance Shrinks for the Encore

Numbers of both competitors and fans diminished for the 2001 encore, but the on-track excitement remained nonstop. Among the late-model set, Scott Bloomquist passed Freddy Smith on the final lap to claim a $10,000 Thursday-night feature. "I had it, and I just gave Scott too much room," Smith lamented years later. The victory gave fans a preview of Bloomquist's $20,000 Saturday-night triumph in a 60-lap feature. Starting on the pole, Bloomquist charged past Billy Moyer on lap 32 and led to the checkers. Steve Francis got around Moyer for 2nd place; Bill Frye and Ray Cook rounded out the top five.

"Once we got rolling, the car is really strong and the engine runs extremely good on the top end," Bloomquist said. Jimmy Mars beat out Freddy Smith in a feature scheduled for Friday but completed in the wee hours of Saturday due to rain.

Scott Bloomquist (No. 0) races against Billy Moyer (No. 21) during the 2001 late-model portion of Bristol's Dirt Weeks. Bloomquist won two of three feature races that weekend and still considers Bristol among his most memorable victories. (David Crigger Photo, Courtesy Bristol Herald Courier*)*

Sprint cars attracted somewhat smaller crowds, compared to the previous year, for the doubleheader show that saw Donny Schatz hold off Jeff Shepard and defending champion Sammy Swindell in Friday's 25-lap A-Main. "The racetrack was a lot better than we expected. I was a little skeptical," Schatz said.

When the lights came on Saturday night, Swindell went back to back, claiming the 30-lap feature for the second-straight year as a crowd of about 25,000 cheered. Swindell mixed it up with Jeff Shepard over the final 10 laps. "Jeff is a guy you can race with and race clean. We gave each other room tonight," Swindell said. "There's not too many guys you can do that with, but that's the way racing should be."

Despite being highly entertaining, dirt racing never returned to Bristol due to a combination of cost, lower attendance, and the problem of cleanup issues on the massive aluminum grandstands and nearly every other surface. Years later, 2001 winner Bloomquist said that the Bristol events remain a "really big deal" and that fans still talk about the times Bristol ran dirt.

Whether he saw the handwriting on the red-clay-stained walls or he simply had a premonition, Swindell said in 2001, "This was a lot of fun. I don't know if fans will get to see many more races like this."

Wood Brothers: A First

An emotional Elliott Sadler gushed thanks after earning his initial trip to a NASCAR premier series Victory Lane at the 2001 Food City 500. Then he paused, allowing the

It was a throwback finish to the 2001 Food City 500 as the Wood Brothers battled the Pettys. Elliott Sadler (No. 21) gave the Wood Brothers their first Bristol victory over John Andretti (No. 43), who was driving a Dodge for Richard Petty. (Jason Davis Photo, Courtesy Bristol Herald Courier)

An excited Elliott Sadler sprays champagne after clinching his first NASCAR premier series victory in the 2001 Food City 500. Sadler's Wood Brothers team gambled that track position would be worth more than fresh tires, a gamble that ultimately paid off. (Photo Courtesy **Bristol Herald Courier***)*

words to sink in after learning that his first victory was also the first for team founders Glen and Leonard Wood and sons Eddie and Len Wood at Bristol Motor Speedway.

"Wow, I had no idea," a stunned Sadler said. "It's an even bigger honor to give the Wood Brothers their first Bristol win." A native of southern Virginia like the Woods, Sadler briefly looked puzzled, trying to grasp the idea that one of the sport's most successful operations hadn't tasted victory at one of its most historic tracks until Bristol's 40th-anniversary season.

Earning that victory required crew chief Pat Tryson to make a clutch pit call, leaving Sadler out on older tires and opting for track position as he made his final pit stop with about 160 laps remaining. Sadler did the rest, taking the lead from Kevin Harvick on lap 431 and holding off John Andretti by .426 second. It was a surreal stretch run for longtime fans since Andretti wheeled a No. 43 Dodge owned by Richard Petty, inspiring visions of David Pearson and the King battling for the win much as they did throughout the 1960s and 1970s.

"It was very special at the time," co-owner Eddie Wood recalled years later in a press release. "It was like the old days, with both of us up front at the end."

Of the 2001 race's challengers, Andretti appeared to have a much better chance of winning. After qualifying a solid 11th, the former IndyCar regular led three times for 51 laps on the brisk April afternoon. In the final 100 laps, Kevin Harvick appeared most likely to visit Victory Lane, but a cut tire forced his Chevrolet to pit road and opened the door for Sadler, who used a provisional to start from the 38th position

Flanked by second-generation brothers Eddie and Len Wood, Elliott Sadler soaks up the moment after capturing his first premier series victory and the legendary racing family's first win at Bristol Motor Speedway in the 2001 Food City 500. (Photo Courtesy Bristol Herald Courier)

and overcame a backstretch pit stall to fight his way into contention. The victory ended a string of 52 winless Bristol starts and represented the team's first NASCAR victory anywhere since 1993.

"I remember we were there a long time after the race," Eddie Wood said, explaining that the post-race interviews and other commitments kept them busy until well past dark. "We were parked about a mile and a half away, at the same place we always park. Somebody offered us a ride on a golf cart, and my brother Len said he wanted to walk. He said we'd made that walk with our heads hung low a lot of times, and he wanted to make that same walk now that we finally had a good finish."

The team's Bristol jinx was so bad that eight drivers delivered just seven top-five finishes over four decades, and their most recent top-five finish prior to Sadler's 2001 victory was Cale Yarborough's 3rd-place run in 1970. Their cars registered just seven lead-lap finishes over that 40-year period, and they fell out of 12 races due to crashes or mechanical failures, with a driver lineup that included Yarborough (who went on to win nine times at Bristol for Junior Johnson), Marvin Panch, Kyle Petty, Neil Bonnett, Dale Jarrett, Morgan Shepherd, and Michael Waltrip.

The Woods' most successful driver was David Pearson, but that combination never entered a single Bristol race, as the Woods and Pearson typically only ran the superspeedways.

Struggles have continued for the Wood Brothers in 20 Bristol races since Sadler took the team to Victory Lane, as six drivers have combined for just two top-five runs and only five finishes on the same lap with the leader.

Bristol also marked the first time that Eddie Wood accompanied his family to a race since he attended the 1967 Volunteer 500.

"I rode over there in the truck with my dad. We got there before daylight on Thursday and had to wait in line to sign in," Wood recalled. Once inside the track, Glen Wood told his son that there were some important people he needed to meet. "He took me across the infield and introduced me to Lee Petty, Richard Petty, Maurice Petty, and Dale Inman back when I was 16 years old. They were the first racing people I'd met other than the men who drove our race cars."

Wood said Maurice Petty gave him a playful pop to the chest; and Inman shook his hand while squeezing his arm so hard that he dropped to his knees in an initiation of sorts into the racing fraternity. That weekend in 1967, Petty scored his first Bristol win as part of his remarkable 27 victories that season; Cale Yarborough, driving for the Woods at that time, dropped out with a blown engine after just 59 laps.

Dale Earnhardt Jr.: It's Bristol, Baby!

Smiling, sweaty, and soaked with his sponsor's product (Budweiser beer), 29-year-old Dale Earnhardt Jr. uttered three little words to sum up the relief and utter joy that surely accompany conquering racing's most unforgiving track. Standing in Victory Lane, the third-generation driver couldn't contain his excitement.

"This is one of the biggest wins of my career," Earnhardt exclaimed. When asked why, he blurted, "It's Bristol, baby!" Earnhardt joined one of the sport's most exclusive clubs, where only 31 other men at that time had earned NASCAR premier series

Dale Earnhardt Jr. celebrates his 2004 Bristol night-race victory with a burnout next to the wall at the start-finish line. He became the first driver to sweep both races in a single weekend at Bristol after also winning the Friday-night Food City 250. (Andre Teague Photo, Courtesy **Bristol Herald Courier***)*

wins in 87 previous Bristol races. One of those men was his famous father, a nine-time Bristol winner.

"I came to a lot of races here when my dad drove. He made this place magical to an Earnhardt fan, me being one of those. I might not have done it like he did, but it was pretty damn close," Earnhardt said after a dominant performance where he led six times for 295 laps and bested 2nd-place finisher Ryan Newman by more than 4 seconds.

His victory occurred five years to the day after Dale Sr. punted Terry Labonte aside on the final lap of the 1999 night race to register his ninth and final Bristol triumph. By snatching his second Bristol win in less than 24 hours, Dale Jr. surpassed even his father, becoming the first driver to sweep both the former Busch Series and Cup Series races in a single Bristol weekend since companion races began in 1982.

"He had some great races here. That's why this place is so magical to me. I've wanted to win here so bad. I never thought I would win a Busch race and a Cup race the same weekend," the prodigal son said later in the track press box. "Wherever he is at, he's laughing. He had to enjoy this butt kicking. I thought Friday's win was cool. This is almost too much."

If that weren't enough, the Cup victory shattered a terrible two-month slump and allowed Earnhardt's team to stay in 3rd place in the points standings just weeks before NASCAR's first championship chase began. Over the nine races preceding Bristol, the team's average finish was a paltry 18.4. Earnhardt called the team "tough as nails," but crew chief Tony Eury Sr. was even more succinct. "We needed this," he said.

2004 Sharpie 500

After qualifying on the pole for the Food City 250, Earnhardt started in a miserable 30th slot for the Sharpie 500. He rolled out to qualify just before Jeff Gordon, but his best lap was 3 mph slower than Gordon's pole-winning 14.930/128.520 lap, which narrowly missed eclipsing Ryan Newman's track record.

However, the No. 8 team found something during final practice and wound up 15th on the speed chart, a tick behind Gordon, and that translated into speed during the race. When the green flag waved, Earnhardt steamed through the 43-car field much as his father often did. He brought the full-house crowd of 160,000, a majority clad in red, to their collective feet when he passed Rusty Wallace for the lead on lap 64. After two more stints at the front, Earnhardt got shuffled as far back as 17th during a pit-stop sequence but retook the lead on lap 240 and paced the field

Dale Earnhardt celebrates in Victory Lane after winning the 2004 Sharpie 500. When asked why he was so excited, he replied, "It's Bristol, baby!" The win came exactly five years after his father's final Bristol win. (David Crigger Photo, Courtesy Bristol Herald Courier)

for the next 156 circuits. He remained among the leaders for the remainder of the night.

Jimmie Johnson, who started in the back of the pack after rolling out the backup car, took the top spot from Earnhardt and led briefly during the race's ninth and final caution. Dale reclaimed the lead for good by passing Jeff Burton on lap 415 and then paced the final 85 circuits. Johnson called his 3rd-place finish "almost like a win." Burton and Elliott Sadler followed him. With only nine caution periods to slow a frenetic pace, just six other drivers managed to finish on the same lap with the leader.

"I'm wore out," Earnhardt said. "We had some long green-flag runs, and I think it wore everybody out. We stayed with it, though. This is awesome for our team. We worked for this one."

2004 Food City 250

Earnhardt, who in 1997 earned his first Busch Series front-row start at Bristol aboard one of hometown car owner Ed Whitaker's Chevrolets, kicked off his weekend sweep by winning the Food City 250 pole in a Chevrolet prepared by his own Chance 2 team. Among the last cars onto the track, Earnhardt reset the series track qualifying record with a 15.160/126.570.

Once the green flag flew, the massive crowd of 120,000 watched Earnhardt lead four times for 125 laps, including the final 17 and an overtime shootout with former Busch Series rival Matt Kenseth. The Wisconsin native only led in the first half of the race, but he worked his way up to 2nd place and got his shot when Tony Raines and Jay Sauter came together in Turn 4, bringing out the night's 13th and final caution on lap 249. After a quick cleanup, NASCAR put the field back under green on lap 255.

"My car was sliding around out there," Earnhardt said. "I was worried [that] I got a bunch of stuff on my tires, but Matt did a good job. To be honest, Kenseth could have run all over me. I was chugging through the corners on that lap just trying to keep my car on the bottom, but Matt laid off me."

A deadpan Kenseth noted that the "crowd seemed to enjoy the outcome" but admitted that he had his own issues. "If I hadn't spun the tires on the last restart, I think I would have had a shot at Dale Jr., but we needed one more lap."

Busch Brothers: Snow Angels and Dominance

Crewmembers and a few drivers engaged in a friendly snowball fight on Bristol's backstretch pit road during a break in the 2006 Sharpie Mini 300. Some considered it a good idea to lob a few toward the grandstands filled with fans waiting for the race to resume. At first, a few snowballs came back. Drivers Kyle Busch and Robby Gordon got into the act, tossing snowballs toward the Turn 3 grandstands, but they and the others soon learned a valuable lesson in military strategy: Challenging an opponent with superior numbers on higher ground is never a good idea. With Christmas music blasting from the public-address speakers, hundreds, perhaps a thousand, fans returned fire, and the avalanche of snowballs temporarily cleared pit road.

Track-drying equipment was on the track during Bristol's March 2006 race weekend, but it was no match for the snow showers that fell that afternoon, delaying the Sharpie Mini 300. Snow caused more than a 1-hour delay, but the race was finally completed. (David Crigger Photo, Courtesy Bristol Herald Courier)

NASCAR officials walk toward shelter after intense storms caused a brief whiteout and delayed the running of the Sharpie Mini 300 in March 2006. (Earl Neikirk Photo, Courtesy **Bristol Herald Courier***)*

Meanwhile, Reed Sorensen's team constructed a snowman complete with helmet on pit road, and baseball bats typically reserved for clearing wrinkled fenders away from tires returned to their sort-of intended purpose, smashing snowballs during a 79-minute red-flag period.

More than a decade after it occurred, the 2006 snow delay remains a part of Bristol lore. Fans may not recall that Kyle Busch eventually scored his first of many wins on the high-banked oval once the snow stopped falling in Saturday's 300-lap test, at that time the longest distance run by drivers in NASCAR's former Busch Series. They may also not remember that his older brother, Kurt, turned it into a family sweep by notching his 5th Bristol victory in just 11 starts, the most prolific beginning in Bristol Motor Speedway history. What most may remember is Kurt Busch climbing out of his Penske Racing Dodge Charger and mimicking a snow angel on the start-finish line after claiming the checkered flag in the Food City 500.

Only flurries marked the running of the 2006 Food City 500, but that didn't stop race winner Kurt Busch from celebrating by imitating making snow angels on the start-finish line. Busch earned his fifth Bristol premier series win and his first during a stint for Penske Racing. (Andre Teague Photo, Courtesy **Bristol Herald Courier***)*

Crewmembers made snowballs and found other ways to amuse themselves when a brief snowstorm temporarily brought the Bristol action to a halt in March 2006. (Andre Teague Photo, Courtesy Bristol Herald Courier*)*

2006 Sharpie Mini 300

Weather wreaked havoc that late March weekend, starting with rain washing out premier series qualifying and practice on Friday. Cars got on the racetrack briefly on Saturday for a hastily rescheduled one-hour practice session, but a snow shower brought qualifying to a halt, forcing the field to line up based on the previous season's car-owner points. That meant the younger Busch would have work to do, starting 20th in the 43-car field.

Kyle Busch was still outside the top 10 when the snow returned, prompting NASCAR to wave the red flag on lap 32. Once action resumed, Busch cracked the top 10 before lap 100 and the top 5 by the race's midway point. He raced among the leaders for the rest of the day but took his first lead by passing Greg Biffle with just 11 laps remaining. From there, he had to fend off pole sitter Kevin Harvick's Chevrolet, edging by him by a half second after Biffle fell from contention with a tire problem.

"It's Bristol, baby! And I love it," Busch told reporters afterward. "It's where my brother always wins, so it's great for me to do it. I wasn't sure if I was going to be able to hold Harvick off, but I was able to do that. I looked up twice, and all I saw was his car number because he was so far up my butt. I kept trying to hit my marks and hang on."

Reflecting on the surreal, snowy day, the Las Vegas native called it the craziest thing. "You see that kind of thing up north with the Modified races at the start of a season or maybe at the end of the season. For it to snow today, that was pretty weird. To be able to throw some snowballs at the fans was a great thing."

Sunday's snow flurries lacked the intensity of Saturday's storm, but even the forecast and frosty temperatures hovering near 40 degrees Fahrenheit didn't deter a bundled sellout crowd of 160,000 from settling in, and they weren't disappointed.

2006 Food City 500

The Food City 500 appeared to belong to either Tony Stewart or Matt Kenseth, who combined to lead eight times for 369 laps. In the end, however, Stewart was shuffled back to a 12th-place finish, and Kenseth could do no better than 3rd. Kurt Busch, on the other hand, overcame a series of misfortunes that saw him lead just three times for 33 laps.

After starting 9th, Busch streaked to the lead by lap 57 before a cut passenger-side rear tire forced him to pit road four laps later. Busch fell two laps down to then-leader Stewart and couldn't communicate with his crew due to a broken radio. By the time the race's seventh caution flew for a four-car crash on lap 188, Busch had erased the deficit and, after a brief red-flag period, was able to switch radios.

He pushed his No. 2 Dodge into the second spot by the race's midway point and briefly took the lead on lap 386 but mostly ran glued to the rear bumper of former teammate Kenseth. With just four laps remaining, Busch said it was "time to go" and tapped Kenseth's red, white, and blue Ford entering Turn 1. Busch drove into the space previously occupied by Kenseth, followed quickly by Kevin Harvick. Kenseth gathered it up and forced his way in front of Jeff Gordon's Chevrolet, but a lap later Gordon bumped Kenseth and took over 3rd place.

On the final lap, Kenseth returned the favor entering Turn 1, punting Gordon's Chevrolet aside and roaring to a 3rd-place finish behind Busch and Harvick. A visibly agitated Gordon climbed from his car on the frontstretch pit road and rushed toward Kenseth, who stepped up to say something, only to have Gordon shove him backward with both hands. Crewmembers and NASCAR officials quickly intervened.

"We got a little bit tight there at the end, and Kenseth got shuffled out. I got to him a couple of times and showed him my nose, and he shut the door on me, and the next time I got an opportunity, I moved him, but I didn't wreck him," Gordon said afterward. "We went down into [Turn] 1, and he just wrecked me."

Kenseth took responsibility, saying, "I did wreck him, but it wasn't intentional."

The win was Busch's fifth at Bristol but his first during a stint driving for Roger Penske and the *Blue Deuce* team that Rusty Wallace wheeled to multiple Bristol Motor Speedway victories.

"This racing is awesome; fans dig it," Busch said afterward. "That's the big thing about Bristol: You have to come to race hard. You have to be able to hoist up the trophy at the end of the day without any grudges." The unapologetic winner said that tagging Kenseth to take the lead was unavoidable because both were on worn-out tires, but his former teammate didn't see it that way.

"I wouldn't have done that to him," Kenseth said. "I would have passed him the right way. He just knocked me out of the way."

Johnson & Johnson: In Search of the Win

Allen Johnson has likely run more laps down Thunder Valley than any other racer in the modern-day Pro Stock category. Living an hour south of the track in Greeneville, Tennessee, he sometimes used the facility for off-week testing and, as he became a force in the category, collected his share of round wins. However, his frustrating string of losses in the Thunder Valley Nationals has prompted a love-hate relationship when the tour rolls into town.

Besides being close to home, the original Bristol track was the site of Johnson's first national-event victory, when he wheeled his father Roy's Dodge Challenger to the 1981 IHRA Spring Nationals Super Stock Eliminator title. Roy's career included multiple victories and championships.

Allen ascended to the Pro Stock class in 1999, coinciding with Bristol's makeover and return to the NHRA for the Winston No Bull Showdown. The race included a full 16-car Pro Stock field where Johnson slid into the ninth slot and then employed a bit of holeshot magic to trailer the quicker cars of Mark Pawuk and Warren Johnson before redlighting against Troy Coughlin in the semifinals.

Amazingly, he again qualified ninth at the second Showdown, winning over Mark Osborne before falling to Ron Krisher in round two.

The next nine seasons and first nine iterations of the Thunder Valley Nationals were pure frustration for Johnson and his father, who produced the Hemi

Roy Johnson launches his Formula Super Stock Challenger in the early 1970s. The Johnson family traces much of its earliest success to Bristol, where Roy campaigned a series of Dodge vehicles, winning two national events and bringing championships home to East Tennessee. (John Beach Photo)

horsepower in the team's engine shop. From 2001 through 2006, Johnson either lost in the first round or failed to qualify. The team broke the ice with a first-round win at the 2007 event but exited in the second round. The script was much the same in 2008 and 2009, during a time when the team typically won between one and three national events every year.

"Coming to Bristol is a challenge all its own, but to come here and win is just a phenomenal challenge," Johnson admitted during a prerace media conference. "If we could pull that off, it would be great for the sport, great for Pro Stock, and great for Bristol. We'll keep working at it as hard as we can go."

That effort, along with Roy's horsepower, bore fruit at the 2010 race, as Allen put the team's Dodge Avenger atop the qualifying chart before thundering into the semifinals and a matchup with Rickie Jones. Johnson blamed himself for selecting the right lane after his car got out of shape and he shut off; Jones's engine failed down track. "I think I could have beaten him," Johnson said afterward.

Fate also denied Johnson in 2011 after he again qualified 1st in the 16-car show and then loaded Steve Kent and Jason Line in the early rounds. Paired with friend and rival Erica Enders in the semifinals, Enders took a slim .006 away from the line and won 6.692/205 to 6.692/205. "What got us is when the car took a sharp right turn in third gear and got out of the groove, which you can't let happen at this track," Johnson said.

Allen didn't know disappointment until the 2012 Thunder Valley Nationals. He played King Kong through four rounds of qualifying and throughout

Pro Stock standout Allen Johnson (left) speaks with Bristol Executive Vice President and General Manager Jerry Caldwell during a press conference promoting the 2016 NHRA Thunder Valley Nationals. Johnson has endured a series of stinging losses at Bristol, including the 2012 edition where he lost a dead heat to Mike Edwards. (Photo by Earl Neikirk, Courtesy Bristol Herald Courier)

eliminations, setting low ET and top speed, and being the quickest car in every session. He was never seriously challenged in eliminations, besting Shane Gray, Ronnie Humphrey, and Jason Line and rolling into the trophy round with lane choice over Mike Edwards, who was seeking his fourth consecutive Thunder Valley Nationals Pro Stock title.

Johnson picked the right lane and left on a solid .018 reaction, but Edwards was better at .005, and that opened the door because Johnson made his slowest run of the weekend at 6.661/207.05. Edwards was slower at 6.674/206.16, but his reaction-time advantage gave him the slimmest of margins and the closest win in NHRA history. The finish-line camera couldn't pick a winner as the cars crossed the finish line locked together, but Edwards tripped the timer by a millisecond.

"I really wanted to give that to my dad for Father's Day and to my employees and crew. I really wanted to give them the excitement of a win here at home," a frustrated Johnson said.

Matt Hagan: Hunting the Groove at Bristol

Funny Car champion Matt Hagan's first brush with the sound and fury of nitromethane-fueled race cars came as a youngster at the original Thunder Valley.

"A friend of mine took me, and I had no idea what to expect," Hagan recalled. "The first time the fuelers took off, I about peed my pants. I was like, 'What was that?' The guy just had a big old grin on his face, and I was scared to death. I never dreamed of being able to sit in one and drive one. It was just a sport I watched and I liked. It's crazy to think I came from some little town bracket racing at Elk Creek [Dragway] to where I am today."

Years later, in his second season steering a temperamental Pro Modified down the current incarnation of Bristol Dragway, Hagan was happy and a bit relieved to qualify for the 16-car field at the 2006 Thunder Valley Nationals.

A Southwest Virginia cattle farmer from nearby Christiansburg and veteran of IHRA's Pro Modified wars, Hagan qualified his 1963 Corvette 11th at Bristol at 6.25/229.12. He escaped a first-round tilt with Joshua Hernandez's higher qualified *Dr. Moon's Rage* Camaro when the Texas driver drew a redlight start. Hagan's 6.28/225 was good enough to advance, but his second session of 6.32/216 was no match for eventual runner-up Joey Martin's Mustang.

Hagan couldn't have guessed that weekend, his first wheeling a professional-class machine at his home track on the NHRA trail, would establish a frustrating pattern.

Qualifying for the Thunder Valley Nationals was a cinch, but making any real headway in eliminations seemed impossible.

Fast forward to 2009, and Hagan was back at Thunder Valley in the midst of his first season of driving a nitro Funny Car for former world champion Don Schumacher. An 11th-hour entry sponsored by his family's auto dealerships, Hagan's rig was nestled in Nitro Alley with a fully stocked trailer where he received tune-up information from his well-heeled teammates. The nitro rookie immediately made his presence known.

His opening-round 4.21-second blast left him second quickest on the speed chart in Bristol's first 1,000-foot national event. He leapt to a 4.139/295 run in the Friday-night session that stood fourth best for the weekend, trailing only Ashley Force Hood, Tim Wilkerson, and Del Worsham. Hagan was to race former world champion Tony Pedregon's Jimmie Johnson Foundation machine in the opening round, but a clamp came off an oil line, forcing Hagan to forfeit the run.

The Thunder Valley Nationals was held on Father's Day weekend for the first time in 2010, and Hagan returned to Bristol's familiar confines in 3rd place in NHRA points, riding the momentum of his first two national-event wins at Houston and Joliet.

Hagan thundered to the third spot on the qualifying ladder with a Friday-night 4.185/292.58 blast that narrowly missed catching Ashley Force Hood's and Cruz Pedregon's nearly identical 4.15s.

Everyone slowed in eliminations, and Hagan barely escaped the first round and upset-minded Jeff Arend. Hagan took .04 at the tree and needed it, besting Arend's Kalitta Racing DHL Toyota Solara 4.27 to 4.29 at the stripe. Although Hagan won the round, he lost lane choice to John Force, whose first-round 4.24 knocked off Cory Lee and kept Force in the preferred right lane. Force slowed to a 4.29/291, but it was low ET of the second round and enough to load Hagan's Dodge, which slowed to a 4.35/274. Force marched on to score the victory and take the points lead later that afternoon.

Hagan couldn't have known that he was in the midst of his first world championship season when the 2011 tour rolled back into Bristol in mid-June. His focus at that moment was on ending his inability to claim Bristol's "Wally" trophy.

His focus appeared to be working, as he snagged the second spot in qualifying with a thundering 4.082 best effort at 308 mph. His 4.14/305 opening-round blast was enough to put away Cory Lee's early-shutoff 7.76 and gain lane choice against second-round foe Jeff Arend. The first pair out of the tunnel had a pedal fest before Arend avenged his 2010 loss, sending Hagan to the showers, 4.65/278 to 5.34/268.

Amazingly, Hagan continued living a version of *Groundhog Day,* enduring two more frustrating outings where Bristol race days ended in the second round. In 2012, crew chief Tommy DeLago tuned his Dodge to a sixth-best qualifying effort and convincing first-round win over Cruz Pedregon. However, Hagan was no match for teammate Jack Beckman, losing 4.10/310 to 4.14/299, while another teammate, Ron Capps, took home his third Bristol trophy.

In 2013, Hagan posted the third-quickest qualifying effort at 4.04/317.05, matching teammate Jack Beckman for top speed of the event. Surely, this would be the year, right? Unfortunately, not. After punching out Tony Pedregon in the opening set, Hagan lined up against John Force, who had secured lane choice by .04 second. At the green it was all Force, who carried .02 away from the line and closed out Hagan 4.16/305 to 4.19/304, in one of the day's best matchups.

Breaking That Second-Round Jinx

It was 2014 and Hagan's sixth Bristol start in Funny Car when he finally broke the second-round jinx, and he did it by beating the fastest guy on the property. After qualifying 8th and blasting Jim Head in round one, Hagan drew top qualifier Del Worsham, who steamrolled the field with a Friday-night qualifying blast of 3.992/319. Del proved to be vulnerable on race day, losing lane choice to Hagan by .03 second.

The breakthrough second-round victory came via a huge starting-line advantage and a 4.21/287 that withstood Worsham's 4.20/299. The bad news was that the 4.20 lost lane choice for the semifinal tussle with teammate Tommy Johnson Jr. That was enough for Johnson's *Make A Wish* Dodge, which steamed to a victory over Hagan in the day's tightest Funny Car contest, 4.201/305 to 4.209/293.

Hagan overcame the Bristol disappointment later that season, catching fire and scoring three playoff wins to earn his second NHRA world championship in the 2014 campaign.

The night before the 2015 Thunder Valley Nationals, the reigning world champion made an autograph appearance at a local sporting-goods retailer on behalf of sponsor Rocky boots, which adorned the sides and hood of his Dodge Charger. It was fitting, since the farmer finally did some serious stomping all weekend.

Dodging rain showers, Hagan's 3.996/322 effort narrowly missed beating John Force's 3.978/323 for the top spot in the 16-car field. On race day, Hagan bested Jeff Diehl with a 4.124/308.78 that secured lane choice over Cruz Pedregon by .001 second. Hagan took full advantage, winning handily, 4.139/300 to Pedregon's

4.163/287. With the .13 ensuring him lane choice against teammate Jack Beckman, the two staged a titanic semifinal tilt won by Hagan 4.201/302.55 to 4.214/295.27 after he grabbed a significant holeshot.

Although Hagan's ET was good enough to advance, he surrendered lane choice to another teammate. Ron Capps was in search of his fourth Bristol trophy after besting Robert Hight, top qualifier John Force, and Tony Pedregon in the semis with a 4.183/304. Capps selected the right lane, but Hagan mastered the left, taking .035 second at the start and sealing the deal with 4.164/303 to Capps' 4.186/307 moments before a massive thunderstorm interrupted the balance of final eliminations.

"Everybody wants to win Indy, and it's great, but I wanted to win Bristol more than I did Indy," Hagan said in a subsequent interview. "It's so special to me. This is my home track, and I have thousands of fans and friends and people that come out. To have my wife there, my kids there, and my father there on Father's Day, I was sobbing like a little girl. It was so cool. That, to me, is what memories are made of. This is one of the most special races I've ever won. Deep down, this was the one I wanted."

He acknowledged that it was tough to turn those Bristol misfortunes around.

"This race I've had bad luck, and sometimes you can't get it all together," Hagan said. "In drag racing, there are a lot more downs than there are ups. I consider myself the biggest cheerleader out there. I have to keep my team and their morale up and the guys moving forward and working hard to know that we're gonna be on top at the end."

Beyond family, Hagan deeply appreciates his Bristol fans and the facility's racing heritage. "It's so close to home. Where I live is two hours away, and you have so many folks that come out and support you. You want to win and put on a great show for folks you see all the time.

"Bristol is the heart of racing. You look at where NASCAR and drag racing got going, and it all happened here in this area, for the East Coast, and people realize that. They appreciate all that Bruton [Smith] is doing, and you see people who save up all year, and they spend their vacation to come out and watch you race. We've got a lot of love at Bristol, a lot of fans, a lot of friends."

Fast Women

Thunder Valley has been the scene of success for female drag racers since the inaugural 1965 NHRA Springnationals, where Michigan racer Nancy McCormack won her class. In the years that followed, many notable women, including Shirley

More than a half-dozen women have captured national-event victories in a variety of Sportsman classes throughout Bristol's rich history. The first female to win Bristol back to back was Malinda Bertozzi, who captured the 8.90 class at both the 1995 Spring and Fall Nationals. (Bryan Epps Photo)

Shahan, Pro Stock racer Shay Nichols, and Funny Car pioneers Paula Murphy and Della Woods, raced at Thunder Valley. They paved the way for Alcohol Funny Car standouts Carol "Bunny" Burkett, Carol Henson, Roberta Schultz, and Melinda Green. Female Top Fuel pilots including Lucille Lee, Lori Johns, Kim LaHaie, Rhonda Hartman-Smith, Danielle DePorter, and Cristen Powell competed at Bristol in the 1980s and 1990s, with both LaHaie and Hartman-Smith reaching final rounds.

Thunder Valley's switch back to NHRA sanction brought another swell of top female racers who enjoyed their greatest success yet. Alexis DeJoria, Leah Pritchett, and Hillary Will all made marks in the nitro classes, highlighted by DeJoria scoring her first nitro Funny Car final round with a runner-up finish to Ron Capps at the 2012 Thunder Valley Nationals.

Drag racing's array of Sportsman classes have also produced multiple female winners at Bristol, including two-time 8.90 eliminator winner Malinda Bertozzi, former Modified champion Ann Peto, and, more recently, Jennifer White, Emily Lewis, and Lauren Freer. Grandmother Cleo Chandler failed to win class at Bristol; she cultivated many fans while racing her Stock Eliminator Chevrolet in her 70s.

Decades before Danica Patrick turned a tire at Bristol Motor Speedway, IndyCar standout Janet Guthrie recorded finishes of 6th and 11th in NASCAR premier series races on the world's fastest half-mile. Patrick was also not the first woman to compete in the former Busch Series at Bristol; Shawna Robinson and Patty Moise had forged that path.

From Tina Gordon to Tammy Jo Kirk, who competed at Bristol in both the NASCAR Xfinity and Truck series, and from Johanna Long to Jennifer Jo Cobb, Erin Crocker, and Deborah Renshaw, Bristol has hosted many female racers. Kirk qualified 10th for the 1997 truck race, then registered a decent 19th-place finish. She returned to finish 13th in 1998. Long scored a 15th-place finish in Bristol's 2011 Truck series race.

The number of female competitors has risen each year that the NASCAR K&N Series has competed at Bristol Motor Speedway. From a single female in that first race in 2012, the number grew, and the women weren't back markers. Kenzie Ruston raced to a strong 11th-place finish in 2013, a result matched by rookie Dominique Van Wieringen in 2016.

Danica Patrick

Patrick earned a 9th-place run in the 2015 Food City 500, her fifth career premier series top-10 finish. That matched a 9th-place lead-lap run in the 2012 Food City 250, her third and most recent Bristol start in what is now the NASCAR Xfinity Series.

In the traditionally male-dominated NASCAR world, female drivers remain a distinct minority, hardly a novelty but still uncommon. Unlike predecessors Robinson and Moise, Patrick has been a lightning rod for fans who seemingly either cheer or abhor her presence behind the wheels of cars fielded by Stewart-Haas Racing.

During her first visit to Bristol in March 2011, Patrick made a point to see the track in person the day before she steered a stock car around its high-banked high-speed corners, her first outing away from speedways at least 1.5 miles in length. "I thought, I better see this place firsthand, at least to be able to sleep on a visual of it," she said during a press conference. "I kind of wonder how they run at any short track, let alone one like this."

She completed 248 laps in her first Bristol outing before contact with Ryan Truex sent her into the wall and out of contention. She wasted no time, however, mastering the Bristol stare as Truex circled past her steaming countenance. Although Bristol's tight quarters were unlike anything she'd ever raced on, Patrick has, at times, found a Bristol comfort zone. Her average finish is eight positions better than her average starting spot, but she has only one lead-lap finish through 11 races.

Bristol was one of four races Patrick ran in her introduction to NASCAR's premier series through an arrangement with car owner Tommy Baldwin. In August 2012, she had a top-20 run going late in the race before contact with Regan Smith ended her day. Exiting the car, Patrick flipped Smith the bird and then walked up the track apron; when he cycled past again under caution, she stopped to point her finger at him before walking to the ambulance.

Janet Guthrie waits inside her team's truck to get back behind the wheel of her Chevrolet. She started both of Bristol's NASCAR premier series races in 1977, earning finishes of 11th and 6th, her best NASCAR outcomes. (Photo Courtesy Bristol Motor Speedway)

"We're all racing hard," a frustrated Patrick said afterward. "This is Bristol, and this is why people love this track: because you see a lot of that, and you see tempers flare."

Janet Guthrie

An aerospace engineer and pilot, Guthrie became the first woman to qualify and race in both the Indianapolis 500 and Daytona 500 during a brief four-year racing career. She qualified for all 19 NASCAR races she entered during the 1977 season in Chevrolets owned by Lynda Ferreri. In 33 premier series races, Guthrie's 9th-place start in Bristol's 1977 Volunteer 400 equaled a career best, and her 6th-place finish in the same race was her best NASCAR showing.

"There isn't anything like Bristol. It's like a teacup for a giant," Guthrie told interviewer Tom Netherland decades later, adding that she cherished that finish. "We hit the setup right and, boy, was it fun."

Shawna Robinson

Janet Guthrie was a role model for Shawna Robinson, a Des Moines, Iowa, native who worked her way up through the short tracks and even diesel-truck racing. She competed four times at Bristol in a career that spanned from the 1980s to the 2000s. Robinson had four starts in the former Busch Series, scoring a best finish of 14th in 1993. In fact, her last series start came in the 2005 Sharpie 250, where a multicar accident relegated her to a disappointing 39th place.

Robinson became the first woman to win a NASCAR touring-series race with three victories and two straight 3rd-place points finishes in the former Dash series,

Shawna Robinson is strapped in and about to roll onto the track at Bristol Motor Speedway. Robinson, who was the first female to win in a NASCAR touring series, made four Bristol starts in the Xfinity Series and finished a solid 14th in 1993. (David McGee Photo)

but the series didn't appear at Bristol during her two-year tenure there. She also never started a premier series race at Bristol.

Patty Moise

Moise, of Jacksonville, Florida, made 13 Bristol starts in the former Busch Series between 1987 and 1998, earning four top-20 finishes. She racked up one top-10 finish at Bristol Motor Speedway, running 10th in the 1998 Moore's Snacks 250, a lap behind the pace of race winner Elliott Sadler.

Moise made history during the August 1994 Food City 250 when she and her husband, Elton Sawyer, became the first married couple to compete against each other at the Bristol oval. For the record, Moise out-qualified Sawyer, but her run from the 13th-place starting spot was spoiled by a blown engine that relegated her to 24th as Sawyer finished 14th. That trend continued for the five other times that the couple raced each other at Bristol, with Sawyer posting a higher finish each time, including a 4th-place run versus his wife's 10th-place showing in 1998.

Shirley Muldowney

While women continue chipping away at oval racing relevance, they have long been part of the equation in major-league drag racing. Iconic Shirley Muldowney provided the driving force, long ago showing that women could compete at the sport's uppermost level and that they could also win races and championships against their male counterparts. Just ask some of the sport's icons, such as Don Garlits, Don Prudhomme, and Connie Kalitta, about facing the three-time world champion.

Muldowney competed sparingly at Bristol through most of the 1970s and 1980s while pursuing NHRA championships. She made quite an impression at Bristol during its final years of IHRA sanction, establishing track records and advancing to two Top Fuel final rounds.

Three-time drag racing world champion Shirley Muldowney blasts off the Thunder Valley starting line with the candles lit. Muldowney advanced to two Bristol finals in the latter stage of her amazing career and reset Bristol's track record. (David McGee Photo)

Shirley Muldowney earned a pair of runner-up finishes when matched with Doug Herbert in the finals of Bristol's 1995 Spring Nationals and the 1996 Fall Nationals, a race in which she reset the track speed record.

The Force Girls

Although John Force's daughters, Ashley, Courtney, and Brittany, have, at this writing, failed to follow their world-champion father into the Bristol Winner's Circle, Ashley and Brittany have logged number-one qualifying efforts. Ashley was the Thunder Valley Nationals top Funny Car qualifier in back-to-back seasons in 2009 and 2010. She set low ET in 2009 and top speed in 2010, and in 2009 she reached the semifinals. Brittany set low ET and was top qualifier in Top Fuel in 2014 before being upset in the first round by Chris Karamesines.

Melanie Troxel

The female racer who not only matched but exceeded her dad's Bristol win total is the versatile Melanie Troxel, the only racer to win the Thunder Valley Nationals in Funny Car and Pro Modified. Mike Troxel earned the Alcohol Dragster trophy at Bristol's 1988 Spring Nationals, but his daughter was in school and couldn't make the trip east from Colorado. Once the NHRA returned to Bristol, Melanie competed in three pro categories: Top Fuel, Funny Car, and Pro Modified.

Three women made the Top Fuel field of the inaugural Thunder Valley Nationals, with Troxel knocking off Shirley Muldowney's *Heart Like a Wheel* entry in round one before losing to eventual race winner Larry Dixon. Rhonda Hartman-Smith qualified a solid 5th in the 16-car show and notched an impressive first-round win over Tony Schumacher.

Melanie Troxel is all smiles after driving the R2B2 Racing turbocharged Corvette to the Pro Modified victory at the 2011 Thunder Valley Nationals. The win was Troxel's second in three seasons after she became the first female to win Funny Car at Bristol in 2008. She was also the fastest qualifier in Top Fuel at the 2006 event. (Chris Haverly Photo)

Troxel qualified atop the 2006 Top Fuel field but was upended in the second round. Two years later, she switched to nitro Funny Car and, after qualifying 11th in the 16-car field, bested Mike Neff aboard one of the Team Force Mustangs in a final round that was run well after 10 p.m. With that victory, Troxel became the 1st woman and 14th driver overall to win NHRA races in both nitro classes.

The race also marked the final time nitro cars raced to the quarter-mile finish line at Bristol, as the NHRA shortened the race distance a month later, following Scott Kalitta's fatal Funny Car crash at Englishtown, New Jersey. Kalitta had been among five drivers, including Jack Beckman and Tommy Johnson Jr., who failed to make 2008's rugged 16-car Bristol field.

Rain plagued the remarkable 2008 Thunder Valley Nationals where Troxel needed three tries to register her initial-round Funny Car win. She and Tony Pedregon had completed their burnouts but were shut off when rain began falling, so their machines were towed back to the pits. More than an hour later, after track drying

Rhonda Hartman-Smith (near lane) squares off with Shirley Muldowney in an all-female Top Fuel matchup during the 1997 Spring Nationals, in which Muldowney emerged the victor. The pair previously clocked Bristol's first side-by-side 4-second runs. (David McGee Photo)

Melanie Troxel burns out in her nitro Funny Car during the 2008 Thunder Valley Nationals. Troxel's first-round victory was her initial-round win in Funny Car. Weather wreaked havoc on the event schedule, but three sets later Troxel was holding the event trophy. (David McGee Photo)

was completed, they rolled out again, completed their burnouts, and were staging to race when, incredibly, showers returned. The third attempt proved to be the charm as Melanie eked out the day's closest contest, 4.816/319.29 to the former world champion's 4.827/319.90.

In the second round, Troxel made more history by defeating Ashley Force, the first time that two women raced in 42 years of NHRA Funny Car action. She advanced to the finals with a semifinal victory over a tire-smoking Jim Head. Underdog Troxel caught a huge break when Neff's John Force Racing team couldn't lift the body after the burnout to make any adjustments to the fuel or clutch systems. She drove her Dodge out of early tire shake and to the finish line as Neff's engine exploded at about the 300-foot mark.

"That was a great day," she said. "I knew he was having troubles over there, and the only thing that crossed my mind was that I didn't win on a bye. I saw him out there on me, but I was reeling him in when he just disappeared."

After her Funny Car team's sponsorship dried up, Troxel jumped into the incredibly challenging Pro Modified class and promptly wheeled the turbocharged R2B2 Racing Corvette to the 2011 Thunder Valley Nationals title, knocking off teammate Leah Pruett-LeDuc (now Pritchett) in the semifinals. Troxel also established low ET and a track record along the way. More than five years later, three of her runs on that weekend remain among the fastest Pro Mod passes in Thunder Valley history.

"They're crossed up, sideways, and really a handful to drive," Troxel said of the unpredictable Pro Mods. "There is a lot of horsepower in a suspension car, and that makes the difference. Nitro cars, Top Fuel dragsters, and Funny Cars have a lot more horsepower, but there is no suspension. When the car gets out of the groove and you have to make an adjustment with the steering wheel, that suspension amplifies what you're doing. That's what makes them unpredictable."

Troxel credits Muldowney with blazing a trail for all other female racers to follow.

"I think the thing that really sets drag racing apart is the number of females involved in the sport," Troxel said. "Certainly, you go back to Shirley Muldowney: She won three championships and kicked the door open and sped the whole process up. We're past the novelty point of women interested in drag racing. Now women are getting into drag racing and winning races."

Erica Enders

Two-time NHRA Pro Stock world champion Erica Enders (now Enders-Stevens) advanced to three consecutive final rounds at the Thunder Valley Nationals and counted Bristol victories in 2014 and 2015 toward her historic consecutive championship seasons.

Enders became the first woman to reach a Pro Stock final in 2005 and the first to earn a Pro Stock national-event victory in 2012. While neither of those milestones occurred at Bristol, that initial victory nearly arrived in the 2011 Thunder Valley Nationals finals. After qualifying fourth quickest, she stormed into the finals holding lane choice against defending champion Mike Edwards. Enders took a .005-second advantage away from the starting line but lost traction in second gear and was forced to settle for runner-up.

Teamed with Richard Freeman's Elite Motorsports team in 2014, the Houston native

Erica Enders found great success at Bristol's Thunder Valley Nationals, reaching the Pro Stock final rounds in 2011 and 2013 before breaking through for consecutive victories in 2014 and 2015. Both wins coincided with sweeping Pro Stock world titles for both seasons. (Chris Haverly Photo)

settled for nothing less than winning as she put down the likes of Greg Anderson, Jeg Coughlin Jr., and Jonathan Gray for one of the six wins during her 2014 title run. Her profile was even more dominant in 2015, qualifying number one and slaying Chris McGaha in Bristol's second-closest Pro Stock final 6.685/206.95 to 6.689/207.46, one of eight wins in her march to a second championship.

"Bristol is one of my favorite places to race," Enders said. "It's always been good to me."

Aggi Hendriks

Women piloting jet-powered dragsters recorded some of the quickest and fastest runs down Thunder Valley. Aggi Hendriks, the sport's first female jet racer, emerged as the winner of Jet Eliminator at Bristol's 1981 World Jet Championship during her rookie season. The 28-year-old Vancouver, British Columbia, native called her career change "sheer lunacy" but admitted that she loved the speed, sound, and fire that jet cars provide.

Wheeling the radical, lightweight *Odyssey* jet dragster prepared by car owner Wayne Knuth, Hendriks qualified first in an eight-car show of many of the sport's biggest names at 5.82/271.90. On race day, she clocked weekend best times of 5.81/278 before defeating Joe Petro's *Kamikaze* in the finals with a 5.99-second ET, but things really got interesting at 270 mph.

"When I pulled the chutes, the car did a wheelie at the top end, and I could feel that [the] right rear tire was flat," she said afterward. "It wasn't noticeable until the car slowed down!"Among those who followed in her path were Jessica Willard, who ran 295 mph during a Super Chevy race in the early 2000s, and jet Funny Car racer Fran Peppler, with her 280-mph *Rock & Roll Thunder* machine.

Aggi Hendriks became an instant fan favorite during the 1980s, regularly wheeling Wayne Knuth's Odyssey *jet-powered dragster to 5-second runs at more than 270 mph. She won Bristol's 1981 World Jet Nationals title in her rookie season. (David McGee Photo)*

Kyle Busch: A Clean Sweep

A dozen drivers have won Bristol in both of NASCAR's top two touring divisions, but only three (Dale Earnhardt Jr., Kevin Harvick, and Kyle Busch) topped both series races in a single weekend. Darrell Waltrip and Dale Earnhardt Jr. won in both divisions but not during the same weekend as a Cup victory. Rusty Wallace, one of the sport's greatest and Bristol's most successful, competed in both divisions and scored nine Bristol Motor Speedway wins in the premier series but never visited Bristol's Victory Lane in the former Busch Series.

The club is more exclusive for men owning BMS victories in all three of NASCAR's top three divisions since the Truck Series first raced at Bristol in 1995, including just Kyle Busch, Carl Edwards, Kevin Harvick, Brad Keselowski, and Mark Martin.

Winning all three trophies in a single weekend at the sport's most demanding track, the one Kyle Petty compared to flying jet fighters in a gymnasium? Almost unthinkable for any racer. Except for Kyle Busch.

Busch finished 5th the first time he raced with the Truck Series at Bristol in 2005, 6th the following season, after winning the spring Sharpie Mini 300, and a disappointing 15th in 2007, the year he mastered the Food City 500.

That all changed in 2008, when Busch led 145 laps, including the final 132, and won the Wednesday-night Truck shootout over Todd Bodine. Knowing he was entered in the other races, Busch was the first to suggest how cool it would be to sweep, admitting he'd dreamed about it since turning 20 and entering NASCAR's premier series.

He was shut out of leading a single lap in that season's Food City 250 and finished 5th. The following night, he led 415 laps in the Sharpie 500 Cup Series race before a late-race bump-and-run by Carl Edwards relegated him to 2nd place.

Busch returned to the Winner's Circle after scoring his second-straight victory in the 2009 O'Reilly 200 truck race. Any dreams of a sweep were crushed in the Food City 250, as Busch took the lead on lap 52 and was promptly clipped by another car while battling Kevin Harvick for the top spot, dooming him to a 28th-place finish. Busch rebounded nicely the following night, holding off veteran Mark Martin in a thrilling late-race battle to sweep both of that season's Bristol Cup races and earn his third Bristol Cup win.

So close, yet so far. Sweeping the weekend would demand 900 virtually flawless laps.

In 2010, the Las Vegas native qualified his Toyota on the pole for the Wednesday-night O'Reilly 200 truck race but started in the rear after a post-qualifying engine change. Busch sliced through the pack and took the point on lap 91. Once out

An exuberant Kyle Busch (left) can't take his eyes off the 2010 Irwin Tools Night Race trophy while being interviewed by Bristol announcer David McGee. And with good reason, since Busch made NASCAR history by sweeping victories in all three touring-series races, Truck, Xfinity, and Cup, in a single weekend. (Photo Courtesy Bristol Herald Courier)

front, he paced the field through a string of caution flags then held off Aric Almirola in overtime, only to have his truck run out of fuel on the cool-down lap. Afterward, Busch was upbeat about the triple.

"I feel like my chances are pretty good. I almost made it last year. Bristol is always so much fun; I can't wait to get going," he told reporters. The key would be finally winning the Food City 250, which would involve some contact with Brad Keselowski. With the race winding down, Keselowski had the lead, and Busch wanted it. The two leaned on each other twice on lap 219 before Busch emerged with the top spot and pulled away.

"I thought I had him cleared, and I moved up in front of him," Busch said of his pass. "He decided he would just run into the back of me and put me in the fence. That's Brad Keselowski. So I went down into the next corner and dumped him."

The raucous Bristol crowd of 112,000 wasn't bashful afterward, issuing a chorus of boos as Busch did a burnout and emerged from his black Toyota to grab the checkered flag and offer a signature bow. For emphasis, he placed his hand up to his head as if to better hear them, prompting many to boo even louder.

With 500 laps to go, Busch admitted that the sweep "would be pretty cool."

Already on probation for another incident, Keselowski opted not to retaliate on Friday, but he found another way to tweak Busch during prerace driver introductions for Saturday's Irwin Tools Night Race. Busch qualified a mediocre 19th and came on stage to the usual booing. "Y'all are so loving," Busch said during his introduction. "Kyle Busch, driver of the Doublemint Camry and ready to win it again."

Keselowski followed him moments later and, after introducing himself, proclaimed, "Kyle Busch is an ass," which drew predictably enthusiastic cheers from much of the crowd of about 155,000.

Once the green flag was unfurled, Busch needed time to work through the pack, never seeing the front until wresting the lead from Jimmie Johnson on lap 172. Johnson, who was trying to sweep both Bristol Cup races for the season, led five times for 175 laps but dropped from contention just past halfway after getting involved in a backstretch crash with Juan Pablo Montoya.

Busch, all of 25 years old, passed underdog David Reutimann to lead lap 429 and then set sail. Reutimann, who was suffering with a stomach virus, put up a valiant fight, but his Camry was no match for Busch, who roared into the history books. He led four times for 282 laps.

After the checkered flag fell, the expected catcalls were balanced with substantial cheering from savvy fans who understood the weighty accomplishment they'd just witnessed. For those who booed, Busch again placed his hand to his helmet, cupping his ear and drying imaginary tears after his signature start-finish-line bow. In Victory Lane, he held a broom high to signify the accomplishment.

"This is history, and I'm really proud to make it," Busch said. "I love Bristol, and I love winning. To sweep a weekend for the first time is pretty awesome. I've been trying to do this since I got to NASCAR."

As for Keselowski, his Penske Dodge finished where Busch started, in 19th place, and he was never a factor. Asked by the media about his rival's prerace verbal jab, Busch was having none of it. "Who?" Busch playfully asked when quizzed.

"You know, the 12 car," a reporter replied.

"I saw it. I passed it," was the grinning Busch's only response.

Kyle Busch did the unthinkable and repeated the triple sweep in the fall races at Bristol in 2017.

World's Fastest Half-Mile

Bristol Motor Speedway has worn the tagline "World's Fastest Half-Mile" almost since opening in 1961. It was a badge of honor in its infancy, at a time when NASCAR's premier division raced on about a dozen half-mile tracks, and it was a title others coveted.

Throughout the 1960s, Bristol and the Asheville-Weaverville Speedway, a now-defunct track north of Asheville, North Carolina, took turns claiming the half-mile qualifying lap record year after year as NASCAR's Grand National cars became progressively faster. It was a full-on rivalry, once prompting Bristol officials to appeal to NASCAR that Asheville-Weaverville was shorter than Bristol's original, true half-mile distance and shouldn't be able to make the claim.

That pendulum swung in Bristol's favor during the summer of 1969, when its track was reconfigured with much steeper banking (claimed then to be 35 degrees and later 36 degrees), which raised the track qualifying record to more than 103 mph. Although Asheville-Weaverville subsequently fell off the premier series schedule, the new high-banked Bristol's claim put itself into another territory.

The previous battle centered on NASCAR and what was then known as its lumbering Grand National Series. With its new high banks Bristol unintentionally projected itself into a different conversation with Midwest ovals including Winchester and Salem, Indiana, and Dayton, Ohio. These tracks hosted everything from sprint cars to late-model stocks that were lighter and sometimes faster than the bulky NASCAR machines, regularly staking their own claims to the title "world's fastest half-mile."

That budding rivalry hit home in 1982 when Rusty Wallace rocketed an ASA late-model Camaro around the Bristol oval on a 15.912/120.500 qualifying lap. That lap was hailed as the fastest on any half-mile track, bettering Bristol's existing Cup qualifying record by 8 mph. The ASA cars ran even faster the following year, and it took years for Cup cars to surpass the mark.

Bristol staked a new claim when the World of Outlaws winged sprint cars competed during Bristol's 2000 Dirt Weeks, where Sammy Swindell carded a new track-record lap of 13.860/138.442.

Then, during Bristol's 50th anniversary season in 2011, the track hosted a unique speed-trials event on its spring race weekend involving sprint cars, super modifieds, passenger cars, and even a motorcycle. At day's end, Michigan's Jason Blonde overcame bouncing off the outside wall to record an electrifying 13.245/144.871.

That adrenaline-fueled record lasted all of six months. On a cold, windy October Saturday, eight sprint-car drivers bettered Blonde's mark during Bristol's Xtreme Speed Classic. Brian Gerster, an Indiana native who cut his teeth on the high banks

Brian Gerster shattered the half-mile speed record at Bristol in 2011, wheeling his Mopar-powered sprint car to a qualifying lap of 150.585 mph. He won the feature race later that same day. (Randall Perry Photo)

of Salem and Winchester, topped them all, wheeling his winged pavement sprinter around Bristol to a new world-record speed of 150.585 mph.

"It's neat to be the first person to go 150 mph and win this race," Gerster said. "We made our qualifying run on an older tire. If we would have been on a fresher tire, we would have qualified even faster."

Later that day, Gerster won the Xtreme sprint-car feature from the pole. Afterward, he quipped, "To be honest, I never took my foot off the floorboard in the final 10 laps."

Rickie Smith: Tricky Rickie

Nobody could wipe the smile from Rickie Smith's face after the King, North Carolina, native captured Pro Modified at the 2012 Thunder Valley Nationals. Standing near the starting line awaiting the formal trophy-presentation ceremony, a jubilant Smith paused while accepting handshakes, fist bumps, and congratulations to gaze up toward the suites and rows of names comprising Bristol's "Legends of Thunder Valley." A first-ballot inductee and the track's winningest driver, Smith seemed to be making sure his name hadn't been erased in the wake of a lengthy drought.

That afternoon's victory was Smith's 12th at Thunder Valley, tying him with NASCAR star Darrell Waltrip for Bristol trophies, and his first since the dragway was renovated in 1998 and 1999. Smith was a force to be reckoned with at the old Bristol, with 11 wins and 4 runners-up in two Professional and one Sportsman class. Success had been sparse since the transition, with only 1 Thunder Valley Nationals runner-up a decade before, in 2002.

Smith's voice cracked discussing his inclusion in the Legends listing. "That, to me, is probably more important than all the championships I won," Smith said. "To be put up there with Larry Carrier and Don Garlits and Bruton Smith. To get that kind of respect, how much better does it get?"

Veteran Rickie Smith makes a point while talking with others during a break in racing at an American Drag Racing League event at Bristol in 2012. By that time, he'd already been inducted into the Legends of Thunder Valley. (David McGee Photo)

Rickie Smith reasserted his dominance at Thunder Valley by returning to the Winner's Circle at the 2012 Thunder Valley Nationals with this nitrous oxide–aided, 900-ci Pro Modified Camaro. For an encore, Smith won Pro Modified again in both 2013 and 2015. (David McGee Photo)

The victory also completed his comeback from a horrific 2011 Thunder Valley Nationals qualifying crash that left him hospitalized with a broken left knee. Running in the left lane, Smith's Pro Modified Camaro got out of the groove before midtrack, but he stayed in the throttle. As the car approached the finish line, it drifted farther to the left. Smith tried to correct, swerving into the right lane but hit Pete Farber's car before slamming into the guard wall.

"I might have just drove the car too far that day, and it had been my fault," Smith recalled. "I've wrecked cars before, but that's the first time I've come away hurt. I had my foot up on the clutch pedal. When you shut off, you push the clutch in and pull the chutes. I did that right, but when I saw I was going to hit the wall, I must have gotten my leg locked. When I hit the wall, my hip moved just enough that it jammed that big [leg] bone up through my knee."

Back for More

Back in the saddle the following year, his race-winning profile included carding the quickest time during all three qualifying sessions, resetting the track ET record twice, and defeating Don Walsh in Sunday's final round.

Smith added to his legacy in 2013 by repeating his march to the Thunder Valley trophy, but the task was Herculean. He spun a bearing in his only engine during Friday qualifying and worked until Saturday morning to complete repairs. After making the show, he appeared to lose in Saturday's first round, but opponent Chris Juliano experienced a violent finish-line nitrous explosion and bypassed the scales, allowing Smith back into the show. With that door open, Smith stormed into Sunday's finals, knocking off veteran Troy Coughlin Sr. on a trademark holeshot, 5.991 to 5.984.

By the time the 2015 Bristol race rolled around, Smith was a two-time NHRA Pro Modified world champion, and he entered Bristol with a new car and something to prove. After struggling in the previous event and with 30 Pro Mods on the property, Smith qualified 7th and overcame Jim Whitely's first-round reaction advantage to win a close one, 5.977 to 5.984. He faced top qualifier Bob Rahaim's Corvette in the finals, but Rahaim fouled and Smith carded his seventh-straight 5.9 of the weekend, at 5.944/244.52.

"You have fans in the stands, and they come to watch these cars go to the finish line, so I try to give the people that paid money what they came to see," Smith told reporters afterward.

Smith has connected with fans since his days of wheeling Keith Fowler's all-conquering *Country Shindig* Ford Maverick in the nearly forgotten Super Modified class. He's a tenacious competitor who long ago embraced a refuse-to-lose mentality through his years as a Pro Stock independent battling titans such as Bob Glidden, Lee Shepherd, and Warren Johnson and then enjoyed a career rebirth in the 1990s racing in Pro Modified. Along the way, Smith earned the "Tricky Rickie" nickname for his starting-line acumen, cutting great reaction times while breaking the concentration of his opponents.

Nowhere is his legacy greater than at Thunder Valley.

"I love to run up here in these mountains," Smith said. "It's a special place in the valley. Back in the day, Bristol and Rockingham [North Carolina] were about two hours from home, and they were our two home tracks. You get a lot of people coming from home supporting you; it puts the pressure on you. Back in the IHRA days they

Rickie Smith (near lane) races his Keith Fowler–owned The Oak Ridge Boys *Mustang II against Bob Glidden during the 1980 Spring Nationals. Smith earned runner-up that weekend to Warren Johnson but bounced back to earn his first Bristol Pro Stock victory later that season. (John Beach Photo)*

used to tell me, I don't know if it was true or not, they'd get more calls to see if I was running Pro Stock than about the fuel cars."

His success began at the 1976 Spring Nationals, when he almost won a Super Modified eliminator final round to John Bray. His first Bristol win came a year later, when he beat legendary Herb McCandless for the 1977 Spring Nationals Super Modified trophy. Smith ventured into Pro Stock the following season and, despite a steep learning curve, was the quickest qualifier at the 1978 Spring Nationals.

Smith became the first Pro Stocker to record a 7-second run in 1980. He finished runner-up to Warren Johnson at that season's Spring Nationals and won Bristol at that August's Summer Nationals, the first of eight Pro Stock victories at Bristol, including five in the 1980s. Some of those victories stand out more than others.

1987 Spring Nationals

Prerace buzz for the 1987 Spring Nationals centered on the return of Top Fuel dragsters to Bristol after a three-year hiatus, but the event's television commercials featured a smiling Rickie Smith. His eventual Pro Stock victory, capped by a celebratory soaking when teammates doused him with a cooler of ice water on the ESPN broadcast, was certainly one for the highlight reel. Wheeling his Jerry Bickel–built Ford Thunderbird, Smith qualified 1st in the 16-car field, set low ET of every round of eliminations, and took the trophy by defeating fellow North Carolinian Terry Adams in the final.

Smith took a giant step toward his third IHRA world championship with a final-round 7.421/193.34 victory over Adams, who shook the tires and shut off. His path included wins over Sam Carroll, Gary Hajek, and Darrell Alderman. He beat the latter, aboard Jerry Haas's Camaro, in the semifinals, 7.40 to 7.42. "Alderman gave me a fit all last year, and I knew I'd have to be at my best against him," Smith told the media after the race.

With the front wheels high in the air, Rickie Smith launches his Ford Thunderbird during the 1987 Spring Nationals. Smith dominated the weekend, qualifying 1st in the 16-car field, running low ET of every round, and beating Terry Adams in the finals. (David McGee Photo)

1992 Spring Nationals

Smith's next Spring Nationals victory occurred five years later during the 1992 event that saw him win what was, for many years, Bristol's closest Pro Stock final. He had abandoned Fords by that time, and his STP Pontiac Trans Am was resplendent in Petty blue and day-glow red, much like Richard Petty's NASCAR ride in his final season. At Thunder Valley, Smith didn't have the weekend's dominant car, but he was its dominant driver.

Twenty-year-old Kentucky phenom Billy Huff and Virginia's Jim Revis appeared to be that weekend's favorites, but Smith was quick to remind them whose house they were playing in. After surprisingly easy wins over Billy Ewing and Craig Hankinson, Smith set down reigning world champion Doug Kirk in the semifinals 7.095/195.86 to 7.131/194.93. Huff was a tick quicker, at 7.087 in his semifinal victory over Jerry Yeoman. After losing lane choice, Smith was the first to leave in the final-round showdown, edging out Huff's Chevrolet 7.122/195 to 7.122/196.

1997 Spring Nationals

After participating in a few uncharacteristically mediocre Pro Stock seasons, Smith made the leap to Pro Modified for the 1997 season, but his victory at that year's Spring Nationals was far from easy, as 52 cars attempted to qualify. Wheeling a 1963 Corvette, Smith qualified 4th in the 16-car field. On race day, Smith advanced to the finals and a matchup with 1995 world champion Tommy Mauney. Saving his best for last, Smith unloaded a 6.498/215.34 that set low ET and top speed of the event and reset both ends of Thunder Valley's track record.

Rickie Smith made the switch to Pro Modified for the 1997 season, and, not surprisingly, his first national-event win came during Bristol's Spring Nationals. In the final round, Smith (near lane) took down former world champion Tommy Mauney in an all-Corvette battle. (David McGee Photo)

"We fought the car all weekend, but in the final round the car ran the best [it had] all weekend," a relieved Smith said in a post-race interview. "When I put it into second gear against Tommy, it was real smooth."

Dustups and Nail-Biting Finishes

Although many of Bristol's early race victories were measured in laps, that certainly isn't the case today. Whether it involves a bump-and-run, a late-race charge, or side-by-side door-to-door action, the battles of Bristol most often go to those unafraid to seize victory.

2002 Food City 500: Busch and Spencer

Young Kurt Busch muscled past leader Jimmy Spencer with a bump-and-run maneuver and then had to run and hide for the final 56 laps of the 2002 Food City 500 to collect his first career NASCAR premier series victory.

Busch had been pacing the field before Spencer dove beneath him as they entered Turn 1. They made contact off Turn 2, with Spencer leading lap 444. Busch quickly used a crossover to get beneath Spencer. Exiting Turn 2, Busch tapped the driver-side rear bumper of Spencer's Dodge, charged low, and retook the lead. Spencer wrestled for control after the two leaders bumped doors on the backstretch. From there, Busch had to navigate lapped traffic and withstand a late-race restart with 15 laps remaining before beating Spencer to the line for his first career victory.

"This is unreal. This is Victory Lane," Busch said to the shouts and cheers of his team as they christened Bristol's new building.

Kurt Busch (No. 97) pulls into the lead after bumping Jimmy Spencer (No. 41) out of his way in the latter stages of the 2002 Food City 500. Busch went on to capture his first premier series win that day; Spencer finished 2nd. (Jason Davis Photo, Courtesy **Bristol Herald Courier)**

Spencer was understandably less enthusiastic. "I never forget. The only thing is, when I smash back, he won't finish."

The race even featured some post-race excitement that didn't involve the leader on the cool-down lap. Dale Earnhardt Jr. angrily bumped Robby Gordon on the track, and Gordon returned the favor on pit road. Earnhardt later explained, "Damn [number] 31 wouldn't get out of the way; [the] lap-down car racing the leaders with 10 laps to go."

Gordon's response was simple: "I don't know what I did to make him mad, but nobody runs into me."

2007 and 2008 Food City 500: Burton

Jeff Burton declined to call his 2008 Food City 500 victory redemption, but the Virginia native was more than happy to hoist the Bristol trophy after leading Richard Childress Racing teammates Kevin Harvick and Clint Bowyer to the overtime victory. The win was Burton's 20th time entering a premier series Victory Lane and the next-to-last win of his 22-year career. Even better, it erased the criticism he received in 2007 for not stealing the victory from Kyle Busch.

In the 2007 Food City 500, David Ragan's lap-499 spin brought out the 15th caution in the debut of NASCAR's Car of Tomorrow. Burton restarted 3rd behind late-race leader Kyle Busch for a green-white-checker finish. Burton charged to 2nd on the restart and reached Busch's rear bumper twice but opted not to spin him, getting the nose of his Chevrolet even with

Driver Jeff Burton (left) and sponsor Steve Smith hold up the trophy after Burton led a 1-2-3 finish for Richard Childress Racing to win the 2008 edition of the Food City 500. First place was one spot better than Burton finished the previous year. (Earl Neikirk Photo, Courtesy **Bristol Herald Courier***)*

Busch's door at the start-finish line. "I wanted to win really badly, but if you knock him out of the win, you didn't win. That's my opinion," Burton said afterward.

The following year, Burton raced from 6th to 2nd before a late-race caution involving Kevin Harvick and Tony Stewart. On the green-white-checker restart, Burton dashed by leader Denny Hamlin on the high side undeterred; teammates Harvick and Bowyer ran 2nd and 3rd, respectively. "I thought, 'Oh no, not again.' [It was the] same scenario as last year," Burton said of the restart, "but something happened to Denny, and we were there."

Burton led only the race's final two laps, but that was two more than the previous year. "We're not going to stand in here and say we had the fastest car all day. We had good pit stops. We had good strategy. We did all the little things well, and, a lot of times, the big things take care of themselves," Burton said.

2008 Sharpie 500: Busch and Edwards

Late-race fireworks between Kyle Busch and Carl Edwards were only a preview of what happened after the checkered flag fell on the 2008 Sharpie 500. Busch had been enjoying a dominant night, passing Edwards for the early lead and pacing the next 415 laps before the night's third debris caution erased a 2-second lead with 38 laps remaining.

Back under green, Edwards chased Busch for two laps before using the bump-and-run tactic, moving the leader aside to take the top spot on lap 470. Busch recovered and returned the favor entering Turn 3. Busch got to Edwards's inside but was unable to pass and soon had to deal with the challenge of 3rd-place driver Denny Hamlin. Edwards sprinted away as the teammates battled for the runner-up spot, winning by nearly 2 seconds.

Retaliation arrived after Edwards slowed on the cool-down lap. Busch drove up and tagged the rear of Edwards's Ford and then banged doors before pulling away. Edwards responded by turning hard left down the track and spinning Busch's Toyota as they exited Turn 2. NASCAR responded by inviting Busch for a visit as Edwards did his traditional victory backflip off the door of his Ford, much to the delight of the fans.

A frustrated Busch called Edwards "Mr. Ed" and predicted that his rival would say he "didn't mean to race that way." Edwards, however, was unapologetic in picking up his sixth win of that season. "I just had to ask myself, 'Would he do that to me?' And he has before, so I hit him. It's just racing. I guess he wasn't happy about it," he said.

Asked about his post-race response, a grinning Edwards said that the "steering wheel slipped out of my hand."

2008 Food City 500: Stewart and Burton

Tony Stewart led more laps at Bristol than at any other NASCAR premier series track during a remarkable career that included 49 wins and 3 championships. And although Stewart did win at Bristol in the 2001 night race, the sheer number of times the Indiana native had the fastest car, appeared to have the field covered, and just ran into bum luck are a whole other matter.

Stewart snagged the pole in only his second Bristol start and led 225 circuits in the epic August 1999 night race. At the finish, he escaped Terry Labonte's last-lap misfortune to finish 5th. Stewart led 133 laps the following August before finishing 2nd to Rusty Wallace.

To make his lone visit to Bristol's Victory Lane, Stewart and his Joe Gibbs Pontiac had to overcome a mediocre 18th-place starting spot. After spending the first half of the race working through the pack, he first led lap 352 and then battled with premier series points leader Jeff Gordon during the race's final segment. Stewart took the top spot for good on lap 432 and outran rookie Kevin Harvick and Gordon to the checkers, winning by a half second.

"I've been wanting to win a race at Bristol all my life. This is my favorite racetrack," the winner said. "It's just awesome to win here."

Following a string of subpar Bristol runs, Stewart started on the pole in March 2006 when rain washed out qualifying and the race started on points. He led 245 circuits on a day marked by cold temperatures and snow flurries. Stewart's car became more and more loose, and he eventually fell out of the top 10 and finished 12th.

Stewart led more than half the race, 257 laps, the following spring in the debut of NASCAR's Car of Tomorrow, but a broken fuel-pump cable put him behind the wall for 21 laps, and he could only manage a miserable 35th-place finish.

Unbelievably, Stewart again led the most laps for the third consecutive year in the 2008 Food City 500 with nothing to show for it. After starting 6th, he led 267 laps, including in the closing laps, but contact with Kevin Harvick on lap 497 sent Stewart spinning and opened the door for eventual winner Jeff Burton. Harvick took the blame for the crash, but that did little to cool Stewart's frustration.

2009 Food City 500: Busch and Martin

A determined Kyle Busch assuaged his frustrations over dominating but not claiming Bristol's 2008 night race by recording another dominant and winning performance in the 2009 Food City 500. The contest even went into overtime, with Busch withstanding the charge of teammate Denny Hamlin. Even so, that finish

Kyle Busch (No. 18) had to withstand a furious late-race charge from Mark Martin (No. 5) and a green-white-checker finish to win the 2009 Sharpie 500 at Bristol. (Earl Neikirk Photo, Courtesy Bristol Herald Courier*)*

couldn't hold a candle to the closing laps of the night race, which appeared to be the property of either Mark Martin or Jimmie Johnson.

This was Bristol and, with less than 100 laps remaining, Busch worked himself into contention, taking the lead for the first time by passing Michael Waltrip on lap 433 following the race's 7th of 12 cautions.

Martin, who was making his 1,000th NASCAR series start, slid into the second spot and began stalking Busch over the race's final 40 circuits, running the bottom groove while Busch opted for a slightly higher line. Busch maintained the top spot through three more restarts, but the last one, which followed a nearly 11-minute red-flag cleanup for a Waltrip crash and some rain, set up a wild four-lap scramble to the checkered flag.

Martin pulled even with Busch as the pair crossed the start-finish line with two laps remaining. Busch eased slightly ahead, but Martin fought back on the bottom as they charged to the white flag. Busch never wavered and moved ahead as they roared down the backstretch. Martin ran up to Busch's rear bumper but couldn't seal the deal. "He gave me room; I just couldn't pass him," Martin said afterward. "I felt that was a great battle at the end. He gave me more than enough room. We just couldn't get it done. I managed to get the crowd on its feet."

Busch, who handed the checkered flag to a fan standing at the fence and then backed his car from the start-finish stripe to Turn 3 before entering Victory Lane, complimented Martin. "It's fun when you're able to race against guys you respect and that respect you. It was a blast. I can't say enough about Mark," Busch said. "I'm sorry he came home 2nd, because I know how he feels. He raced me clean, and I gave it everything I had."

Jimmie Johnson speaks during a press conference at a 2006 test session at Bristol Motor Speedway. After several frustrating tries, Johnson finally earned his first Bristol victory during the 2010 Food City 500 by outrunning a trio of Fords in the final laps. (David McGee Photo)

2010 Food City 500: Johnson Breaks Through

The Fords of Roush-Fenway Racing held the top three spots on a late restart with 10 laps remaining in the 2010 Food City 500. Greg Biffle lined up behind the pace car with Matt Kenseth to his inside and Carl Edwards just behind, flanked by Tony Stewart. All received two fresh tires on their last pit stop; crew chiefs for Kurt Busch, in 5th place, and Jimmie Johnson, in 6th, opted to change all four. Biffle led the restart, but Johnson emerged from a three-wide battle to pull into the runner-up spot after just one lap.

Stewart held the bottom and Biffle held the top, with Johnson between them. Stewart worked by to lead lap 493, but his time at the front was brief; Johnson blasted past on the outside as they crossed the stripe with six laps remaining. From there, Johnson pulled away to post his 50th career premier series victory by 10 car lengths over Stewart, who held off Busch's pole-winning Dodge.

An emotional Johnson celebrated by throwing his car into a slide before pulling down next to pit wall and burning out in front of his crew. He then performed a burnout all the way up the ramp of the Victory Lane building, exited the car, and threw the faux groceries out of the Food City bag in every direction. "It's just amazing to finally get a win at Bristol," Johnson said. "We've struggled here so much."

2012 Irwin Tools 500: Stewart and Kenseth

At the 2012 Irwin Tools Night Race, Tony Stewart was again knocked out of contention while leading, and that's when things got interesting.

Midway through the race, many of the leaders pitted under caution on a long, hot night, but Stewart and Matt Kenseth were among those who remained on track. Back under green, Kenseth took the lead with Stewart racing to the high side as they

Matt Kenseth (No. 17) and Tony Stewart crash together on the frontstretch while battling for the lead in the 2012 Bristol night race. Stewart displayed his displeasure with Kenseth by throwing his helmet at Kenseth's car. (Drew Hierwarter Photo)

exited Turn 2. Kenseth fought back to his inside and ran the middle groove through Turn 3 and Turn 4, with the leaders banging doors exiting the corner. Both slid sideways across the start-finish line with white smoke boiling from their tires. Kenseth hit the inside frontstretch wall first, damaging the driver-side front corner; Stewart's Chevy backed into the wall and came to rest on the apron.

As Kenseth's car limped away, Stewart climbed from his Chevrolet clutching his helmet. He started walking toward the ambulance but stopped when Kenseth's green and white Ford appeared on the frontstretch pit road. Stewart took a few steps and launched a perfect, two-handed helmet strike that bounced off the center of Kenseth's hood. A scowling Stewart turned back toward the ambulance, raised his left arm, and made a circular motion toward the crowd, which was already cheering wildly.

Kenseth didn't apologize for refusing to lift, saying Stewart had roughed him up twice before. "I learned my lesson there," Stewart fumed to the media, after exiting the infield care center. "I'm gonna run over him every chance I get from now until the end of the year. Every chance."

2015 Irwin Tools Night Race: Logano and Harvick

Joey Logano and Kevin Harvick staged a stunning battle of cat and mouse over the final 40 laps of the 2015 Irwin Tools Night Race that saw Logano deftly lead the veteran beneath, above, and around lapped traffic to claim his second consecutive night-race win.

The top groove was Logano's preferred line all night, but with slower cars often filling that space, he dipped in and out of the high line, running most of the final laps along the bottom and forcing Harvick to also abandon the faster lane. Harvick closed right up to Logano's rear bumper at least a dozen times, only to see the yellow Ford pull away.

Harvick charged harder into the corners; Logano backed up the corners but was faster off and able to pull away on the straights. At one point, with 27 laps to go, Harvick drove low off Turn 4 and Logano dove off the banking, missing the nose of his Chevrolet by inches. Just when it appeared that Logano would extend the lead, he caught another slower car, and Harvick reeled him back in. Harvick turned up the pressure over the final five laps, positioning his car in the top groove and closing within a single car length as they raced into Turns 1 and 2, but Logano was consistently faster on the corner exit. At the finish, Harvick's Chevrolet trailed by a single car length.

Logano's post-race burnout blew out the driver-side rear tire but not his enthusiasm. "He'd drive in so hard and almost get to my back bumper, and then I'd drive off really good. It's kind of interesting to watch races like that, when two cars are a similar speed but in two completely different ways," Logano said. "What's so fun about Bristol is [that] you can drive the car about five or six different ways and make it fast, so it's fun to race here."

Asked about Harvick and some of their previous run-ins, Logano said that he didn't care if he had to "beat his sister" to win at Bristol.

"There were a couple times it was pretty close," Harvick said, "but I just couldn't get close enough to do what I needed to do at the end to make something happen."

APPENDIX I

Bristol Motor Speedway NASCAR Cup Series Winners

Year	Spring Winner	Car	Summer Winner	Car
1961	Jack Smith	Pontiac	Joe Weatherly	Pontiac
1962	Bobby Johns	Pontiac	Jim Paschal	Plymouth
1963	Fireball Roberts	Ford	Fred Lorenzen	Ford
1964	Fred Lorenzen	Ford	Fred Lorenzen	Ford
1965	Junior Johnson	Ford	Ned Jarrett	Ford
1966	Dick Hutcherson	Ford	Paul Goldsmith	Plymouth
1967	David Pearson	Dodge	Richard Petty	Plymouth
1968	David Pearson	Ford	David Pearson	Ford
1969	Bobby Allison	Dodge	David Pearson	Ford
1970	Donnie Allison	Ford	Bobby Allison	Dodge
1971	David Pearson	Ford	Charlie Glotzbach	Chevrolet
1972	Bobby Allison	Chevrolet	Bobby Allison	Chevrolet
1973	Cale Yarborough	Chevrolet	Benny Parsons	Chevrolet
1974	Cale Yarborough	Chevrolet	Cale Yarborough	Chevrolet
1975	Richard Petty	Dodge	Richard Petty	Dodge
1976	Cale Yarborough	Chevrolet	Cale Yarborough	Chevrolet
1977	Cale Yarborough	Chevrolet	Cale Yarborough	Chevrolet
1978	Darrell Waltrip	Chevrolet	Cale Yarborough	Oldsmobile
1979	Dale Earnhardt	Chevrolet	Darrell Waltrip	Chevrolet
1980	Dale Earnhardt	Chevrolet	Cale Yarborough	Chevrolet
1981	Darrell Waltrip	Buick	Darrell Waltrip	Buick
1982	Darrell Waltrip	Buick	Darrell Waltrip	Buick
1983	Darrell Waltrip	Chevrolet	Darrell Waltrip	Chevrolet
1984	Darrell Waltrip	Chevrolet	Terry Labonte	Chevrolet
1985	Dale Earnhardt	Chevrolet	Dale Earnhardt	Chevrolet
1986	Rusty Wallace	Pontiac	Darrell Waltrip	Chevrolet
1987	Dale Earnhardt	Chevrolet	Dale Earnhardt	Chevrolet

Bristol Motor Speedway NASCAR Cup Series Winners

Year	Spring Winner	Car	Summer Winner	Car
1988	Bill Elliott	Ford	Dale Earnhardt	Chevrolet
1989	Rusty Wallace	Pontiac	Darrell Waltrip	Chevrolet
1990	Davey Allison	Ford	Ernie Irvan	Chevrolet
1991	Rusty Wallace	Pontiac	Alan Kulwicki	Ford
1992	Alan Kulwicki	Ford	Darrell Waltrip	Chevrolet
1993	Rusty Wallace	Pontiac	Mark Martin	Ford
1994	Dale Earnhardt	Chevrolet	Rusty Wallace	Ford
1995	Jeff Gordon	Chevrolet	Terry Labonte	Chevrolet
1996	Jeff Gordon	Chevrolet	Rusty Wallace	Ford
1997	Jeff Gordon	Chevrolet	Dale Jarrett	Ford
1998	Jeff Gordon	Chevrolet	Mark Martin	Ford
1999	Rusty Wallace	Ford	Dale Earnhardt	Chevrolet
2000	Rusty Wallace	Ford	Rusty Wallace	Ford
2001	Elliott Sadler	Ford	Tony Stewart	Pontiac
2002	Kurt Busch	Ford	Jeff Gordon	Chevrolet
2003	Kurt Busch	Ford	Kurt Busch	Ford
2004	Kurt Busch	Ford	Dale Earnhardt Jr.	Chevrolet
2005	Kevin Harvick	Chevrolet	Matt Kenseth	Ford
2006	Kurt Busch	Dodge	Matt Kenseth	Ford
2007	Kyle Busch	Chevrolet	Carl Edwards	Ford
2008	Jeff Burton	Chevrolet	Carl Edwards	Ford
2009	Kyle Busch	Toyota	Kyle Busch	Toyota
2010	Jimmie Johnson	Chevrolet	Kyle Busch	Toyota
2011	Kyle Busch	Toyota	Brad Keselowski	Dodge
2012	Brad Keselowski	Dodge	Denny Hamlin	Toyota
2013	Kasey Kahne	Chevrolet	Matt Kenseth	Toyota
2014	Carl Edwards	Ford	Joey Logano	Ford
2015	Matt Kenseth	Toyota	Joey Logano	Ford
2016	Carl Edwards	Toyota	Kevin Harvick	Chevrolet
2017	Jimmie Johnson	Chevrolet	Kyle Busch	Toyota

	NASCAR Xfinity Series Winners			
Year	Spring Winner	Car	Summer Winner	Car
1982	Phil Parsons	Pontiac	Jack Ingram	Pontiac
1983	Morgan Shepherd	Oldsmobile	Sam Ard	Oldsmobile
1984	Morgan Shepherd	Pontiac	No race	
1985	Darrell Waltrip	Chevrolet	Brett Bodine	Pontiac
1986	Morgan Shepherd	Buick	Brett Bodine	Oldsmobile
1987	Morgan Shepherd	Buick	Larry Pearson	Chevrolet
1988	Dale Earnhardt	Chevrolet	Larry Pearson	Chevrolet
1989	Rick Wilson	Oldsmobile	Mark Martin	Ford
1990	L. D. Ottinger	Oldsmobile	Rick Mast	Buick
1991	Bobby Labonte	Oldsmobile	Dale Jarrett	Pontiac
1992	Harry Gant	Buick	Todd Bodine	Buick
1993	Michael Waltrip	Pontiac	Todd Bodine	Chevrolet
1994	David Green	Chevrolet	Kenny Wallace	Ford
1995	Steve Grissom	Chevrolet	Steve Grissom	Chevrolet
1996	Mark Martin	Ford	Jeff Fuller	Chevrolet
1997	Jeff Burton	Ford	Jimmy Spencer	Chevrolet
1998	Elliott Sadler	Chevrolet	Kevin Lepage	Chevrolet
1999	Jason Keller	Chevrolet	Matt Kenseth	Chevrolet
2000	Sterling Marlin	Chevrolet	Kevin Harvick	Chevrolet
2001	Matt Kenseth	Chevrolet	Kevin Harvick	Chevrolet
2002	Jeff Green	Chevrolet	Jimmy Spencer	Chevrolet
2003	Kevin Harvick	Chevrolet	Michael Waltrip	Chevrolet
2004	Martin Truex Jr.	Chevrolet	Dale Earnhardt Jr.	Chevrolet
2005	Kevin Harvick	Chevrolet	Ryan Newman	Dodge
2006	Kyle Busch	Chevrolet	Matt Kenseth	Ford
2007	Carl Edwards	Ford	Kasey Kahne	Dodge
2008	Clint Bowyer	Chevrolet	Brad Keselowski	Chevrolet
2009	Kevin Harvick	Chevrolet	David Ragan	Ford
2010	Justin Allgaier	Dodge	Kyle Busch	Toyota

NASCAR Xfinity Series Winners				
Year	Spring Winner	Car	Summer Winner	Car
2011	Kyle Busch	Toyota	Kyle Busch	Toyota
2012	Elliott Sadler	Chevrolet	Joey Logano	Toyota
2013	Kyle Busch	Toyota	Kyle Busch	Toyota
2014	Kyle Busch	Toyota	Ryan Blaney	Ford
2015	Joey Logano	Ford	Kyle Busch	Toyota
2016	Erik Jones	Toyota	Austin Dillon	Chevrolet
2017	Erik Jones	Toyota	Kyle Busch	Toyota

NASCAR Truck Series Winners		
Year	Winner	Truck
1995	Joe Ruttman	Ford
1996	Rick Carelli	Chevrolet
1997	Ron Hornaday Jr.	Chevrolet
1998	Ron Hornaday Jr.	Chevrolet
1999	Jack Sprague	Chevrolet
2003	Travis Kvapil	Chevrolet
2004	Carl Edwards	Ford
2005	Mike Skinner	Toyota
2006	Mark Martin	Ford
2007	Johnny Benson	Toyota
2008	Kyle Busch	Toyota
2009	Kyle Busch	Toyota
2010	Kyle Busch	Toyota
2011	Kevin Harvick	Chevrolet
2012	Timothy Peters	Toyota
2013	Kyle Busch	Toyota
2014	Brad Keselowski	Ford
2015	Ryan Blaney	Ford
2016	Ben Kennedy	Chevrolet
2017	Kyle Busch	Toyota

APPENDIX II

Bristol Dragway National Event Winners				
Year	Top Fuel	Funny Car	Pro Stock	Pro Modified
1965	Maynard Rupp	Not contested	Not contested	Not contested
1966	Jimmy Nix	Not contested	Not contested	Not contested
1967	Don Prudhomme	Tommy Grove	Not contested	Not contested
1968	Chris Karamesines	Bob Sullivan	Not contested	Not contested
1968*	Not contested	Ray Alley	Not contested	Not contested
1969	Leroy Goldstein	Danny Ongais	Bill Jenkins	Not contested
1969*	Jim Nicoll	Terry Hedrick	Gary Kimball	Not contested
1970	Richard Tharp	Gene Snow	Ronnie Sox	Not contested
1970*	Pete Robinson	Gene Snow	Don Nicholson	Not contested
1971	Mike Martini	Don Schumacher	Ronnie Sox	Not contested
1971*	Ronnie Martin	Gary Dyer	Ronnie Sox	Not contested
1972	Don Garlits	Don Schumacher	Bill Jenkins	Not contested
1972*	Pat Dakin	Don Schumacher	Don Carlton	Not contested
1973	Marvin Schwartz	Bill Leavitt	Don Carlton	Not contested
1973*	Not contested	Dale Emery	Don Nicholson	Not contested
1974	Dale Funk	Billy Meyer	Reid Whisnant	Not contested
1974*	Paul Longenecker	Shirl Greer	Wayne Gapp	Not contested
1975	Don Garlits	Gene Snow	Scott Shafiroff	Not contested
1975*	Don Garlits	Shirl Greer	Wally Booth	Not contested
1976	Billy Graham	Gary Burgin	Bob Glidden	Not contested
1976*	Don Garlits	Larry LaDue	Bob Glidden	Not contested
1977	Jeb Allen	Dale Pulde	Pat Musi	Not contested
1977*	Not contested	Roy Harris	Not contested	Not contested
1978	Johnny Abbott	Pete Williams	Lee Edwards	Not contested
1978*	Not contested	Pete Williams	Not contested	Not contested
1979	Dave Settles	Dale Pulde	Warren Johnson	Not contested
1980	Bobby Hilton	Billy Meyer	Warren Johnson	Not contested

Bristol Dragway National Event Winners

Year	Top Fuel	Funny Car	Pro Stock	Pro Modified
1980*	Richard Tharp	Paul Smith	Rickie Smith	Not contested
1981	Jeb Allen	Billy Meyer	Warren Johnson	Not contested
1981*	Gary Beck	Raymond Beadle	Ronnie Sox	Not contested
1982	Jerry Ruth	Raymond Beadle	Lee Shepherd	Not contested
1982*	Connie Kalitta	Dale Pulde	Rickie Smith	Not contested
1983	Gary Beck	Mark Oswald	Rickie Smith	Not contested
1983*	Joe Amato	Mark Oswald	Lee Shepherd	Not contested
1984	Not contested	Billy Meyer	Lee Shepherd	Not contested
1984*	Not contested	Mark Oswald	Lee Shepherd	Not contested
1985	Not contested	Dale Pulde	Bruce Allen	Not contested
1985*	Not contested	Dale Pulde	Bob Glidden	Not contested
1986	Not contested	Tim Grose	Darrell Alderman	Not contested
1986*	Not contested	Mark Oswald	Bob Glidden	Not contested
1987	Hank Endres	Mike Dunn	Rickie Smith	Not contested
1987*	Jack Ostrander	Paul Smith	Doug Kirk	Not contested
1988	Joe Amato	Mark Oswald	Warren Johnson	Not contested
1988*	Eddie Hill	Ed McCulloch	Warren Johnson	Not contested
1989	Jim Head	Tony McCallum	Warren Johnson	Not contested
1989*	Earl Whiting	Chuck Etchells	Rickie Smith	Not contested
1990	John Carey	K. C. Spurlock	Tommy Mauney	Mike Ashley
1990*	Gene Snow	D. A. Santucci	Rickie Smith	Ronnie Sox
1991	Gene Snow	Not contested	Harold Denton	Scotty Cannon
1991*	Gene Snow	Not contested	Billy Ewing	Ed Hoover
1992	Doug Herbert	Del Worsham	Rickie Smith	Michael Martin
1992*	Bruce Larson	Not contested	Jerry Yeoman	Tim McAmis
1993	Doug Herbert	Not contested	Rickie Smith	Scotty Cannon
1993*	Richard Langson	Not contested	Roy Hill	Bill Kuhlmann
1994	Jim Bailey	Not contested	Robert Patrick	Carl Moyer
1994*	Doug Herbert	Not contested	Billy Huff	Shannon Jenkins

Bristol Dragway National Event Winners			
Year	Top Fuel	Funny Car	Pro Stock	Pro Modified
1995	Doug Herbert	Not contested	Roy Hill	Tommy Mauney
1995*	Dave Bieneman	Not contested	Mike Bell	Scotty Cannon
1996	Wayne Bailey	Not contested	Richie Stevens	Scotty Cannon
1996*	Doug Herbert	Not contested	David Jenkins	Shannon Jenkins
1997	Doug Herbert	Not contested	Angelo Alesci	Rickie Smith
1997*	Paul Romine	Not contested	Tony Gillig	Shannon Jenkins
1999	Not contested	John Force**	Jeg Coughlin Jr.	Not contested
2000	Cory McClenathan**	Not contested	Troy Coughlin	Not contested
2001	Doug Kalitta	Ron Capps	Greg Anderson	Quain Stott
2002	Larry Dixon	Whit Bazemore	Warren Johnson	Thomas Patterson
2003	Brandon Bernstein	Del Worsham	Kurt Johnson	Fred Hahn
2004	Tony Schumacher	John Force	Greg Anderson	Al Billes
2005	Doug Kalitta	Gary Scelzi	Warren Johnson	Mike Ashley
2006	Doug Kalitta	Ron Capps	Jason Line	Jay Payne
2007	Brandon Bernstein	John Force	Jeg Coughlin Jr.	Josh Hernandez
2008	Tony Schumacher	Melanie Troxel	Dave Connolly	Steve Engel
2009	Tony Schumacher	Del Worsham	Mike Edwards	Burton Auxier
2010	Tony Schumacher	John Force	Mike Edwards	Von Smith
2011	Larry Dixon	Robert Hight	Mike Edwards	Melanie Troxel
2012	Tony Schumacher	Ron Capps	Mike Edwards	Rickie Smith
2013	Steve Torrence	John Force	Rodger Brogdon	Rickie Smith
2014	Shawn Langdon	Tommy Johnson Jr.	Erica Enders	Pete Farber
2015	Richie Crampton	Matt Hagan	Erica Enders	Rickie Smith
2016	Shawn Langdon	Tommy Johnson Jr.	Jason Line	Mike Castellana
2017	Clay Millican	Ron Capps	Alex Laughlin	Troy Coughlin

* All-American, Summer or Fall Nationals
** All-star format, Top Fuel versus Funny Car

INDEX

A

A Life in NASCAR: Real Men Work in the Pits, 92
ABC's *Wide World of Sports*, 49, 53, 54
Abraham, Bill, 51
Adams, Joe Bill, 25
Adams, Terry, 146, 211
AHRA Grand American tour, 78
AHRA U.S. Open Nationals, 79
Alderman, Darrell, 132, 145, 211
All Pro Series, 109
All-American World Championships, 71, 76–79
All-American Nationals, 81
Allen, Bruce, 133
Allen, Jeb, 103, 115, 116
Allen, Johnny, 20–22, 25, 92
Alley, Ray, 12, 76, 79, 170, 192
Allison, Bobby, 24, 63, 89, 91, 93–100, 105, 107, 108, 110, 111–113, 137, 138
Allison, Davey, 110, 111, 126, 139–144
Allison, Donnie, 95, 97
Almirola, Aric, 205
Alugard, 124
Amato, Joe, 119
American Hot Rod Association, 32, 33, 43, 46, 65–68
American Speed Association, 109, 110–113, 124, 147, 148, 207
Anderson, Greg, 203
Andretti, John, 179, 180
Andrews, Clester, 48
Arciero, Sarge, 87
Arend, Jeff, 192
Arfons, Art, 68, 71, 76, 77, 79, 82
Arfons, Walt, 77
Armstrong, Dale, 121
Arons, Dick, 53
Arp, Skip, 177, 178
ARTGO, 113

Ashley, Mike, 130, 192, 199, 201
Aussie Raider, 122
Austin, John, 86
Austin, Ted, 76, 77
Automobile Racing Club of America, 63

B

Babb, Shannon, 178
Bailey, Jim, 154
Baker, Buck, 19
Baker, Buddy, 19, 21, 91, 93, 95–98
Baker, Gary, 96, 123
Baldwin, Tommy, 196
Balough, Gary, 106
Balzano, Mike, 178
Barbin, Walt, 103, 104
Bare, Booper, 178
Bazemore, Whit, 169, 170
Beachcomber, 52
Beadle, Raymond, 103, 104, 117, 118, 122, 124, 126, 158
Beam, Herman, 21, 69, 137
Beck, Gary, 118
Beckman, Jack, 193, 194, 200
Beebe, Tim, 87
Bell, Mike, 52, 158, 159
Bergler, Al, 51, 54
Berlo Vending Company, 14
Bernstein, Kenny, 79, 101, 104, 117, 119, 121, 122, 168, 170
Bertozzi, Malinda, 195
Beswick, Arnie, 46
Bickel, Jerry, 211
Bickle, Rich, 113
Biffle, Greg, 187, 218
Big Daddy, 39, 72, 73, 84
Biggers, Don, 76
Billboard, 54
Blakely, Glen, 43
Blaney, Dale, 114, 176, 177
Blonde, Jason, 207

Bloody Mary, 77, 79
Bloomquist, Scott, 178, 179
Blue Deuce, 188
Blue Max, 81, 83, 104, 118, 122, 124, 158
Bodine, Geoff, 125, 126
Bodine, Todd, 204
Boninfante, Nick, 169
Bonner, Phil, 43, 48
Bonnett, Neil, 111, 125, 181
Bonneville Salt Flats, 71
Borkes, Robert, 43
Bounty Hunter, 40
Bowyer, Clint, 214, 215
Bracken, J. D., 138
Bradford, Jerome, 104, 131, 132, 156
Brady, Malcolm, 24, 25
Brand X Eliminator, 43
Brannan, Dick, 43, 48
Branstner, Dick, 45
Bray, John, 211
Brewer, Tim, 106
Brissette, Jim, 152, 155
Bristol Herald Courier, 27, 32, 38
Brooks, Dick, 91, 95
Brooks, Mark, 149
Brown, Perk, 23
Brown, Vic, 67, 76
Bryant, Jim, 128, 129
Budweiser King, 101, 121
Budweiser 200, 139, 140
Budweiser 500, 147, 148
Burkett, Carol, 195
Burkhart, Mike, 76
Burnett, Ed, 57
Burton, Jeff, 184, 214–216
Busch Series, 97, 138, 139, 150, 195, 197, 198, 204
Busch 500, 105, 107, 108, 135, 183, 184
Busch, Kurt, 175, 187, 218
Busch, Kyle, 185–187, 204–206, 213, 214–217
Byrd, Jeff, 165, 166, 176

C

Cajun Cuda, 70
Callier, Fritz, 71, 78
Caminito, Jerry, 120
Campbell, Charlie, 149
Candies, Paul, 68, 101, 103, 115–118, 122
Cannon, Scotty, 127, 130
Capps, Ron, 170, 193, 195
Car Craft, 58, 66, 67, 70
Car of Tomorrow, 214, 216
Carlton, Don, 79, 83, 85, 160
Carpenter, Charles, 127, 128, 129
Carrecia, Eddie, 71
Carrier, Chris, 139, 140
Carrier, Larry, 12, 14, 16, 17, 21, 24, 28, 33, 34, 37, 42, 54, 61, 64–66, 71, 75, 77, 78–81, 87, 88, 96, 102, 112, 123, 145, 149, 164, 165, 208
Carroll, Sam, 39, 211
Carter, Winnie, 14
Casto & Boggs, 78
Chadwick, Kelly, 76
Chandler, Cleo, 195
Channellock Challenge, 176
Childress, Richard, 127, 135, 214
Chrisman, Art, 58
Christian, Ray, 43
Circle Track, 112
Clark, Ed, 123
Clark, Roy, 114
Clement, Frank G., 55
Cobb, Jennifer Jo, 196
Coca-Cola, 89
Coil, Austin, 122, 170
Coleman, Bob, 76
Collett, Gordon, 42, 52, 75
Collins, John, 119, 121
Colvin, Bob, 19
Comeaux, Jerry, 60
Comet Cyclone, 43
Cook, Ray, 67, 178

Cotton Picker, 45, 46
Couch, Buster, 32, 33
Couch, Randy, 112
Coughlin, Jeg Jr., 203
Coughlin, Troy, 189
Coughlin, Troy Sr., 209
Country Shindig, 210
Courage of Australia, 84, 85
Cowin, Graeme, 122
Creitz, Bob, 71, 76
Crocker, Erin, 196
Crouse, Eddie, 22
Cunningham, J. T., 43
Curb, Mike, 100
Cyclops, 77, 82

D

Dallenbach, Wally, 174
Davis, Preston, 83, 179, 213
DeJoria, Alexis, 195
DeLago, Tommy, 193
DeNoble, Ray, 41
Denton, Harold, 131, 145, 146
DePorter, Danielle, 195
DeWitt, L. G., 79
Diehl, Jeff, 193
Dieringer, Darel, 59
DiGard Racing, 105
Dirt Weeks, 175, 178, 207
Dixie Drag Chanpionships, 76
Dixie Twister, 68
Dixon, Ed, 146
Dixon, Larry, 199
Dodson, Barry, 124, 126
Dr. Moon's Rage, 191
Drag News, 73, 74, 151
Drag Racing, 38
Drag Review, 86, 102, 134
Drolema, Jack, 110
Duncan, Dan, 149
Durbin, John, 38
Dye, Wayne, 46

E

Earles, H. Clay, 19
Earnhardt, Dale Sr., 100, 102, 105, 108, 124, 125, 127, 135, 136, 138, 139, 144, 160, 161, 164, 166, 168, 171, 174
Earnhardt, Dale Jr., 175, 182–185, 204, 214
Earnhardt, Ralph, 22, 24, 97
Eckstrand, Al, 43, 56
Economacki, Chris, 21
Eddy, Mike, 111, 112
Edwards, Carl, 204, 215, 218
Edwards, Lee, 131
Edwards, Mike, 190, 191, 202
Elder, Jake, 98
Ellington, Buford, 16
Enders, Erica, 190, 202, 203
Engine Masters, 79
English, Bill, 86
Entertainment and Sports Programming Network, 123, 126, 164, 211
Etchells, Chuck, 170
Eury, Tony Sr., 183
Evernham, Ray, 160
Ewing, Billy, 132, 133, 212
Exodus, 77

F

43 Jr., 38, 46, 47
Faifer, Frank, 154
Fall Nationals, 74, 121, 129, 130, 132–134, 153, 154, 158, 195, 199
Fanning, Vicky, 155
Farber, Pete, 209
Farmer, Charles, 24, 25, 191, 193
Farndon, Fred, 41
Faubel, Bud, 43, 56
Fedderly, Bernie, 170
Ferreri, Lynda, 196
Finchum, Chad, 140
Firecracker 400, 31
Flemke, Eddie, 24

Flickinger, Larry, 113, 114
Flock, Tim, 59
Flying Carpet, 43
Food City 250, 182–184, 196, 198, 204, 205
Food City 500, 128, 148, 160–163, 175, 179, 181, 186, 188, 196, 204, 213, 214, 216, 218
Force, Ashley Hood, 192, 199, 201
Force, Brittany, 199
Force, Courtney, 199
Force, John, 119, 169–171, 193, 194, 199, 200, 201
Ford Charger, 56, 58
Frakes, Bill, 85
Frakes, Robert, 86, 87
France, William H. G., 13, 14, 26, 28
Francis, Steve, 177, 178
Frank, Chub, 55, 132, 154, 178
Frazier, Larry, 152
Fredrick, Bill, 85
Freeman, Jim, 26
Freeman, Richard, 202
Freer, Lauren, 195
Freight Train, 53
Frye, Bill, 178
Funk, Dale, 85, 87

G

Gant, Harry, 138, 139
Garlits Chassis Special, 39
Garlits, Don, 39, 72–74, 78, 84, 87, 199, 208
Gemini Cricket, 68
Gerster, Brian, 207, 208
Gibbs, Joe, 148, 170, 216
Glidden, Bob, 104, 130–134, 155, 210
Glotzbach, Charlie, 87–90, 93
Glover, Gene, 93, 136, 138
Glover, Tony, 136
Godman, Ray, 39, 54, 83
Going Thing, 70
Golden Commandos, 43, 56
Golden Rod, 27, 28

Golden, Bill, 44
Goldfinger, 43
Goldstein, Leroy, 67, 70
Goodsell, Ron, 40
Goodyear, 50, 64, 126
Gordon, Jeff, 42, 52, 75, 127, 139, 160–164, 174, 183, 188, 216
Gordon, Robby, 175, 185, 214
Gordon, Tina, 196
Gossage, Eddie, 123
Graham, Marvin, 87, 116
Gray, Jonathan, 203
Gray, Shane, 191
Green Monster, 71, 77, 79
Green, David, 150, 151, 154
Green, George, 21, 23, 137
Green, Melinda, 195
Greene, Bob, 44
Greer, Ed, 76
Greer, Shirl, 43
Griffen, Pee Wee, 25
Griffith, Chuck, 51
Grimes, Hoyt, 75
Grose, Tim, 120
Grotheer, Don, 50, 53
Groundhog Day, 193
Grove, Tommy, 56, 57, 58
Guthrie, Janet, 94, 196

H

Haas, Jerry, 211
Hagan, Matt, 191–194
Hagen, John, 53
Hajek, Gary, 211
Hall, Barney, 21, 31, 44, 60, 64, 125
Hamby, Mike, 119, 120
Hamilton, Pete, 95
Hamlin, Denny, 215, 217
Hammond, Jeff, 92, 106, 107
Hamrick, Hal, 17, 26, 32, 33, 37
Hankinson, Craig, 212
Harmon, Bob, 109
Harrell, Dick, 68, 69, 70, 76, 78
Harrop, Bob, 43

Hartman-Smith, Rhonda, 155, 195, 199, 200
Harvick, Kevin, 180, 187, 188, 204, 214–216, 219, 220
Hassler, Friday, 24, 25, 63, 89, 93
Hatcher, Earl, 23
Hatten, Woody, 65
Hav-A-Tampa, 177
Hawaiian Punch, 117
Hayter, Fred, 19, 21
Head, Jim, 119, 120, 122, 169, 193, 201
Heart Like a Wheel, 199
Hedrick, Terry, 77, 78
Henard, Ron, 19, 137
Henderson Motorsports, 139
Henderson, Charlie, 138, 139, 140
Hendriks, Aggi, 203
Henson, Carol, 195
Herbert, Chet, 151
Herbert, Doris, 151
Herbert, Doug, 151–155, 199
Hernandez, Joshua, 191
Hester, Lanny, 96, 99, 123
Hight, Robert, 194
Hill, Roy, 15, 23, 35, 104, 129, 131, 132, 155–160
Hilton, Bobby, 103, 104, 115
Hmiel, Gordy, 127, 129, 130
Hodgdon, Warner, 100, 108, 111, 123, 145, 165
Hoefer, Bill, 43
Holcomb, Richard, 86
Holman, John, 29, 48, 61, 140
Honker, 43, 56
Hood, Ronnie, 21, 26, 63, 100, 129, 192, 193, 219
Hoover, Tom, 40, 41
Hornish, Sam Jr., 175
Hot Rod, 32, 33, 44, 54, 68, 70, 80
Hot Wheels, 79
Householder, Ronny, 45
Houston, Tommy, 150, 151, 192, 202
Howard, Richard, 87, 89, 91
Howell, Jay, 45

Huff, Billy, 212
Hugger, 77
Hughes, Julius, 51, 75
Hughes, Leonard, 69, 70, 101, 115, 116
Hulk, 156
Humbert, Dick, 79
Hume, Jim, 119
Humphrey, Ronnie, 191
Hunter, Jim, 40, 88
Hurst Hairy Oldsmobile, 52
Hurst Hemi Under Glass, 44
Hurst Performance, 44
Hutcherson, Dick, 32, 60, 61, 137
Hylton, James, 89, 93

I

Iaconio, Frank, 132
Ingersoll, Buddy, 134
Ingram, Jack, 138
Inman, Dale, 45, 182
International Hot Rod Association, 80–87, 101–104, 113–123, 127, 130, 131, 133, 134, 145, 151–156, 158, 159, 189, 191, 210, 211
Irvan, Ernie, 135, 136, 141, 143, 143
Irwin Tools Night Race, 205, 218, 219
Irwin, Tommy, 19, 205, 218, 219
Isaac, Bobby, 24, 25, 63, 89, 91, 95

J

Jackson, Keith, 54
Jade Grenade, 87
Jarrett, Dale, 138
Jarrett, Ned, 19, 21, 31, 32, 48, 93, 148, 163, 181
Jellen, Peter, 149
Jenkins, Bill, 50, 53, 70, 84, 130
Johns, Bobby, 152, 195
Johns, Lori, 152, 195
Johnson, Allen, 190
Johnson, Don, 62
Johnson, Jimmie, 184, 192, 206, 217, 218

Johnson, Joe Lee, 22
Johnson, Junior, 19, 21, 25, 30, 31, 32, 87–92, 93, 96, 105, 107, 108, 144, 155, 181
Johnson, Jurt, 157
Johnson, Rick, 117, 119
Johnson, Roy, 189
Johnson, Tommy Jr., 170, 193, 200
Johnson, Warren, 104, 131, 132, 156, 157, 189–191, 210, 211
Jones, Rickie, 190
Jones, Ted, 130, 145
Joniec, Al, 43, 48, 51, 57
Juliano, Chris, 209

K

Kaase, Jon, 131
Kahne, Kasey, 175
Kalitta, Conrad, 37, 38, 40, 41, 48, 103, 117, 192, 199
Kalitta, Doug, 113, 169, 170
Kalitta, Scott, 200
Kamikaze, 203
Karamesines, Chris, 40, 41, 67, 68, 78, 155, 199
Kelley, Dallas, 21
Kelly, Earl, 43
Kenseth, Matt, 184, 185, 188, 189, 218, 219
Kent, Steve, 190
Kentucky Moonshiner, 86
Keselowski, Brad, 204, 206
Kimball, Larry, 78
King, A. J., 48, 59, 60, 71, 73, 78, 91, 121, 138, 180, 190, 208
King, Herman, 25, 26, 137
King, Jimmy, 71, 73, 78
Kinser, Mark, 176
Kinser, Steve, 176
Kirk, Doug, 158, 212
Kirk, Tammy Jo, 196
Kisha, Larry, 79
Knuth, Wayne, 79, 203

Kodak, 136
Koffel, Dave, 57
Konigshofer, John, 160
Krisher, Ron, 189
Kristek, J. E., 71
Kuhlmann, Bill, 127, 128, 130
Kulwicki, Alan, 110–112, 136, 142, 144, 147–149

L

Labonte, Terry, 97, 107, 108, 136, 161, 164, 171, 174, 183, 216
LaHaie, Kim, 152, 153, 195
Lancaster, A. J., 57
Land, W. L., 13, 14, 35, 47, 71, 79, 85, 114
Landy, Dick, 50, 71, 155
Langson, Richard, 154
LaPorte, Val, 41
Lawton, Bill, 43, 48, 57, 58
Leavitt, Bill, 85
Lee, Alison, 103, 115
Lee, Cory, 192
Lee, Lucille, 195
Legends of Thunder Valley, 171, 208
Lemons, T. C., 73
Leong, Roland, 117
Leslie, Tracy, 150
Lewis, Emily, 195
Lewis, Paul, 13, 21, 31, 137, 138
Lilly, Judy, 53
Lindamood, Roger, 43
Lindley, Butch, 138
Line, Jason, 157, 190, 191
Lippencott, Floyd Jr., 53
Little Red Wagon, 44, 45
Litton, Bruce, 155
Living Air 100, 177
Livingston, John, 68
Logano, Joey, 219, 220
Lombardo, John, 119, 122
Long, Johanna, 196
Lorenzen, Fred, 11, 19, 28–32, 48, 93

Lunati, Joe, 75
Lund, DeWayne, 19, 21, 22, 29, 63
Lundberg, Jon, 66
Lyall, Dave, 70, 77, 79

M

Mac, Cory, 170
Mad Dog IV, 26, 27
Mader, Dave III, 113
Make A Wish, 193
Malco Gasser, 53
Malone, Art, 27, 28, 40, 41
Mancini, Ron, 53
Mangler, 39
Marcis, Dave, 94, 95, 97, 107
Markwalter, Fred, 34, 35
Marlin, Clifton, 24
Marlin, Sterling, 136, 141, 144, 147, 148, 163
Mars, Jimmy, 178
Martin-McClure Motorsports, 140
Martin, Joey, 191
Martin, Mark, 110, 126, 136, 143, 144, 150, 151, 161, 174, 204, 216, 217
Martini, Mike, 83
Mauney, Tommy, 146, 212
Maybeck, Jim, 78
Mayfield, Jeremy, 174
McCandless, Herb, 43, 68, 79, 155, 211
McClenathan, Cory, 169, 170
McClure, Ed, 136
McClure, Eric, 140
McClure, Jack, 85
McClure, Jerry, 140
McClure, Larry, 136, 143
McClure, Teddy, 136
McCormack, Nancy, 194
McCulloch, Ed, 119, 122
McDowell, Dale, 177, 178
McDuffie, J. D., 91, 95, 97
McEwen, Tom, 52, 117, 119, 121
McGaha, Chris, 203

McGee, David, 205
McMahan, Bill, 137
Mears, Casey, 175
Meyer, Billy, 86, 101, 103, 104, 117, 119, 121, 122, 145
Meyer, Randy, 152
Miller Brewing, 119
Miller, Butch, 110–12
Miller, Ed, 79
Miller, Sam, 87
Minton, Fencil, 88
Moise, Patty, 195, 196, 198
Monaghan, Fran, 68
Montgomery, Bob, 21, 53, 54
Montgomery, George, 53
Montoya, Juan Pablo, 206
Moody, Ralph, 29, 32, 48, 61
Mooneyham, Gene, 66, 83
Moore, Bud, 63, 98, 106, 107, 125
Moore, Carl, 12, 17, 22, 28, 32, 33, 37, 54, 66, 80, 81, 95, 96, 165
Moore, Pat, 130
Moore's Snacks 250, 198
Mopar Missile, 85
Moran, Donnie, 178
Morrison, Buddy, 132, 133
Mortimer, Gale, 57
Morton, Bill, 21–25, 137
Motown Missile, 83
Motz, Bob, 77, 82
Mountain Dew, 106, 107
Moyer, Billy, 178
Muldowney, Shirley, 154, 155, 198–200, 202
Mulligan, John, 67
Mullins, Bill, 75, 76
Muravez, Bob, 52, 53
Murphy, Paula, 195
Musgrave, Ted, 163
Musi, Pat, 104
Myers, Bob, 92, 112
Myl, Tom, 53

N

Nab, Herb, 88, 90, 97
Nabors, Tim, 146, 159
NASCAR, 11–13, 15, 20, 22, 26, 28, 32, 36, 38, 44, 45, 47, 48, 59, 62, 64, 68, 72, 75, 86, 94, 97, 100, 101, 105, 107, 110, 111, 113, 123, 128, 131, 136, 140, 142, 143, 145, 147, 149, 150, 156, 158, 160, 162, 164, 166, 168, 172, 174, 176, 179, 184, 186, 188, 194, 196, 204, 208, 212, 214, 217, 217
National Dragster, 34, 36, 38, 42, 50
National Hot Rod Association, 11–32, 34, 37, 38, 42–58, 65, 66, 68, 71, 72, 75, 76, 78, 81, 102, 113, 117, 119, 130–132, 151, 152, 156, 157, 169, 175, 189–195, 199–202, 209
National 400, 12
Natural High, 113
Neff, Mike, 200, 201
Netherland, Tom, 197
Newman, Ryan, 183
Nichols, Shay, 195
Nicholson, Don, 43, 58, 70, 76, 79, 130, 131, 155
Nicoll, Jim, 71, 78, 82
Nix, Jimmy, 39, 40, 41, 51
Norris, Paul, 48
Not Quite Over The Hill Gang, 129

O

Oak Ridge Boys, 104, 210
Odyssey, 75, 79, 203
Ongais, Danny, 39, 41, 51, 68–70, 78, 101
O'Riley 200, 204
Osborne, Mark, 189
Osiecki, Bob, 26, 27, 28
Osterlund, Rod, 97, 100
Ostrander, Jack, 152, 153
Oswald, Mark, 103, 104, 115–119, 122
Ottinger, L. D., 93, 138

Outlawed, 46
Owens, Cotton, 19, 45, 61, 62

P

Panch, Marvin, 31, 32, 181
Parks, Wally, 28, 32, 34, 49, 54, 65
Parsons, Benny, 91, 93, 94, 95, 97, 138
Party Time, 134, 144, 146
Paschal, Jim, 19, 21, 29, 93
Patrick, Danica, 195, 196, 197
Patrick, Robert, 160
Pawuk, Mark, 189
Paxson, John, 85
Peacock, Charley, 41
Pearson, David, 19, 20, 44–47, 60–65, 93, 99, 110, 111, 137, 138, 177, 180, 181
Pedregon, Cruz, 169, 192, 194
Pedregon, Tony, 192, 193, 194, 200
Penske, Roger, 140, 142, 175, 186, 188, 206
Peppler, Fran, 203
Pepsi, 107
Performance Racing Network, 98
Peters, John, 53
Peto, Ann, 195
Petty, Kyle, 181
Petty, Lee, 21, 93, 182
Petty, Maurice, 59, 182
Petty, Richard, 19, 20, 21, 29–31, 38, 44, 46, 47, 59, 60, 62, 64, 89–91, 93, 95, 98, 105, 179, 182, 212
Peyton, R. L., 51, 66, 67
Phillips, Carlton, 160
Pieri, Mark, 51
Pink, Ed, 52
Piquet, Nelson Jr., 140
Pistone, Tom, 31
Pizzi, Tony, 53
Platt, Hubert, 46, 53, 68, 77
Poole, Barrie, 53
Poole, Ronnie, 115
Pope, R. G., 14, 16
Pott, John, 119, 120, 122

Potter, E. J., 77, 79
Potter, Mike, 98
Powell, Cristen, 169, 195
Pritchett, Leah, 195, 201
Prudhomme, Don, 52, 70, 78, 79, 117–121, 199
Pruett-LeDuc, Leah, 201
Prussian, 40, 41, 51
Pugh, John, 119
Pulde, Dale, 117, 119–122
Punch, Jerry, 117, 126
Purcell, Pat, 13, 17

R

R.J. Reynolds, 87, 96, 133, 165
Rackemann, Don, 74
Radford, Paul, 23, 25
Raffa, John, 66
Ragan, David, 214
Rahaim, Bob, 210
Raines, Tony, 184
Rambunctious, 71, 78
Ramchargers, 39, 41, 52, 70
Randall, Tex, 40, 41, 207
Ranier, Harry, 97
Rawls, Gene, 15
Reed, John, 75, 186
Reehl, Robert, 152
Reher, David, 132, 133
Renshaw, Deborah, 196
Reuther, Bob, 24
Reutimann, David, 206
Revell Models, 127
Revis, Jim, 212
Richert, Doug, 99
Richmond, Tim, 59, 105, 124
Ridley, Jody, 111
Robbins, Marty, 60
Roberts, Glenn, 19, 21, 22, 29, 30, 48
Roberts, Johnny, 24
Robinson, Pete, 42, 52, 76, 78
Robinson, Shawna, 195, 197, 198
Rock & Roll Thunder, 203
Rodder and Super Stock, 45

Rossi, Mario, 63, 94
Roulston, Dan, 38
Rudd, Ricky, 105, 125, 136, 143, 174
Runyon, Ronnie, 76, 78
Rupp, Maynard, 39–42, 57, 58, 75
Rush, Ken, 26
Ruston, Kenzie, 196
Ruth, Duane, 145
Ruth, Jerry, 117
Ruth, Jim, 130, 134, 144–146, 158
Ruth, Rick, 145

S

Sadler, Elliott, 179–181, 184, 198
Sauter, Jay, 184
Sauter, Jim, 112
Sawyer, Elton, 198
Scelzi, Gary, 169, 170
Schartman, Eddie, 43, 58, 67
Schatz, Donny, 176, 179
Schmidt, Harry, 81, 83
Schmitt, Mike, 43, 51, 75
Schubeck, Joe, 40, 52
Schultz, Roberta, 122, 195
Schumacher, Don, 83, 84, 157
Schumacher, Tony, 113, 199
Schwartz, Marvin, 39, 41, 73, 85
Scott, Wendell, 19, 129, 178, 200
Seabrook, Charley, 47
Segrini, Al, 117, 122
Selley, Bill, 103, 104
Senneker, Bob, 111
Shadinger, Pete, 43, 47
Shafiroff, Scott, 129
Shahan, Shirley, 195
Sharpie 250, 197
Sharpie 500, 183, 184, 204, 215–217
Sharpie Mini 300, 185, 187, 204
Shaver, Steve, 178
Shepard, Jeff, 179
Shepherd, Lee, 130, 132, 133, 138, 139, 181, 210
Shepherd, Morgan, 11
Shipley, Phyllis, 44

Shrewsberry, Bill, 43
Shroyer, Dick, 76, 77
Sibley, Fred, 57
Slitten, Dan, 107, 116, 119, 121, 123
Smart, Jody, 116, 119, 121
Smith, Freddy, 177, 178
Smith, Jack, 17, 20, 21, 22, 92
Smith, Lee, 57
Smith, Michael, 152
Smith, O. Bruton, 12, 135, 146, 164, 165, 166, 168, 169, 194, 208
Smith, Paul, 119
Smith, Regan, 196
Smith, Rickie, 104, 131–134, 145
Smith, Stevie, 176
Sneden, Tom, 57
Snow, Gene, 56, 70, 71, 76, 78, 175, 185–187, 216
Sorensen, Reed, 175, 186
Southeastern 400, 91
Southeastern 500, 11, 24, 26, 27, 29–31, 38, 61–64, 88, 90, 91, 94, 97, 99, 100, 102, 106, 137
Sox & Martin, 50, 53, 56, 57, 70, 77, 79, 83
Sox, Ronnie, 43, 56, 68, 70, 71, 77, 79, 83, 104, 130, 132, 155
Spehar, Ted, 6, 83, 85
Spencer, G. C., 22, 93, 95, 136
Spencer, Jimmy, 174, 213, 214
Spring Nationals, 34, 55, 66, 73, 78, 81–86, 101–103, 115–120, 128–133, 145, 151–157, 160, 189, 199, 200, 210–212
Springnationals, 33, 34, 36, 40, 42, 44, 45, 47–58, 65, 75, 194
Squier, Ken, 99
Stacy, Nelson, 19, 25, 137
Stahl, Jere, 50, 51, 53
Stardust, 83
Stebbins, Bill, 85, 86
Steffey, Roy, 40, 41, 58
Stepp, Billy, 79
Stevens, Richie, 157, 159

Stewart, Cliff, 124
Stewart, Tony, 174, 188, 215, 216, 218, 219
Stiles, Bill, 50
Stock Car Racing, 28, 38, 48, 88, 92, 96
Strickler, Dave, 42, 43, 55, 58
Sullivan, Bob, 68, 76
Summer Nationals, 115, 131, 145, 211
Sun Drop, 102
Sunoco Pro Stock Shootout, 158
Super Cyclops, 82
Super Shaker, 78
Super Stock, 45, 65, 115, 128, 129
Swamp Rat 13, 73
Swindell, Sammy, 176, 177, 179, 207
Swingle, Connie, 73, 74

T

Tanner, Bill, 78
Tarr, Don, 95
Tatroe, Bob, 77
Teague, Brad, 138, 139, 175, 182, 186, 187
Tharp, Richard, 71, 73, 81, 83, 103, 104, 115, 118
Thomas, Mark, 159, 160
Thompson, Dean, 132
Thompson, Jimmy, 23
Thompson, Mickey, 68, 70, 78, 101
Tice, Jim, 65, 67, 71, 76, 77, 79, 80
Trickle, Dick, 110, 113, 126
Troxel, Melanie, 199, 200, 201, 202
Troxel, Mike, 199
Truex, Ryan, 196
Tryson, Pat, 180
Turbonique, 79
Turner, Curtis, 12, 88, 144

U

Ulrey, John, 43
Unitas, Johnny, 82
United Drag Racers Association, 32
Utsman, Dub, 21

Utsman, John A., 91, 93–96, 138
Utsman, Layman, 21
Utsman, Sherman, 21, 23

V

Valleydale 500, 97, 105, 107, 109, 124, 126, 136, 140–142, 144
Van Wieringen, Dominique, 196
Vandergriff, Rob, 76
Vanderwoude, Al, 50, 51, 53, 75
Vanke, Arlen, 50, 51, 53, 75
Vaughn, Linda, 11, 52
Vest, Dick, 51
Volunteer 300, 109, 112
Volunteer 400, 95, 196
Volunteer 500, 16, 18, 20, 22, 23, 29, 31, 47, 59, 60, 62, 64, 88, 89, 95, 137, 138, 182
Vulcan Shuttle, 115

W

Wallace, Kenny, 163
Wallace, Russ, 110
Wallace, Rusty, 110, 111, 124, 126, 128, 136, 140, 143, 149, 158, 161, 163, 183, 188, 204, 207, 216
Wallace, Wendell, 177, 178
Walsh, Don, 209
Waltrip, Darrell, 91, 97, 99, 105, 110, 124, 127, 140, 143, 147, 161, 163, 174, 204, 208
Waltrip, Michael, 127, 175, 181, 217
War Eagle, 119, 120
Warrior, 119, 120, 122, 160
Weatherly, Joe, 19, 21, 28
Welborn, Bob, 19, 21
West, Johnny, 23, 65, 170
Westerdale, Don, 39, 41, 52
Whisnant, Reid, 86
Whitaker, Ed, 138, 139, 184
White, Jennifer, 195
White, Rex, 12, 19, 21
Whitely, Jim, 210

Wiebe, John, 74, 78
Wiggins, Blake, 127, 130
Wilkerson, Tim, 192
Will, Hillary, 195
Willard, Jessica, 203
Williamson, Charlie, 23
Williford, Steve, 145, 146
Wilson, Rick, 110, 136, 139, 140
Winston, 91, 102, 110, 112, 123, 147, 150, 168, 169, 171, 189
Winston No Bull Showdown, 169, 189
Winter Nationals, 43, 46
Winternationals, 43, 49
Wood, Bobby, 76, 77
Wood, Danny, 176
Wood, Eddie, 180, 182
Wood, Glen, 22, 182
Wood, Len, 180, 181
Wood, Leonard, 180
Woods, Della, 58, 76, 180, 182, 195
Woosley, Glen, 41
World 600, 12, 86, 87, 88
World Finals, 50, 58, 81
World of Outlaws, 176, 177, 207
Worsham, Del, 192, 193
Wynn's Charger, 72

X

Xtreme Speed Classic, 207

Y

Yarborough, Cale, 62–64, 90–92, 94–96, 98–100, 127, 138, 181, 182
Yarbrough, LeeRoy, 62, 75, 95
Yates, Robert, 141, 143
Yeoman, Jerry, 212
Yunick, Smokey, 21

Z

Zervakis, Emanuel, 21
Zink, Cliff, 39, 41

Additional books that may interest you...

1001 DRAG RACING FACTS: The Golden Age of Top Fuel, Funny Cars, Door Slammers & More *by Doug Boyce* Spanning the 1950s through the 1970s, this book is packed with well-researched drag racing facts that even some of the most hard-core drag racing fans might be surprised to learn. Covered are all the popular classes of drag racing of the era, including Top Fuelers, Funny Cars, Pro Stocks, and Eliminators including Gassers and Altereds, Stocks, Super Stocks, and more. Softbound, 6 x 9 inches, 416 pages, 125 photos. *Item # CT539*

LINDA VAUGHN: The First Lady of Motorsports *by Linda Vaugh with Rob Kinnan* For the first time ever, Linda Vaughn allows her fans a behind-the-scenes look at her career in motorsports and promotion through her personal photographic archive and other photos. Linda tells the story of individual images recounting countless stories from her amazing memory. She recounts events with racing personalities and automotive icons from George Hurst to Richard Petty to Mario Andretti to Don Garlits. Through her 50-plus years in Motorsports, Linda has lived it all, been everywhere, and met everyone. If you are a fan of Linda this will be a great addition to your library! Hardbound, 8.5 x 11 inches, 224 pages, over 300 color and almost 200 B/W photos. *Item # CT555*

MATCH RACE MAYHEM Drag Racing's Grudges, Rivalries and Big-Money Showdowns *by Doug Boyce* During the golden age of drag racing, fans didn't care as much about class racing as much as they wanted to see scores settled and interesting match-ups. Match races were also a great way to feature wildly popular cars that no longer had a class in which to compete, yet the fans still wanted to see them. So popular were these races that many track promoters didn't bother to promote class racing at all. Instead, they used the match races as headliners, similar to the marquee at your local arena or a billboard in Las Vegas, all resulting in putting more fans in the stands. And the drivers loved it too. Many of the most popular pro drivers quit class racing altogether just to go match racing. Softbound, 8.5 x 11 inches, 176 pages, 201 color and 96 b/w photos. *Part # CT582*

1001 NASCAR FACTS: Cars, Tracks, Milestones, Personalities *by John Close* Covered in depth are 65+ years of the cars, tracks, milestones, and personalities that have made this sport what it is today. With this book you will be racing through the pages and absorbing information that will make you a walking encyclopedia of NASCAR knowledge. Softbound, 6 x 9 inches, 416 pages, 110 photos. *Part # CT584*

www.cartechbooks.com or 1-800-551-4754